MODELS & PROTOTYPES

モデリング テクニック

Yoshiharu Shimizu

清水吉治（しみず・よしはる）

Takashi Kojima

小島 孝（こじま・たかし）

Masazo Tano

田野雅三（たの・まさぞう）

Shinji Matsuda

松田真次（まつだ・しんじ）

グラフィック社

目次

CONTENTS

装丁・レイアウト：大貫伸樹＋伊藤庸一＋竹田恵子
Book Design: Shinju Onuki + Yoichi Ito + Keiko Takeda

撮影：工藤正志
Photographs: Masashi Kudo

協力：株式会社 *Too*   Tel.03(3440)8941
Collaboration: Too Corporation

Models & Prototypes

First Printing, Dec. 1991
Printed in Japan
ISBN4-7661-0617-2

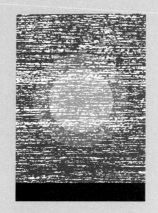

CONCEPT SKETCHING

コンセプトスケッチ

清水吉治
Yoshiharu Shimizu

1. コンセプトスケッチについて
About concept sketching

プロダクトデザイナーが，まとまったコンセプションに基づき自分のイメージを展開し，表示するメディアには，モデル，図面，スケッチなどがある。

スケッチによる表示は，これらのなかでも費用，時間などがかからず経済的で，最も卓越した手段といえる。

スケッチは，デザインプロセスの各ステージに従ってその表示目的や表示方法が違ってくるが，大別すると次の2種類に分類される。

その一つはデザイナーが自分のイメージ，アイディアの確認や展開のために描かれるスケッチで，サムネイルスケッチ，メモスケッチなどとよばれる第三者に伝達する必要のないものと，もう一つはデザイナーが自分のデザイン意図を第三者に伝達し理解を求めるために描かれるスケッチでコンセプトレンダ，レンダリングなどとよばれているものである。

前者は本人だけが理解できればよいスケッチなので，特別のスケッチテクニックはいらないが，後者はその形態，構成，素材，色彩など，誰が見ても理解できるようアトラクティブに描かれていなければならない。

最近は，デザインプロジェクトの多様化にともないデザイン開発サイクルが早くなり，一層のスケッチ省略化がいわれている。

時間のかかるレンダリングを描かないで，コンセプトスケッチなどに描写面での付加価値をつけ完成度をあげ，これをレンダリングやコンセプトレンダとするケースが非常に多い。

こうなるとコンセプトスケッチなどとレンダリングの分類上の境界はないといえる。

このためか，レンダリングを除くプロダクトデザインに関するスケッチを総称して"コンセプトスケッチ"(concept sketches)とよぶ傾向が強まっている。

本書では，コンセプトスケッチの表現法を解説し，できるだけ多くのスケッチサンプルを掲載した。

Product designers use models, plans and sketches to develop and express their own images based on definite concepts.
Above all, the sketching method is the most efficient in the sense that it is the cheapest and least time-consuming.
Two styles of sketching are available, although each stage of the design process has a different purpose and method of expression. One is known as the thumbnail sketch or memo sketch and is drawn by designers to confirm or develop their own image or idea and which does not need to be delivered to a third party. The second is known as the concept render or rendering and this is drawn by designers in order to give a third party a good idea of the concept.
The first style has no specific technique as such sketches are drawn for one's own sake, but the second style must be drawn attractively and be precise in shape, construction, material and color to ensure that it can be understood at a first glance.
Recently the speed of design development cycles have been increased in accordance with diversifications in design projects. Consequently, there is an even larger tendency of sketches being omitted. In many cases the time-consuming process of rendering is omitted and in its place the final value is added to the actual drawing of the concept sketch under the name of a rendering or concept render.
Thus, there is very little distinction between the concept sketches and the renderings. Because of this, perhaps, there is a strong tendency to call all sketches for product design, with the exception of rendering sketches, 'concept sketches'.
This volume contains the largest possible amount of sketch samples with full explanations on how to express the concept sketches.

2. コンセプトスケッチの種類
Styles of concept sketching

プロダクトデザインの現場においては，デザインの目的や内容，種類などにより多種多様なスケッチが描かれるが，ここでは最も代表的ともいえる3種類のコンセプトスケッチについて説明する。

The styles of sketches used in a product design workshop will vary depending on the purpose, content and type of design required, but here I would like to concentrate on the most typical of the three concept sketches.

1) サムネイルスケッチ(thumbnail sketch)，メモスケッチ(memo sketch)

サムネイルスケッチは親指程度の大きさに描く小さなスケッチ，メモスケッチはイメージしたものを記録するための小さなスケッチをいう。

両者とも，デザインプロセス初期の段階に，デザイナーが自分のイメージの展開や確認をしたり，デザインの基本構成を大まかにまとめたりすることを目的に描かれるスケッチで，それを描いたデザイナー本人さえ理解できればよいわけであるから，第三者に見せて伝える性質のものではないといえる。

これらのスケッチはプレゼンテーションを目的としないので，特定のスケッチテクニックをもたないが，描かれたスケッチだけでは記録不足，説明不足の場合には，簡潔な文章をスケッチに書き入れ補足することもある。

なお，浮かんだイメージなどをフリーハンドでクイックスケッチするには，ボールペン，サインペン，細描きマーカー，鉛筆などが一般的で使いやすいだろう。

1) Thumbnail sketch, memo sketch.

A thumbnail sketch is a small sketch drawn in the dimensions of a thumbnail, and a memo sketch is a tiny sketch used to log records of images.

Both are part of the early stage in the drawing process for designers and are used to confirm their own images as well as to organize the rough design of the basic construction.

They are for the sole use of the designer and as long as he himself can understand them they have served their purpose.

It is not necessary for a third party ever to view them.

These sketches have no specific technique involved as they are not drawn for presentation. However, in some cases it might be necessary to insert brief comments if the sketch alone fails to sum up the true intentions of the drawer.

For quick free-hand sketches to record flashed images, a ball-point pen, felt-tip pen, slender marker or a pencil are ideals tools.

A spinning machine represented in a thumbnail sketch. It is a free-hand drawing in a sketch-book using a black ball-point pen and a marker.

A thumbnail sketch of a digital telephone. No specific techniques are required for thumbnail sketches as it is not necessary to offer them for viewing to a third party. This is a quick sketch which records instant images.

A thumbnail sketch of some stationary. Having completed the line drawing with a black ball-point pen and a water felttip pen on layout paper, marker has been used to express an faint image of shading. 60 % of the sketch was completed in the free-hand style, and the remainder with the use of a ruler.

紡績機械のサムネイルスケッチ
スケッチブック用紙に黒ボールペン，マーカーを使い，フリーハンドで描かれている。

デジタルテレフォンのサムネイルスケッチ
第三者に見せる必要がないサムネイルスケッチは，その技法の特定をもたない。

浮かんだイメージを素早くスケッチしていけばよい。

ステーショナリーのサムネイルスケッチ
レイアウトペーパーに黒ボールペン，水性サインペンでラインドローイングのあと，マーカーで簡潔に陰影などを表現した。

スケッチの60％はフリーハンドで，40％は定規類を使って描いた。

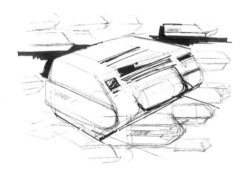

2) プレゼンテーションスケッチ(presentation sketch)

コンセプトに基づき，デザイナーが自分のイメージを展開，発展させまとめた多様なデザインヴァリエーションを第三者に伝達し理解を得たり，それぞれのデザインを比較検討するために描かれるスケッチで，プレゼンテーションラフスケッチ，アイディアプレゼンテーションスケッチ，コンセプトプレゼンテーションスケッチなどとよばれ，おそらくプロダクトデザイナーの描写頻度が最も高いスケッチといえる。

通常，スケッチはパースペクティブ（perspective）で描くが，時には"三面スケッチ"で表現することもある。いずれにせよスケッチは誰が見ても，そのデザイン意図が理解できるようにフォルム，構造，材質などが描写されていなければならない。

さて，デザインプロセスのデザイン検討段階で直面する時間的制約のなかで，プロダクトデザイナーは，完成度が高く，訴求力をともなったプレゼンテーションスケッチを早く，多く描かなければならないし，時にはドラマチックな描写も必要とされる。

2) Presentation sketch.

This style of sketch should be drawn to ensure that a third party is fully aware of the content and can compare the definite design variations which were developed from images based on the concept of the designer. This style is also known as the presentation rough sketch, the idea presentation sketch and the concept presentation sketch, and is probably the most popular drawing used in product design.

Perspective is mainly used for presentation sketches, but sometimes three-dimensional sketching can be used also.

Whichever is chosen from these two methods, the sketch must contain a detailed description of the form, construction and texture in order to allow complete understanding from a brief glance. Product designers are required to produce many presentation sketches, including the occasional dramatic sketch, with excellent results and as much appeal as possible within a limited time period throughout the reviewing stage of the design process.

In order to work within the above conditions, layout paper, Vellum paper or colored paper is recommended for concept presentations.

Tool-wise, markers are the most frequently and practically used, and should be utilized to draw the main sketch. Pastel can be used to color in the sections which have used the detail ellipsis method.

This book concentrates on offering as many sketch demonstrations of the most commonly used detail ellipsis method as is possible.

このような条件にかなうコンセプトプレゼンテーションスケッチを表現するのには，やはりレイアウトペーパー，ヴェラム紙やカラーペーパーなどの上に，簡便性と即乾性という利点で，現在最も使用頻度と実用性の高いマーカーをベースに使い省略法を駆使して描くのが一番よいだろう。
　したがって本書では，プロダクトデザイナーの描写頻度の最も高い，省略法を駆使して描くコンセプトプレゼンテーションスケッチ作例（スケッチデモンストレーション）を多く掲載した。

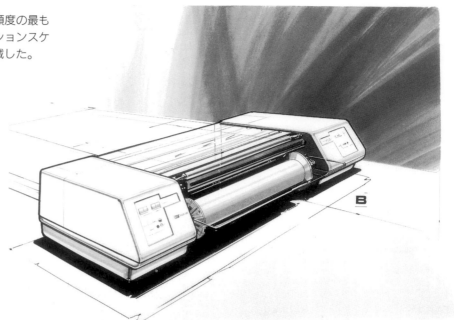

紡績機械のプレゼンテーションスケッチ

A2サイズレイアウトペーパー（PMパッド白）に黒のボールペン，水性サインペンで線描きし，マーカーで陰影，ヴァリューの表現がされている。
デザインを強調したいフロント部分はやや細かく描かれ，その他のところは省略表現となっている。

A presentation sketch of a spinning machine.

This sketch has been drawn on A2 layout paper (white PM pad) with a black ball-point and water felt-tip pen for the line drawing, and marker to express the shadow and values.
The front part has been drawn in slightly slender lines in order to achieve the design accent, and the rest has been drawn in the detail ellipsis method.

3）コンセプトレンダリング（concept rendering）

　レンダリングとは，すでにデザインが決定した製品などのできあがりを想定して描く完成予想スケッチのことで，誰が見ても十分にそのデザイン意図が理解できるように，フォルム，材質，色彩，構造，グラフィックなどが表現されていなければならない。
　このような視覚伝達機能の高いレンダリングは，デザインの依頼主に提示したり，製品企画，生産関係者などにデザイン意図を伝えるために使われる。
　なお，レンダリングはパースペクティブで描くのが一般的であるが，場合によっては正面，側面，上面のいわゆる"3面レンダリング"で表現することもある。
　前述のように，最近は製品の多様化にともない，デザイン開発サイクルも早くなり，デザイナーはスケッチワークに時間をあまりとれなくなってきている。
　このため，時間のかかるレンダリングを描かないで，コンセプトプレゼンテーションスケッチやプレゼンテーションスケッチに，バックグラウンドや若干のディテールなどを描きたしてやや完成度を高め，それを"コンセプトレンダリング"とするケースが増えつつある。

デジタルテレフォンのコンセプトレンダリング

A3サイズレイアウトペーパー（PMパッド白）にマーカー，パステル仕上げ。
（備考）このデジタルテレフォンを基にして，ペーパーモデルが製作された。

A concept rendering of a digital telephone.

A3 layout paper (white PM pad), marker and pastel have been used.
NB : This digital telephone was used to create a paper model version.

3) Concept rendering.

Rendering is to draw a conceptional sketch of the product at its completion. The form, texture, color, structure and graphics should therefore be drawn in great detail to ensure that the design is readily understandable.
This kind of rendering, which requires a high visual quality of communication, is used to present to the client or the people concerned the product design or production.
Incidently, in most cases perspective drawings are used for renderings, but there are also some cases in which three-dimensional drawings will suffice for renderings.
As previously mentioned, the development of design cycles is speeding up in accordance to the current diversity of products and designers cannot afford to spend too much time on sketch work.
Owing to this, many designers have started to leave out the time-consuming rendering work and present the concept presentation sketch or presentation sketches as concept renderings by adding backgrounds and a few details to improve the overall impression of the drawing.

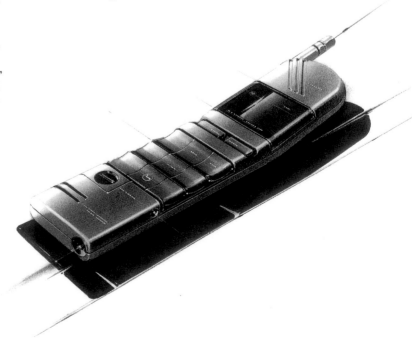

コンセプトスケッチ技法は大別すると，ラインドローイング，ヴァリュースケッチ，ハイライトスケッチの3種類に分けられる。

Concept sketch techniques are largely classified into three styles : line drawing, value sketching and highlight sketching.

1) 線描きスケッチ(line sketching)

線描きスケッチはその簡便さから，あらゆるスケッチのなかで最も一般的な表現技法である。

本来，線描きスケッチは，透視図や形を表現することが主な目的とされ，プレゼンテーション用としてはあまり使われなかったが，スケッチの省略化がいわれるようになってからは，描かれる線の太さのバリエーションを増やしたり，明暗及び影などを簡潔に加えるなど，線描きスケッチであっても描写面での付加価値をつけて，プレゼンテーションが可能なスケッチとする例が増えてきた。

1) Line drawing sketch

The line drawing sketch is the most commonly used sketch among all sketches due to its simplicity.
Initially, line sketches were used more often for perspective drawing or drawing shapes than for presentation purposes, but since the tendency to omit sketches began to increase, a similar increase in the cases of line drawings being created with enough quality for presentation by adding more variations to the lines and including shading and shadows has been noted.

デジタルテレフォンの線描きスケッチ

A3サイズレイアウトペーパー(PMパッド白)に黒水性サインペン，ボールペン，細描きマーカー仕上げ。

太線，細い線など何種類かの線をミックスして描けば，"めりはり"のあるラインスケッチが表現できる。

A line drawing of a digital telephone.

Drawn on A3 layout paper (white PM pad) with black water-color felt-tip pen, ball-point pen and slender marker.
Constrasts within the line drawing can be enjoyed by adding variations to the lines.

パソコンの線描きスケッチ

A3サイズレイアウトペーパー(PMパッド白)に黒水性サインペン，細描きマーカー仕上げ。
備考) 同じ太さの線で描かれたスケッチは，平面的で魅力に欠ける。

太い線，中位の線，細い線など何種類かの線をミックスして描けば，アトラクティブなスケッチ表現になる。

A line sketch of a personal computer.

Drawn on A4 layout peper (white PM pad) with black water-color felt-tip pen and slender marker.
NB : Lines of the same thickness will make the sketch plain and unattractive.
The sketch will be improved by adding variations to the lines ; thick lines, semi-thick lines, slender lines.

外形線（デザインライン）は太くする
The outline (design line) should be drawn in thick lines.

ハイライトラインは細い線で描く
Use thick lines for highlighting.

中位の太さの線で描く
Use semi-thick lines.

外形線（デザインライン）は太くする
Use thick lines to draw the ouline (design lines).

中位の太さの線で描く
Use semi-thick lines.

ハイライトラインは細い線で描く
Use thin lines for the highlights.

人物を配して，パソコンを使っている場面を表現する。
人物は目鼻等を描かない。(表情をださない)
Draw in a person using the personal computer. Omit details such as eyes and nose (facial features are not needed).

2) ヴァリュースケッチ(value sketching)

ヴァリュースケッチとは，表現する物体の各面にそれぞれ明暗の差をつけて立体表現するスケッチであるが，ここでいうヴァリュースケッチは明暗段階づけのほかに，様式化された映りこみ(リフレクション)，シャドウ，バックグラウンドを簡潔に描き入れたアトラクティブなプレゼンテーションスケッチをいう。

実際には，ボールペンやサインペンでラインドローイングし，マーカー，パステル，色鉛筆などいわゆるミックスメディア画材で，省略法を駆使して面やディテールを描きおこしていく。

2) Value sketch.

Under normal conditions a value sketch is a solid delination produced by adding shading on each surface of the object, but here it indicates an attractive presentation sketch with a stylized reflection, shadowing and a background that was briefly added apart from the shading.
In fact, use a ball-point pen and felt-tip pen to complete the line drawing, and then use the so-called mix medium tools such as marker, pastel and colored pencils to fill in the faces and the details by freely using the omit method.

ジェット機のヴァリュースケッチ

A3サイズヴェラム紙にマーカー, 若干のパステル, 白カラーペンシルで描かれている。

A value sketch of a jet plane.

This was drawn on A3 velum paper with markers, a touch of pastel and white colored pencil.

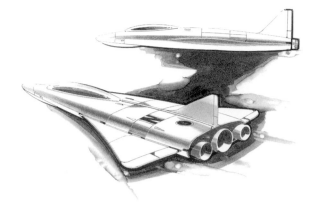

3) ハイライトスケッチ(highlight sketching)

　ダークカラーペーパーに, ハイライトラインやデザインライン(外形線)などを強調して製品を立体的に表現するスケッチをいう。

　通常, 赤色の製品をスケッチするときは赤色のカラーペーパー, 青色の製品をスケッチする場合には青色のスラーペーパーを使い, 白の色鉛筆でラインドローイングし, マーカー, パステル, ポスターカラーなどで簡潔に明暗, リフレクション, シャドウを描き入れて表現する。

　このように, スケッチする製品の色と同色のカラーペーパーにハイライト描写するため, 白い紙に描くより手間が省け, そのぶん早く表現できる利点がある。

3) Highlight sketch

This is a three-dimensional sketch of a product drawn on dark colored paper by emphasizing the highlight and design lines (outlines).
Normally red paper would be used to draw a red product and blue for a blue product. White colored pencil is used to complete the line drawing, and markers, pastel and poster colors to express the brief shades, reflections and shadows.
This sketch has the advantage of reducing time-consuming coloring over sketches drawn on white paper as the paper is the same color as the product.

クリーナーのハイライトスケッチ

A3サイズパントンカラーペーパー(ダークブルー)にマーカー, 若干のパステル, 白カラーペンシルで描かれている。

A highlighted sketch of a vacuum cleaner.

This has been drawn on A3 Pantone color paper (dark blue) with markers, a touch of pastel and white colored pencil.

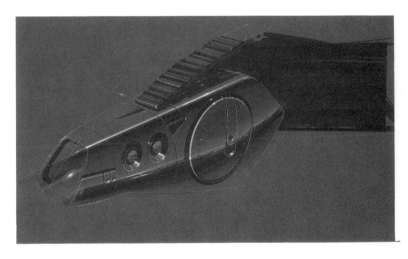

4. コンセプトスケッチ(下図・下絵)の描き方
Drawing methods of concept sketching (Rough plans and drawings)

　デザイナーは, 誰が見てもそのデザイナ意図が理解でき, しかも訴求力のあるプレゼンテーションスケッチ, コンセプトレンダリングを短時間で描かなければならない。

　しかし, 手馴れていないものなどを描くときに, 下図(下絵・アンダーレイ)もなくスケッチすることは相当の経験者でも難しく能率もあがらないので, やはり基本となる形態を大まかにラインドローイングし, その上にレイアウトペーパー等を重ね, デザインバリエーションスケッチを描いていくのが, 最も一般的でやりやすい表現方法といえる。

　次に, その基本となる形態の下図(下絵)の表現方法をいくつか述べておく。

Designers are required to draw clear and appealing presentation sketches and concept renderings so that anyone can understand the contents in the shortest period of time.
However, it is difficult and inefficient to sketch something you are not used to without a rough plan (rough sketch, underlay) even for experienced experts. So, we are brought to the conclusion that the most common way is to produce a rough line drawing of the basic shape and place a piece of layout paper on top of it to work on the design variations.
Here are some examples of rough drawings of basic shapes.

●透視図法で表現する（perspective）

透視図法とは，われわれの目で見ることのできる形態を，平面の上にそのまま再現するテクニックである。

透視図法には様々な方法があるが，ここでは，最も広くプロダクトデザイン関係で使われていると思われる有名な，Jay Doblinの簡略透視図法に基づき，製品のラインドローイングを二つ行ってみた。

● Perspective.

Perspective drawing is the technique of reproducing a visible shape on a plane.
Many kinds of methods are available in perspective drawing, but here we introduce two examples of line drawing work based on the famous simple perspective method by Jay Doblin which is seemingly the most popular method used amongst product designers.

A）45°透視図法で鉛筆けずりを描く

❶水平線（目の高さ・視点）を引き，左右に任意の2点（消点という）VP-L，VP-Rを定めその中心をVCとする。
❷VCから若干の角度をつけて線を引き，VP-L，VP-Rからこの対角線上で交わる任意の角度に透視線を引き，最近角Nを定める。
❸Nから任意の長さのところに対角線を引き，透視線と交わった点をD，Wとする。D，Wより透視線を引いて立方体の底面の透視図ができる。

A) A drawing of a pencil sharpener using a 45° angle perspective.

> *Draw a horizontal line (including the eye-level/visual points) and decide on two points on the line - one on the left, the other on the right - and call them respectively VP-L and VP-R. The point mid-way between is the VC.*
> *Select a slight angle and draw a line from the VC point, then draw a perspective line to the arbitrary angle where the diagonal lines drawn from the VP-L and VP-R points meet. This point is known as N.*
> *Draw a diagonal line from N to the VP points, and where the perspective points meet on this line, mark them as D and W. Using the D and W points, draw perspective lines to mark out the base of the shape.*

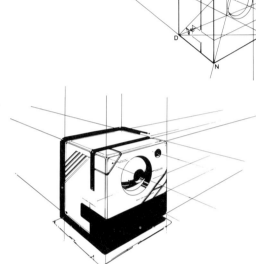

45°透視図法で立方体（鉛筆けずり）を描く
A drawing of a solid body using a 45° angle perspective method.

❹立方体の底面（正方形）の各コーナーから垂直線をたてる。
❺Dから45°の線を引き，Wを回転させて点Eを定める。
❻点Eを通る水平線を引き，立方体の対角面を決める。
❼各点を通る透視線を引いて立方体ができ上がる。
❽完成した立方体をベース（下図・下絵）にして鉛筆けずりを線描きスケッチする。

45°透視図法で作図された立方体をベース（下絵・下図）にして描かれた鉛筆けずりのスケッチ例。
This pencil sharpener has been drawn over the cubic base (rough drawing, rough plan) which was constructed by the use of the 45° angle perspective drawing method.

> *Pull up verticle lines from each corner of the cubic base.*
> *Draw a line from point D at an angle of 45° and set point E by rotating it in a 45° angled arc from point W.*
> *Draw a horizontal line through point E to fix the diagonal plane of the cube.*
> *Join all the points with perspective lines to complete the cube.*
> *Using this completed cube as a base, sketch the pencil sharpener with lines.*

B）30°—60°透視図法でFAXを描く

❶水平線を引き，左右に任意の2点VP-L，VP-Rを定める。
❷VP-L，VP-Rの中心を測点MP-L，MP-LとVP-Lの中心をVCとし，VCとVP-Lの中心に測点MP-Rを定める。
❸点VCより垂直線をおろし，視点から任意の位置に直方体（FAX）の最近角Nを定め，Nを通る測線MLを引く。
❹Nより直方体（FAX）の高さをとりHを定める。
❺Nから測線ML上にFAXの幅をとりWとし，同様にNからFAXの奥行きをとりDとする。

B) A drawing of a facsimile using a 30° - 60° angle perspective drawing method.

> *Draw a horizontal line (visual point) and mark the two VP-L and VP-R points anywhere along it ; one on the left, the other on the right.*
> *Mark the middle points of the line between the VP-L and VP-R points as MP-L, the line between MP-L and VP-L as VC, and the line between VC and VP-L as MP-R.*
> *Lower a verticle line from point VC to fix the nearest angle N of the hexahedron (fax) anywhere from the viewpoint and draw a lateral line MC through N.*
> *Fix the height of the hexahedron (fax), H from N.*
> *Decide on the width of the facsimile on the lateral line M from N and mark it as W. Do the same for the depth and mark it as D.*

30°—60°透視図法で直方体（FAX）を描く。
A hexahedron drawing using the 30° - 60° angle perspective drawing method.

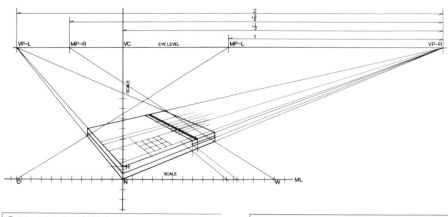

❻N，Hから透視線を引く。
❼MP-RとW，MP-LとDをそれぞれ結ぶ。透視線との交点がFAXの幅と奥行きである。
❽底面のコーナーから垂直線をたてて直方体（FAX）を完成する。

> *Draw a perspective line from N and H.*
> *Join all lines between the points MP-R and W, and MP-L and D. The junctions of the lines with the perspective lines indicate the width and depth of the facsimile.*
> *Put up lines from each corner of the base to complete the hexahedron (facsimile).*

❾完成した直方体をベース（下図・下絵）にしてFAXを線描きスケッチする。

30°－60°透視図法で作図された直方体をベース（下絵・下図）にして描かれたFAXのスケッチ例。
備考）このFAXのデザインをベースにしてペーパーモデルが製作された。

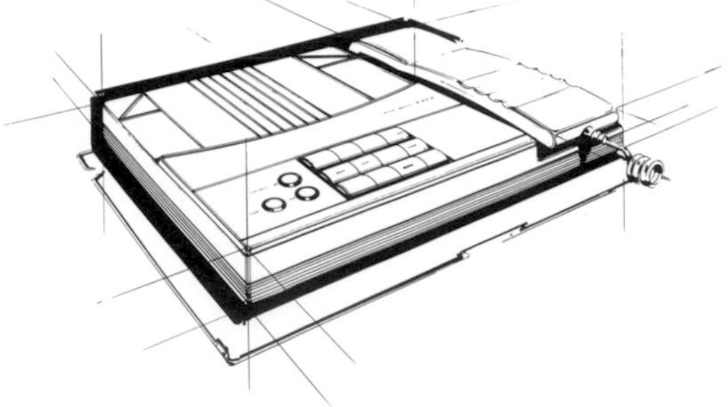

Using this hexahedron as a base (rough plan, rough drawing) draw a line sketch of the facsimile.

✳ This sketch of a facsimile has been drawn over the hexahedron which was constructed by use of the 30° - 60° angle perspective drawing method.
NB : A paper model was made of the facsimile using this design as a reference.

対象物の底面の最近角Nが鋭角になっている悪い透視図の例である。

通常，最近角Nは90°以上（フリーハンドパースの場合も同じ）にとらなければならないとされている。

備考）対象物は視点（作図者の目の位置・VC）から離れるにしたがって，その形体の歪みが目立ってくるので，なるべく視点の近くに位置するのが望ましい。

✳ This is a bad example of a perspective drawing as the nearest base angle of the object has been drawn at an acute angle.
Usually the nearest angle N should be more than 90° (which also applies to free-hand drawing).
NB : It is advisable to construct a perspective drawing not too far from the view point (the eye-level of the designer, VC) as the further the distance from the view point, the worse the shape will become.

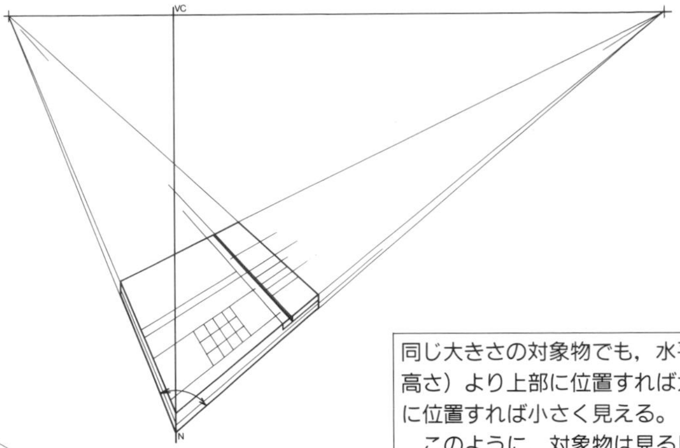

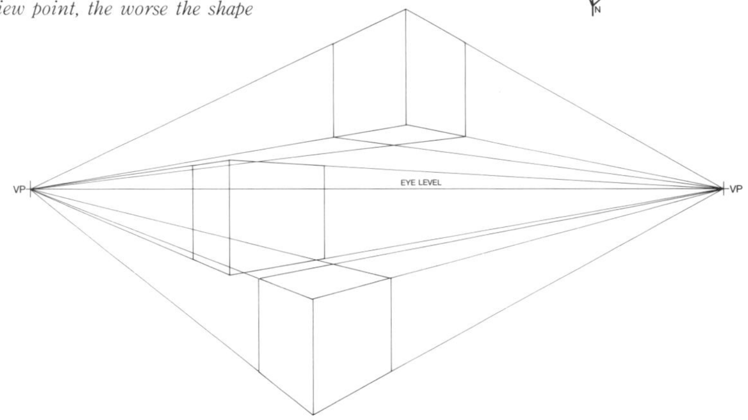

同じ大きさの対象物でも，水平線（視点・目の高さ）より上部に位置すれば大きく見え，下部に位置すれば小さく見える。

　このように，対象物は見る目の高さによって同じ大きさの物でも，スケール感が違ってくる。

　プロダクトデザイナーが描く対象物は一般にそれほど大きくはないので，水平線より下部に位置させて表現するのが適切であろう。

✳ The same object will look bigger if it is constructed above the horizontal line (view point, eye-level) than below.
Thus, the scale of the impression received for the same object can be different depending on the level of the eyes.
Objects drawn by product designers are visually not so big.
Therefore it is more appropriate for them to be drawn below the horizontal line.

●フリーハンドパース（感覚的パース）で表現する

　フリーハンドパースとは，描く対象物の大きさや消点などを"なれ"によって判断しながら描いていく方法で，視覚的に歪みを感じさせない程度に表現するには多少の練習をつまなければならない。

　それには形体の基本である立方体を，水平線，消点の基準にたよらずにフリーハンドで，いろいろの角度から多数描くことが一番いい練習方法だろう。

　ところで，フリーハンドパースは，透視図を作図する手間がかからないのと，表現する対象物が美しく見えるアングルの設定等が容易にできることから，実際のプロダクトデザイン現場でのスケッチワークには欠かせない表現方法の一つであろう。
備考）本書に載せてあるスケッチ作例の多くは，フリーハンドパースがベースとなっている。

●Expression by free-hand perspective (sensuous perspective).

With the free-hand perspective, one needs to guess the size of the object and draw the vanishing point from one's own experience. This takes a little practice until one can attain a visually reasonable shape. The best pratice for this is to draw many hexahedrons freehand from various angles without depending on the horizontal line or vanishing points.
In fact, free-hand perspective drawing is one of the indispensible methods for sketch work in actual product design workshops due to the fact that it requires only a short period of time to construct perspective drawings and offers free angle setting to enable one to choose the most attractive angle of the object to draw.
NB : Most of the examples shown in this book are based on the free-hand perspective method.

●写真，印刷物などをベースにして表現する

　手馴れていない飛行機などを描く場合，下絵もなく表現することは容易ではないので，飛行機などの写真，カタログなどをベースに，最小限に必要な線のみで下図（下絵・アンダーレイ）をつくり，その上にレイアウトペーパーなどを重ねてデザインバリエーションスケッチを表現していく。

● Expression of objects refering to photographs or prints.

It is not easy to draw such objects as aiplanes which one does not get the chance to draw often. So, with the use of a photograph or catalogue of airplanes, draw in the least amount of necessary lines, place a piece of layout paper on top of it and express the variations in design sketches.

ハンディクリーナーをスケッチする
A3サイズレイアウトペーパー（PMパッド白）

　後ろから見たハンディクリーナーを小さく描きいれたが，これによってハンディクリーナーの後部のデザインが大まかに理解できる。

　また，2つのクリーナーをバックグラウンド処理によってジョイントさせ，スケッチ画面構成に"動き"をあたえた。

Sketch of a handy cleaner

A3 layout paper (white PM pad)

A small sketch of the rear view of the handy cleaner has been added. This will enable one to gain a rough idea of the design on the rear area. Movement has also been added to the construction of the sketch by joining the two cleaners with a background treatment.

❶アンダレーレイ（下図・下絵）の上にレイアウトペーパー（PMパッド白）を重ね，ライトグレイカラーペンシルでデザインラインなどをいれていく。

❶*Place a piece of layout paper on top of the underlay (roughplan, rough drawing) and draw in the design lines in light grey colored pencil.*

❷ライトグレイカラーペンシルによって描かれたハンディクリーナーのラインドローイングスケッチ。

❷*A line drawing sketch of the handy cleaner in light grey colored pencil.*

❸クールグレイマーカーNo.5〜8でストラップ部分から描いていく。

❸*Use cool grey markers No.5-8 to start drawing in the strap parts.*

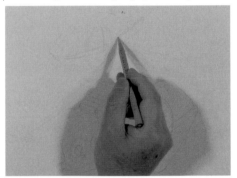

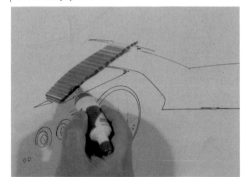

❹クールグレイマーカーNo.7〜黒マーカーでバックグラウンドを塗る。

　2つのクリーナーをバックグラウンドでジョイントさせ，スケッチ画面構成に"動き"をあたえる。

　バックグラウンドを塗った後，黒細描きマーカーでディテールを描いていく。

❹*Paint the background in cool grey marker No. 7 and black marmarker.*
Join the two cleaners with the background to add some movement to the construction of the sketch.

❺クールグレイマーカー，黒マーカーで描かれたハンディクリーナーのスケッチ。

　マーカー処理終了。

❺*A sketch of the handy cleaner drawn in cool grey and black marker. All marker work is now complete.*

❻粉状にしたダークグレイパステルを，重ね折りしたティッシュペーパーまたは白ネルにつけ，ボディーの面を塗っていく。

❻*Apply powdered dark-grey pastel to a double-folded piece of flannel to draw the body.*

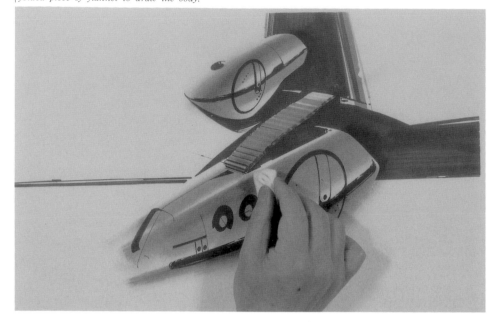

備考）棒状のパステルを粉にする方法。
A）トレーシングペーパーの上で，パステルをこすって粉にする。
B）カッターナイフで削って粉にする。

NB : How to powder stick pastel.
A) Rub the stick pastel against a piece of tracing paper to powder.
B) Use a cutter knife to powder.

C）金アミの上でパステルをこすって粉にする。
C) Rub against a wire net to powder.

❾明るいリフレクション部分やハイライトラインは，鉛筆型消しゴム，練りゴム，消しゴムを使いパステルをふきとって描出する。

❾*Use a pencil eraser, kneaded rubber or eraser to express the light reflection and the highlight lines by wiping off the pastel.*

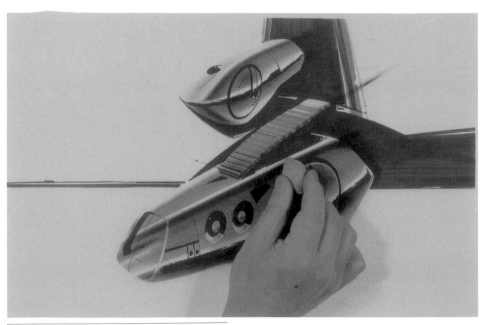

❿スプレーフィキサチーフでパステルやマーカーを定着する。

❿*Apply fixative spray to set the pastel and marker work.*

❼黒のパステルで，クリーナーのボディー稜線に沿って軽く線を引く。

❼*Draw a light line in black pastel along the ridge line of he cleaner body.*

❽パステルで線を引くと粉が線上に残り，それを指でなぞって稜線のぼかしを表現する。

❽*Use a finger to spread the powder left on the line by the astel in order to shade the area.*

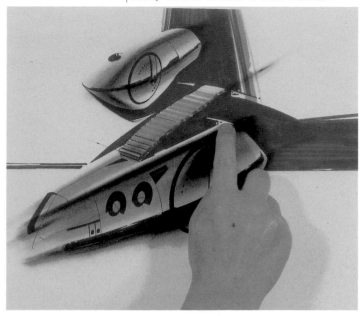

❶❶白のカラーペンシルで，ハイライトライン，ハイライトスポット，デザインライン，ディテールを描く。
　曲線部分はレンダリングカーブ定規を使ったほうが描きやすい。

❶❶*Work on the highlight lines, the highlight spots, the design lines and the details in white pencil. It is easier to draw the curved lines with a rendering curve ruler.*

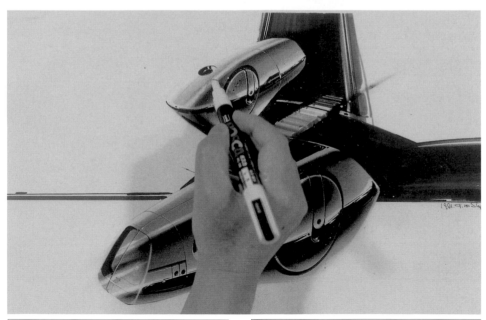

❶❷白のポスターカラーを使ってハイライトライン，ハイライトスポット，デザインラインを強調する。
備考）ここでは，白のポスターカラーを溶いたり，水，絵具皿，筆洗器を準備したりの手間を省くために，スティック状で筆記幅1.0の白ポスターカラーマーカーを使ってハイライトライン，ハイライトスポットなどをいれた。

❶❷*Use white poster color to emphasize the highlight lines, the design lines and the details.*
NB : A stick-type 1.0 thickness white poster color marker has been used here to draw in the highlight lines and design lines in order to eliminate the bother of thinning the white poster color and preparing water, a palette and a jar in which to rinse brushes.

回転部のハイライトラインは楕円
定規を使い，白のカラーペンシル
で描く

*Use an eliptical template and
white color pencil for the highlights on the rotating area.*

クールグレイマーカーNo. 5〜8を
使い，ストラップをラフタッチで
描く

*Draw the strap with a rough
touch in cool grey markers
between No.5-8.*

ボディー上部（稜線）のハイライ
トラインは白のカラーペンシル，
白ポスターカラーで強くいれる

*Use white colored pencil and
white colored poster color to
sharply insert the highlight
lines on the upper part of the
body (ridge line).*

ボディーの明るい部分の外形線（デ
ザインライン）はライトグレイカ
ラーペンシルで，細く，弱くいれ
る

*The outline (design lines) of the
light part of the body should be
drawn thinner and more lightly
with light grey colored pencil.*

粉状にしたダークグレイまたは黒
パステルを，重ね折りしたティッ
シュペーパーなどにつけ，ボディ
ーの面を塗る

*Apply powdered dark grey or
black pastel to a double-folded
tissue paper to paint in the
body.*

白のポスターカラーによるハイラ
イトスポット

*A highlight spot in white poster
color.*

バックグラウンドの描き方に定義
はないが，ここでは2つのクリー
ナーをバックグラウンドでジョン
イトさせて表現し，画面構成に"動
き"をあたえた。クールグレイマ
ーカーNo. 7〜10を使用

*There is no definition of how
the background should be
drawn, but here it has been
drawn to join the two cleaners,
giving a sense of movement to
the sketch. Cool grey markers
between No.7-10 have been
used.*

黒ボールペンや黒細描きマーカー
で，シャープなリフレクションを
ボディーラインに調和するように
いれる

*Use a black ball-point pen or a
fine marker to draw in a sharp
reflection in harmony with the
body line.*

明るいリフレクションは鉛筆型消
しゴムで，パステルをふきとって
描出する

*Use a pencil eraser to express
the light reflection by rubbing
out the pastel.*

ハンディクリーナーをハイライトスケッチする

A3 パントンカラーペーパー（ダークブルー）

Highlighted sketch of a handy cleaner

A3 Pantone color paper (dark blue).

　ハンディクリーナーの一番説明したいボディーの真ん中，操作部分周辺のディテール，リフレクション，ハイライトラインなどを意図的にやや強調して描いてある。

　したがって，あまり見せなくてもよいその他の部分の輪郭線（デザインライン）やハイライトラインなどは，細く弱くいれ，必要以上に描き込み過ぎないようにした。

　スケッチ時間は50分位。

The sketch has been drawn with the intention of slightly emphasizing the details of the area around the operating parts, the reflections and the highlight on the center of the body, the most important part of all.
Therefore, the outline (design lines) and high-light lines and other parts which have reduced importance have been purposely drawn in thinner and lighter.
The entire sketch took approximately 50 minutes.

❶カラーペーパーの上に，明るいパステルのついた下図（裏面にパステルの粉をつける）を重ね，ボールペン等でデザインライン（外形線・輪郭線），ディテールなどを転写する。

　次に，クールグレイマーカーNo.7と黒細描きマーカー，黒マーカーなどを使いストラップ，操作部分のディテール，リフレクション，バックグラウンドを描く。

❷クールグレイマーカー，黒細描きマーカー，黒マーカーなどによって描かれたハンディクリーナーのスケッチ。

❷*A sketch of the handy cleaner drawn in cool grey marker, slender black marker and black marker.*

❶*Place a rough plane powdered with a light pastel (apply the powdered pastel to the reverse side) on top of a piece of color paper and use a ball-point pen to transfer the design lines (the external lines, outlines) and the details.*
Using a No.7 grey marker, a slender marker and a black marker, draw in the strap, the details on the operating part, the reflection and the background.

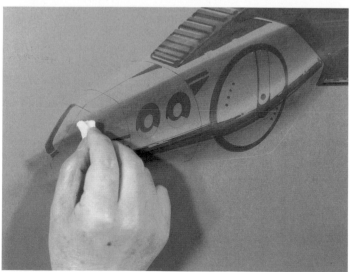

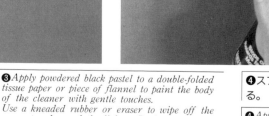

❸粉状にした黒パステルを，重ね折りしたティッシュペーパーまたは白ネルにつけてクリーナーのボディー面をかるく塗っていく。

　パステルのはみだし，明るいリフレクション部分などは練りゴム，消しゴムでふきとる。

❸*Apply powdered black pastel to a double-folded tissue paper or piece of flannel to paint the body of the cleaner with gentle touches.*
Use a kneaded rubber or eraser to wipe off the excess powder and the light reflection part.

❹スプレーフィキサチーフでパステルを定着する。

❹*Apply fixative spray to set the pastel.*

❺黒のパステル処理が終わったハンディクリーナーのスケッチ。

❺ *The sketch with the black pastel process complete.*

❻白のカラーペンシルで，ハイライトライン，ハイライトスポット，デザインライン，ディテールを描く。
　なお，デザインライン，ハイライトラインはレンダリングカーブ定規を，円部分などは楕円定規をそれぞれ使って表現する。

❻ *Draw in the highlight lines, the highlight spots, the design lines and the details in white colored pencil. Additionally use a rendering curve ruler to draw the design lines and highlight lines and an eliptical template for the round parts.*

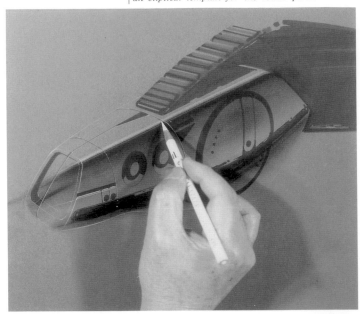

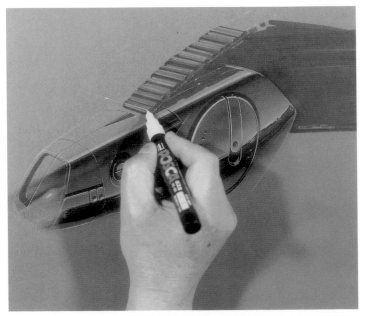

❼白のカラーペンシルによってハイライトライン，デザインライン，ディテールなどが表現されたハンディクリーナーのハイライトスケッチ。

❼ *The sketch with the highlight lines, the design lines and the details expressed with white colored pencil.*

❽白のポスターカラーを使ってハイライトライン，ハイライトスポット，デザインライン，グラフィックインディケーションをいれる。

❽ *Use white poster color to insert the highlight lines, the highlight spots, the design lines and the graphic indications.*

❾完成したハンディクリーナーのハイライトスケッチ。

❾ The completed sketch of the handy cleaner.

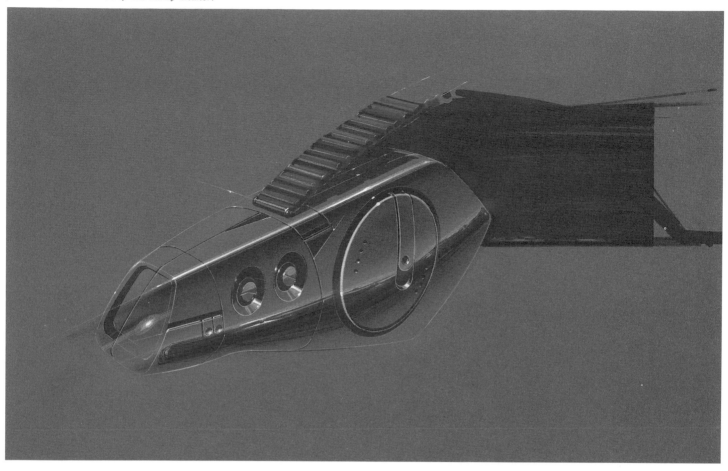

ストラップは，クールグレイマーカーNo.7〜10を使ってラフタッチで表現する

Use colors between cool grey No.5-7 to draw in the strap using a rough touch.

白のポスターカラーによるハイライトスポット

The highlight spot made with white poster color.

ボディー上部（稜線）のハイライトラインは白のカラーペンシル，白ポスターカラーでいれる

Use a white colored pencil and poster color to draw in the highlight lines on the upper body (ridge line).

回転部分のハイライトラインは，楕円定規を使い白のカラーペンシル，白ポスターカラーマーカーでいれる

The highlight on the rotating area should be inserted with the use of an eliptical template, a white colored pencil and a white poster color marker.

粉状にした黒パステルを，重ね折りしたティッシュペーパーにつけ，滑らかなボディー面を描く

Apply powdered black pastel to a double-folded tissue and draw in the smooth surface of the body.

黒のマーカーを使いラフタッチでバックグラウンドを処理する

Treat the background with rough touches of black marker.

白のカラーペンシルでデザインラインを細く，うすくいれる

Draw in the design line thinner and lightly with a white colored pencil.

明るいリフレクションの部分は，鉛筆型消しゴムなどで，パステルをふきとって描出する

Use a pencil eraser to express the light reflection areas by wiping off the pastel.

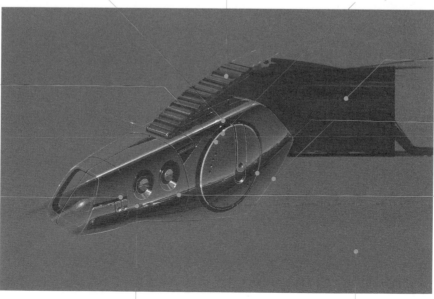

ボディーの暗いリフレクションは，黒ボールペンで線描きし，黒細描きマーカーで塗りつぶす

Use a black ball-point pen to draw the lines of the reflection on the body and paint it out with a slender black marker.

パントンカラーペーパー（ダークブルー）使用

Pantone color paper (dark blue) has been used.

多目的ドームをスケッチする

A3サイズレイアウトペーパー（PMパッド白）

多目的ドーム全体のデザインがよく理解できるように鳥瞰パースで表現，この上部に縮小図を配してスケッチ画面が単調になるのを防いだ。

　まだ建物自体のデザインバリエーションの展開をしている段階のスケッチなので，周囲の環境描写は必要でない。

Sketch of a multi-purpose dome

A3 layout paper (white PM pad)

A birds-eye view perspective is used to draw this sketch in order to offer a clear design of the multi-purpose dome. A plain appearence in the sketch has been avoided by drawing a scale-down of the dome. This is only the stage of working on the design variations of a building, so it is not necessary to draw in the surrounding descriptions.

❶多目的ドームの見せたいところを重点にしてパースアングルを決め，黒のカラーペンシルで大まかなアンダーレイ（下図・下絵）を描く。

❶*Select the perspective angle of the multi-purpose dome - an angle from which you feel it would be best depicted - and draw a rough underlay (rough plan, rough drawing) in black colored pencil.*

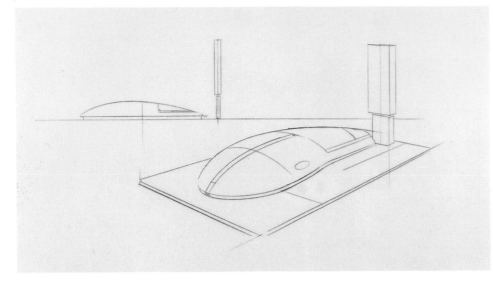

❷下図の上にレイアウトペーパー（PMパッド白）を重ね，0.2ミリ程度の黒水性サインペンで外形線（デザインライン），ディテールを描いていく。

❷*Place the layout paper(white PM pad) on top of the underlay and draw in the external lines (design lines) and the details with an 0.2mm thick black water-color felt-tip pen.*

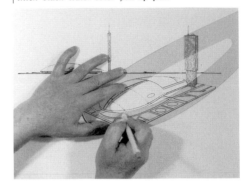

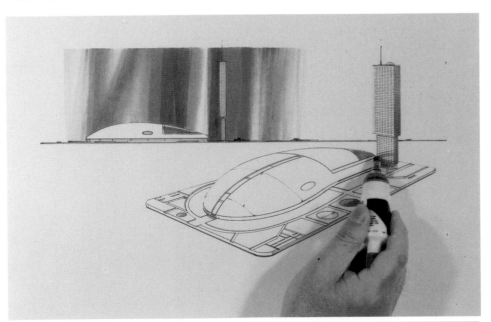

❺クールグレイマーカーNo.5〜7位を使ってリフレクション，その他の部分を描いていく。

❺*Use cool grey markers between No.5-No.7 to draw in the remainder.*

❻黒細描きマーカーで，ドームのシャドウ，分割線などディテールを表現する。

❻*Use a slender black marker to express the details such as shadows and partition lines.*

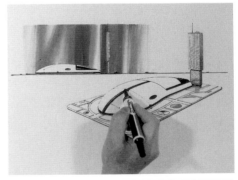

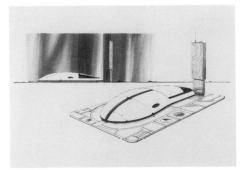

❼クールグレイマーカー，黒マーカーで表現された多目的ドームのスケッチ。

❼*The sketch of the multi-purpose dome expressed with cool grey markers and a black marker.*

❸黒水性サインペンで描かれた多目的ドームの
ラインドローイングスケッチ。

❸*The line drawing sketch of the multi-purpose dome.*

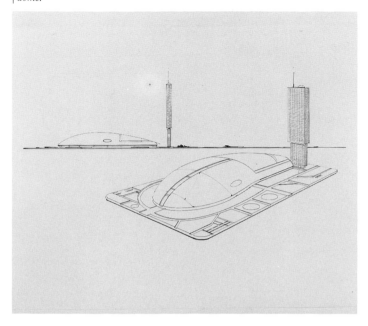

❹ドーム縮小図面部分を任意にマスキングして、
バックグラウンド処理をする。
　ここでは、クールグレイマーカーNo. 4〜6を
使い垂直方向のストロークで描いた。

❹*Mask the scaled-down dome and work on the background. Here the background has been treated with vertical strokes using the color scheme of cool grey markers between No.4-No.6.*

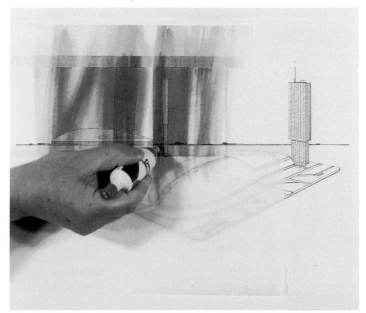

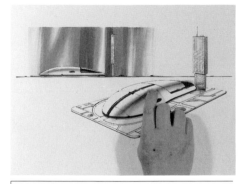

❽黒のパステルでドームのデザインラインに沿
うようにして軽く線を引く。
　パステルで線を引くと粉が線上に残り、それ
を指でなぞって稜線（かなり幅がある）ぼかし
をする。
　パステル処理が終わったら、スプレーフィキ
サチーフでパステルを定着する。

❽*Draw in a gentle line along the design line of the dome in black pastel.*
Use a finger to smear the powder left on the line to shade Toff the ridge line (leaving a good thickness).
When the pastel process is complete, use a fixative spray to permanently a fix the pastel.

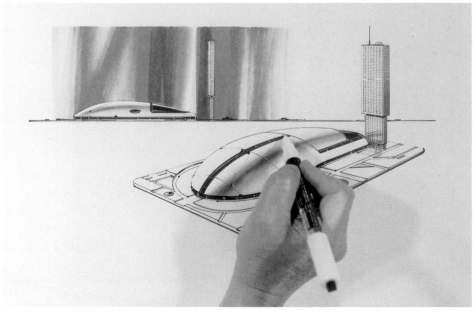

❾白のカラーペンシルで、ハイライトライン、
デザインライン、ディテールを描いたあと、白
のポスターカラーでハイライトライン、ハイラ
イトスポット、デザインラインをタッチアップ
して強調する。

❾*After the highlight lines, the design lines and the details have been drawn in with white colored pencil, go over them with white poster color for additional emphasis.*

多目的ドームの縮小図を付加し，スケッチの構図に"めりはり"をつける。

A scaled-down dome has been added to offer modulation to the construction of the sketch.

多目的ドーム全体のデザインがよく理解できるように，鳥瞰パースで表示する

A birds-eye view perspective method was used to give a clear view of the entire dome.

任意の範囲をマスキングし，クールグレイマーカーNo.4〜6を使い，垂直方向のストロークでバックグラウンドを描く

Mask an arbitrary area and work on the background with the colors No.4-No.6 cool grey.

黒水性サンイペン（0.2ミリ程度）でラインドローイングする
適宜，直線定規やレンダリングカーブ定規を使ってラインドローイングする

Use a black water-color felt-tip pen (0.2mm) for the line drawing. Use a straight ruler and a rendering curve when necessary.

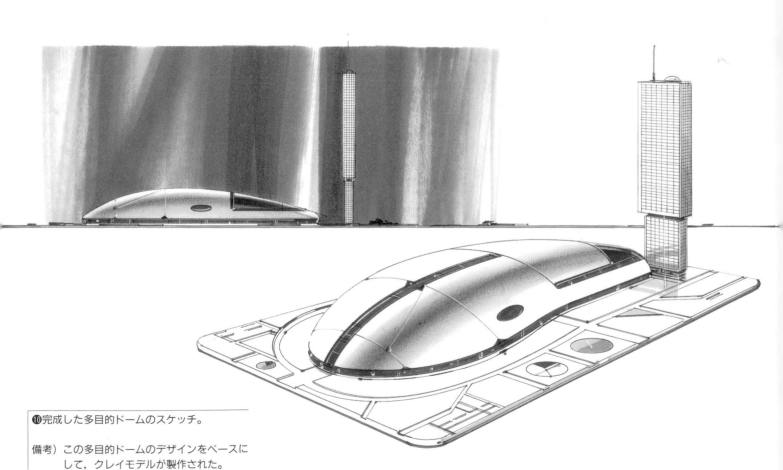

黒の細描きマーカーで，ドームの分割線やディテールを表現する

白のカラーペンシルでハイライトライン等をいれる

Insert the highlights with white colored pencil.

白のポスターカラーでハイライトスポットをいれる

Insert the highlight spots with white poster color.

黒のパステルでドームの曲面に沿うように線を軽く引く
パステルで線を引いたあとに粉が残り，それを指でなぞってドームの曲面のぼかしをする

Draw in a gentle line along the curved surface of the dome with black pastel. Smear the pastel towards the left of the line with a finger during this process to shade off the curved surface of the dome.

❿完成した多目的ドームのスケッチ。

備考）この多目的ドームのデザインをベースにして，クレイモデルが製作された。

❿*The completed sketch of the multi-purpose dome.*
NB : The design of this multi-purpose dome was used to make a clay model.

デジタルテレフォンをハイライトスケッチする

A highlight sketch of a digital telephone.

Ａ３パントンカラーペーパー（グリーン）

A3 Pantone color paper (green)

このスケッチはグリーン（描くデジタルテレフォンと同色）の
パントンカラーペーパーに，白のカラーペンシルでラインドローイングしたあと，マーカーでリフレクション，シャドウなどを描きいれて表現した。

スケッチ時間は50分位。

This sketch was made on green (the same color as the digital telephone) Pantone color paper with a white colored pencil for the line drawing process, followed by marker to express the reflections and shadows.
The sketch took approximately 50 minutes.

❷フリーハンドで描かれたデジタルテレフォン
の透視図の上に，トレーシングペーパーを重ね，
黒のカラーペンシル等で正確な透視図に整えて
いく。

❷Place a piece of tracing paper on top of the free-hand perspective drawing and adjust it to a correct perspective with a black colored pencil.

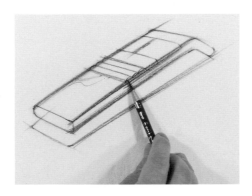

❶デジタルテレフォンのフリーハンド透視図を
描く。

任意の白い紙に，黒カラーペンシル，黒サインペンなど描き易い画材で，デジタルテレフォンが一番美しく見えるパースアングルを選び，フリーハンドパース（感覚的に処理する透視図法）で大まかにラインドローイングをする。

❶Draw a free-hand perspective of the digital telephone.
Select the best angle for the phone and make the rough line drawing on any white paper with something that is easy to draw with, such as black colored pencil or felt-tip pen, using the free-hand perspective method (perspective involving one's own senses).

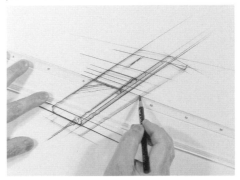

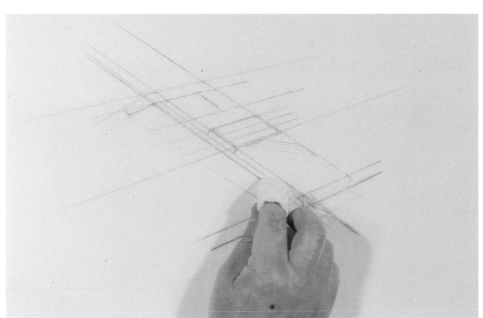

❸描きあがったデジタルテレフォンの下図。

❸The completed rough plan of the digital telephone.

❹下図の裏面に白か明るい色のパステルを塗る。

❹Paint the back of the rough sketch with a light color pastel.

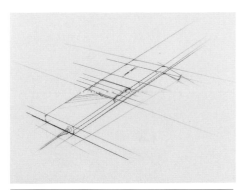

❺パステルの粉が飛ばないように，ティッシュ
ペーパーなどで，パステルを塗った部分をこすりおさえておく。

❺Hold the pastel powder on to the paper by rubbing the area painted with pastel powder to prevent it from flying off.

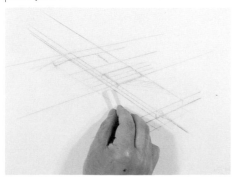

❻ カラーペーパーの上に，パステルのついた下図を重ね，硬い鉛筆かボールペンで外形線，ディテールなどをなぞり描き（転写）する。

❻Place the rough sketch with the pastel on top of the color paper and trace the external lines and etails with a hard pencil or ball-point pen to transfer the sketch.

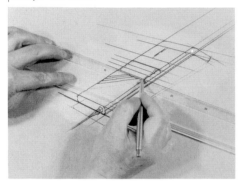

❼ 下図をはがす。
うすく転写されたデジタルテレフォンのデザインライン。

*❼Peel off the rough sketch.
The vague design lines of the digital telephone after being transfered.*

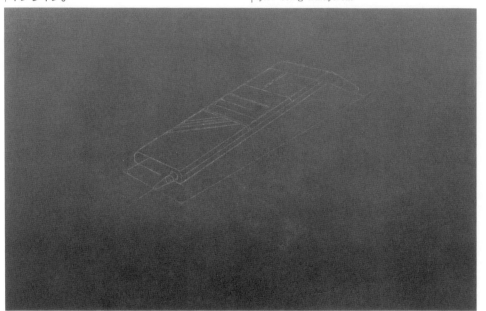

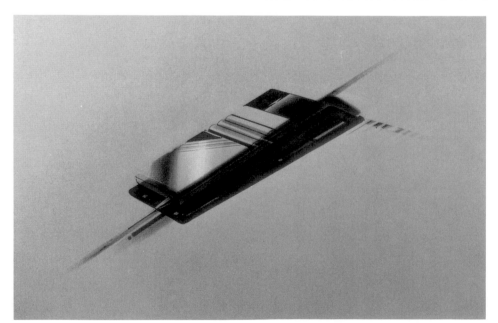

⓫ パステル処理が終わったデジタルテレフォンのスケッチ。

⓫The sketch with the pastel treatment complete.

⓬ スプレーフィキサチーフでパステルを定着する。

⓬Use a spray fixative to permanently afix the pastel.

⓭ 白のカラーペンシルで，デザインライン，ハイライトライン，ディテールを描く。
ハイライトライン，ハイライトスポットなど明るい部分は白を強くいれて表現する。

*⓭Draw in the design lines, the highlight lines and the details with a white colored pencil.
The lighter parts, such as the highlight lines and the highlight spots, should be expressed by emphasizing the white.*

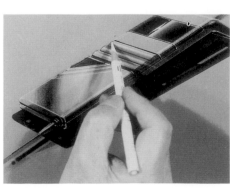

❽黒の細描きマーカーで，リフレクションやキャストシャドウなどを描く。

❽*Draw in the reflections and the cast shadow with a slender black marker.*

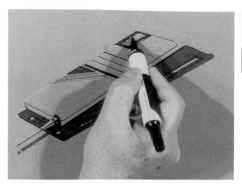

❿黒のパステルで，デジタルテレフォンのボディーの稜線に沿って軽く線を引く。
　パステルで線を引くと粉が線上に残り，それを指や擦筆でなぞって稜線のぼかしをする。

❿*Use a black pastel to draw a gentle line along the ridge line of the digital telephone body. Follow the powder left on the surface with a finger to shade off the ridge line.*

❾粉状にした白パステルを，重ね折りしたティッシュペーパーまたは白ネルにつけ，極めて簡潔にハイライト部分を描写する。

❾*Apply powdered white pastel to a double-folded tissue paper or piece of flannel and draw in the highlight section very briefly.*

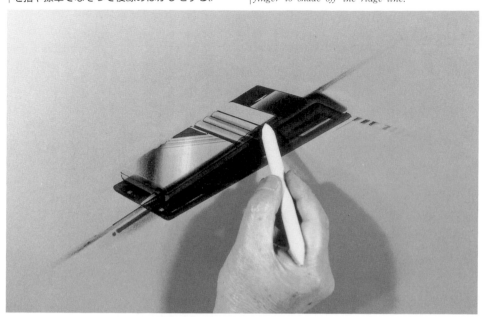

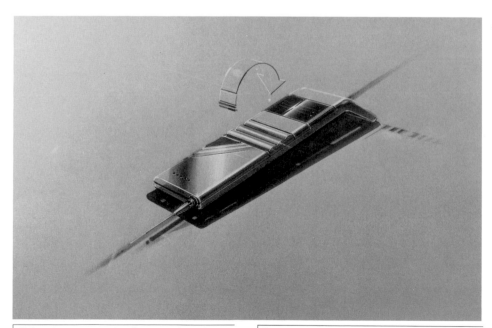

❷白のカラーペンシルによってハイライトライン，デザインライン，ディテールなどがはいったデジタルテレフォンのハイライトスケッチ。

❷*The sketch of the digital telephone with the highlight lines, the design lines and the details completed with white colored pencil.*

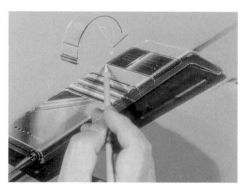

⓯白のポスターカラーを使ってハイライトライン，ハイライトスポット，デザインラインを強調する。
　直線部分は溝引きの手法を使ってシャープに描く。

⓯*Use white poster color to emphasize the highlight lines, highlight spots and design lines. Use a slotted ruler to draw in the sharp straight lines.*

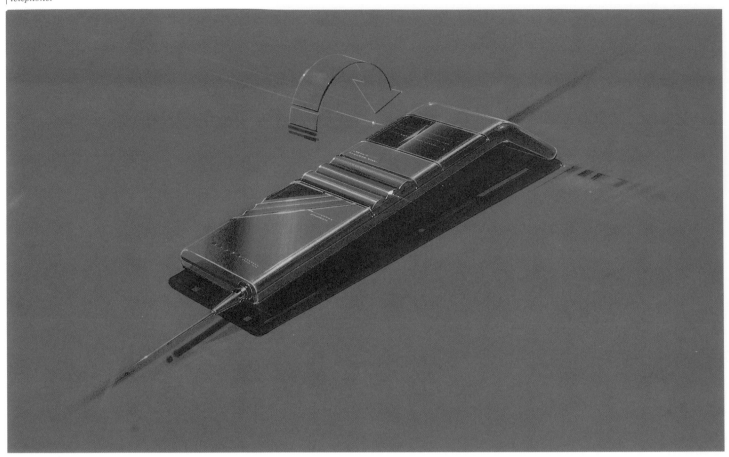

白のカラーペンシルでデザインラ
インを描く

Draw in the design lines with white colored pencil.

白のポスターカラーで文字をいれ
る
注）文字のインディケーションは
簡潔に

Insert the letters with white poster color.
NB : The letter indications should be left brief.

ディスプレイ部やキャストシャド
ウなどは，黒の細描きマーカーで
描く

Use a slender black marker to draw the display and cast shadow.

粉状にした白パステルを，重ね
折りしたティッシュペーパーにつ
け，極めて簡潔にハイライト部分
を表現する

Apply powdered white pastel to a double-folded tissue and express the highlight sections very briefly.

ボディーの稜線のぼかしは黒パス
テルで表現する
パステルで線を引くと粉が線上に
残り，それを指でなぞって稜線の
ぼかしをする

Use black pastel to shade off the ridge line of the body. Run a finger along the pastel line to shade off the ridge.

白のポスターカラーによるハイラ
イトライン

The highlight lines in white poster color.

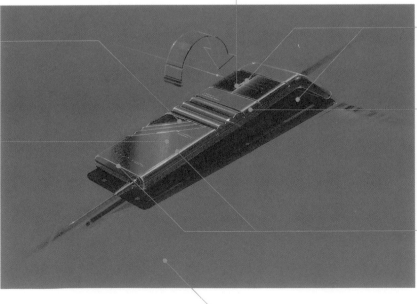

パントンカラーペーパー（グリー
ン）を使用

Pantone color paper (green) has been used.

クルマをスケッチする

A3サイズレイアウトペーパー（PMパッド白）

黒のカラーペンシルでラインドローイングのあと，マーカー，パステルで極めて簡潔にリフレクションやキャストシャドウなどを描きいれたヴァリュースケッチである。

省略法を駆使してのびのびと描いたつもりだが，技法書掲載を意識したためか，スケッチが硬くなった。

Sketch of a car

A3 layout paper (white PM pad)

This is a value sketch with a very simple expression of the reflection and shadow added using marker and pastel after the black colored pencil line drawing process.
My intentions were to produce a free and easy drawing using an abridged method, but unfortunately the sketch has turned out to appear hard. Maybe I was concious of the fact that my drawing techniques would be published.

❶任意の白い紙に，黒の細描きマーカーや黒色鉛筆で，クルマがアトラクティブに見えるパースアングルを設定し，フリーハンドで大まかに線描きする。

❶*Select the most attractive perspective angle for the car and use the free-hand method to create a rough line drawing on any white paper with a slender black marker or a black colored pencil.*

❷フリーハンドで描かれたラインドローイングの上にトレーシングペーパーを重ね，レンダリングカーブ定規を使い（フリーハンドでもよい）黒のカラーペンシルで形体を整えていく。

❷*Place a sheet of tracing paper on top of the free-hand line drawing and use a rendering curve ruler (also possible by free-hand) and a black colored pencil to adjust the shape.*

❸最小限に必要な線だけで完成したアンダーレイ。（下図・下絵）

❸*The completed underlay with the least necessary lines.*

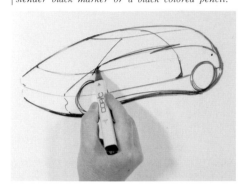

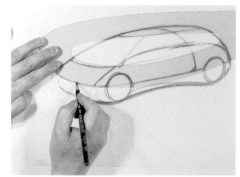

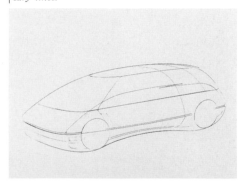

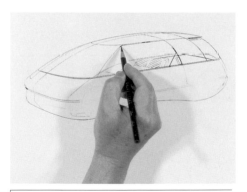

❹アンダーレイの上にレイアウトペーパー（PMパッド白）を重ね，黒カラーペンシルでデザインライン，キャストシャドウなどを線描きする。

ボディーの明るい部分の輪郭線やハイライトラインは細くうすくいれる。

❹*Place a piece of layout paper (white PM pad) on top of the underlay and work on the line drawing design lines and shadows with a black colored pencil. The outlines of the lighter part of the body and the highlights should be drawn thinly and vaguely.*

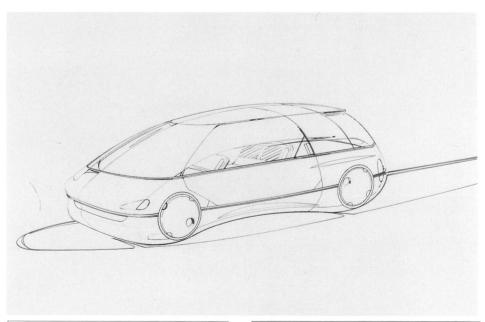

❺黒のカラーペンシルによって描かれたクルマのラインドローイングスケッチ。

❺*The line drawing sketch of the car in black colored pencil.*

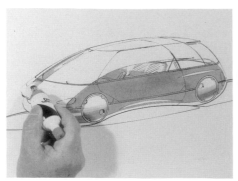

❻クールグレイマーカーNo.4でボディーのリフレクション，インテリア，ディテールを簡潔に描く。

❻*Use a cool grey marker No.4 to draw in the reflection, interior and details briefly.*

❼クールグレイマーカーNo.7〜8でボディーのディテールを描きこむ。

❼*Use a combination of cool grey markers between No.7 and No.8 to draw in the details.*

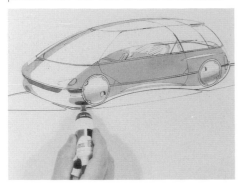

❽黒細描きマーカーでウィンドーのリフレクション，キャストシャドウ，ディテールを描く。
　ウィンドーにリフレクションの入った部分は，クルマのインテリアが透けて見えるように描く。

❽*Draw in the reflections on the window, the cast shadow and the details in a slender black marker.*

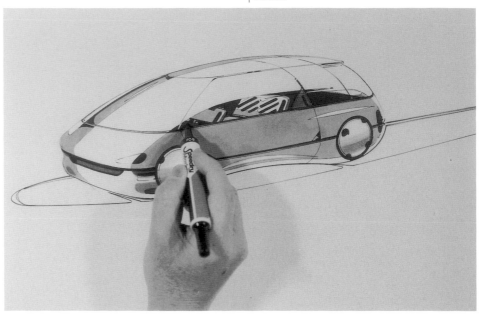

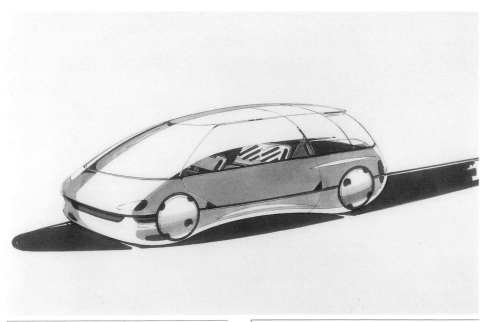

❾クールグレイマーカー，黒マーカーによる処理が終わったスケッチ。

❾*The sketch with the cool grey marker and black marker work complete.*

❿ダークグレイのパステルを粉状にし，重ね折りしたティッシュペーパーまたは白ネルにつけて，ウィンドー前面にかるくリフレクションをいれる。
　練りゴム，消しゴムなどでパステルのはみだしをふきとる。

❿*Apply powdered dark grey pastel to a double-folded tissue or piece of flannel to insert the reflection on the front window with a gentle touch.*
Wipe off the excess pastel with a kneaded rubber or eraser.

❶完成したクルマのスケッチ。
備考）このクルマのデザインをベースにして，
クレイモデルが製作された。

❶*The completed sketch of the car.*
NB : This design was used to make a clay
model.

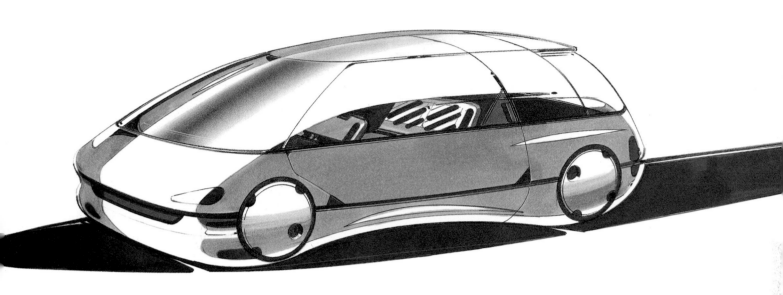

黒のカラーペンシルで，デザイン
ライン（外形線），キャスト・シャド
ウなどをラインドローイングする
ボディーの明るい部分の輪郭線や
ハイライトラインは細く，弱くい
れる
Use a black colored pencil for
the line drawing and design
lines (external lines) and the
shadow.
The outlines of the light areas
of the body and highlight lines
should be thin and vague.

ウィンドーのリフレクション部分
は，室内がすけて見えるように表
現する
The description of the internal
parts should be drawn on the
window reflection to offer a
transparent look.

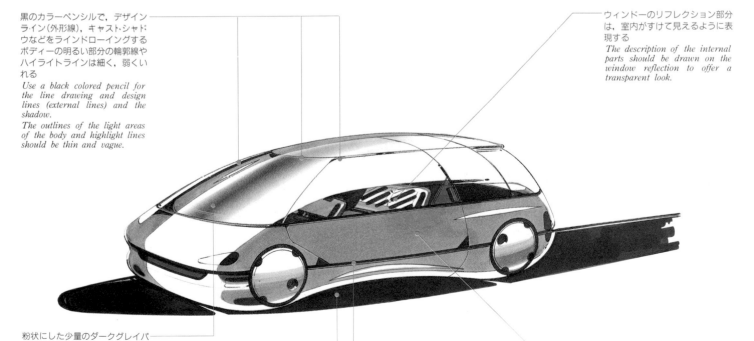

粉状にした少量のダークグレイパ
ステルを，重ね折りしたティッシ
ュペーパーなどにつけ，極めて簡
潔にウィンドー前面のリフレクシ
ョンを描く
Apply a little powdered dark
grey pastel to a double-folded
tissue and draw in the reflection
on the front window very brief-
ly.

黒マーカーでキャストシャドウを
いれ，画面を引き締める
Draw in the cast shadow with a
black marker to tighten up the
picture.

黒の細描きマーカーでディテール
やパーティングラインなどを描く
Use a slender black marker to
draw in the details and the
perspective lines.

クールグレイマーカー№.4でボデ
ィーのリフレクションをいれる
Use cool grey marker No.4 to
draw in the reflection on the
body.

ジェット機をスケッチする

A3サイズヴェラム紙（VR紙）

機体を黒ボールペン，黒水性サインペンでラインドローイングのあと，マーカー，若干のパステルで簡潔に明暗の差をつけて描いたヴァリュースケッチである。

独特なマーカーのぼかし塗りができることと，紙の両面（裏と表）描きで微妙なハーフトーン表現がしやすいことから，ヴェラム紙を使った。

およそ構造を無視して描いた非科学的なジェット機のスケッチだが，デザイン造形処理の練習にはよい題材であろう。

スケッチ時間は50分位。

Sketch of a jet plane

A3 Vellum paper (VR paper)

This is a value sketch with brief shading added with a marker and a touch of pastel after the completion of the line drawing sketch of the airplane with a black ball-point pen.
The Vellum paper was especially chosen here as it allows a special shade-off technique with markers to take place. With the use of delicate drawing on both sides of the paper, half tones can also be easily expressed.
It is a sketch of an unscientific jet plane drawn without respect to its construction, but this is good practice for the formative process of a design.
The sketch took approximately 50 minutes.

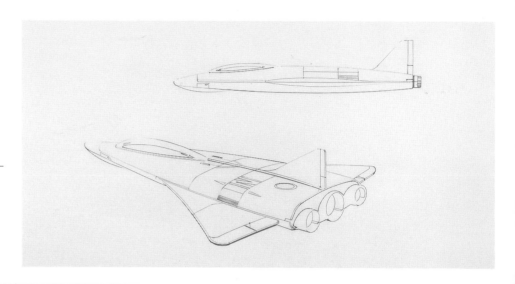

❶アンダーレイ（下絵・下図）の上にヴェラム紙を重ね，黒ボールペン，黒水性サインペンで線描きをする。

機体の明るい部分の外形線（デザインライン）やハイライトラインは細くうすくいれる。

フリーハンドで描きにくい線はカーブ定規などを使って表現する。

❶Place a sheet of Vellum paper on top of the underlay (rough sketch, rough drawing) and use a black ball-point pen and a water color felt-tip pen to do the line drawing.
The external shape lines on the light areas of the plane and the highlight lines should be drawn in with thin and vague lines.
Use a curved ruler to draw the lines which are difficult to attain free-hand.

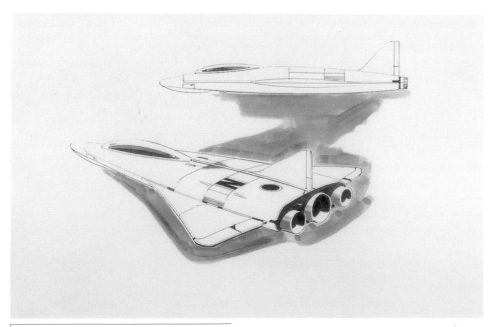

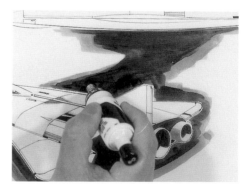

❻ダークグレイマーカーNo.7で処理したバックグラウンドの上から，さらに黒マーカーを塗り画面全体を引き締める。

❻Use a black marker to paint over the background which has already been treated with dark grey marker No.7 in order to tighten up the entire sketch.

❺ダークグレイマーカーNo.7によるバックグラウンド処理終了。
備考）　バックグラウンドの描き方に定義はないが，ここでは二つのジェット機をバックグラウンドでジョイントさせて表現し，"めりはり"と"動き"のある画面構成にした。

❺The background process with the dark grey marker No.7 is now complete.
NB : There is no definition of how the background should be drawn, but here I have joined the two planes with the background to produce a modulation and movement to the picture.

❼黒マーカーによるバックグラウンド処理終了。

❼The background process with black marker is now complete.

❷ヴェラム紙の裏面よりダークグレイマーカー
を塗る。
　マーカーの裏描きで，微妙なハーフトーンを
表現する。

❷*Use a dark grey marker to paint from the back side of the Vellum paper to express the delicate half tones.*

❹バックグラウンドを描く。
　ダークグレイマーカーNo.7で任意にバックグ
ラウンドを塗る。

❹*Draw in the background.*
Use dark grey marker No.7 to paint the background in any style required.

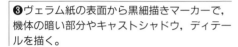

❸ヴェラム紙の表面から黒細描きマーカーで，
機体の暗い部分やキャストシャドウ，ディテー
ルを描く。

❸*Draw in the dark area of the airplane, the cast shadows and the details from the front side of the paper with a slender black marker.*

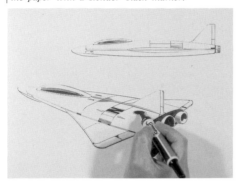

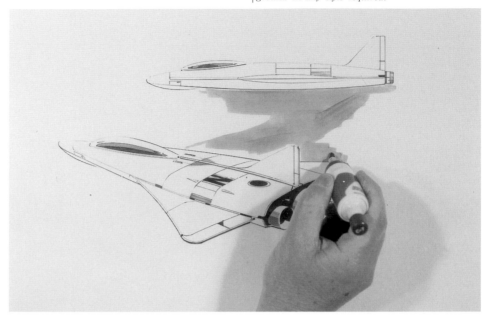

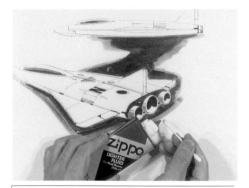

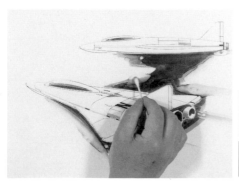

❽綿棒にマーカーの溶剤（ライターオイルまた
はフローマスタークレンザー）を若干しみこま
せる。

❽*Dip an application Q-Tip gently into a marker solution (lighter oil or Flo-Master Cleanser).*

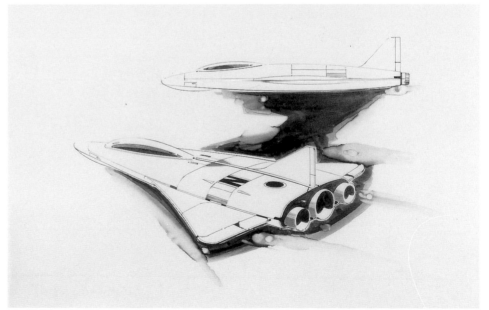

❿バックグラウンド処理すべて終了。

❿*The background process complete.*

❾マーカーの溶剤をしみこませた綿棒で，バッ
クグラウンドの任意の部分をぼかし，雲のイメ
ージを表現する。

❾*Use the Q-Tip with its marker solution to express an image of clouds by shading off any area of the background.*

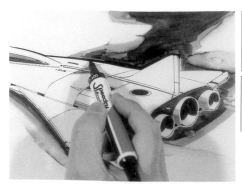

⓫マーカー処理の終わったスケッチ全体をながめ，必要があれば手を加える。
　ここでは，黒細描きマーカーを使って，デザインラインの一部を強調した。

⓫Take an overall view of the sketch with the completed marker work and add extra work if necessary.
Here I have used a slender black marker to emphasize a part of the design lines.

⓬黒のパステルで，ジェット機ボディーの稜線に沿ってかるく線を引く。
備考）フリーハンドでパステルの稜線引きが難しければ，定規を使って描く。

⓬Draw a gentle line along the ridge line of the body of the jet plane with black pastel.
NB : Use a ruler if it is difficult to draw the pastel ridge line free-hand.

⓭パステルで線を引くと，粉がその線上に残り，それを指でさっとなぞると，稜線のぼかしが簡単にできる。

⓭Draw a finger along the pastel ridge line and smear the left-over pastel to the left of the line.

⓮パステルのはみだしや画面の汚れを消しゴムや練りゴムでふきとる。

⓮Rub out the excess pastel and any stains made on the sketch with an eraser or kneaded rubber.

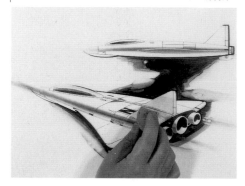

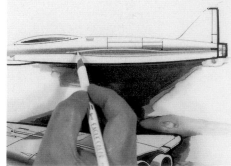

⓯スプレーフィキサチーフでパステルを定着させる。
備考）ここでは，マーカーの塗りむら防止用のマーカースプレーフィキサチーフ（BLAIR-MARKER FIX）を使った。

⓯Spray fixative to hold the pastel.
NB : A marker fixative spray to prevent an uneven coat was used here (Blair Marker Fix).

⓰白のカラーペンシルで，ハイライトライン，デザインラインをいれる。
　デザインライン，ハイライトラインはレンダリングカーブ定規を使って描く。

⓰Use a white colored pencil to draw in the highligh lines and design lines.

⓱最終仕上げ。
　白のポスターカラーで，強いハイライト部分，ハイライトライン，ハイライトスポット，デザインラインなどをいれる。

⓱The final process.
Use white poster color to draw in the sharp highlights, the highlight lines, the highlight spots and the design lines.

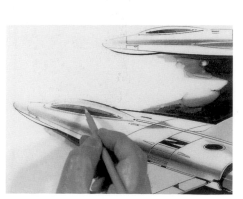

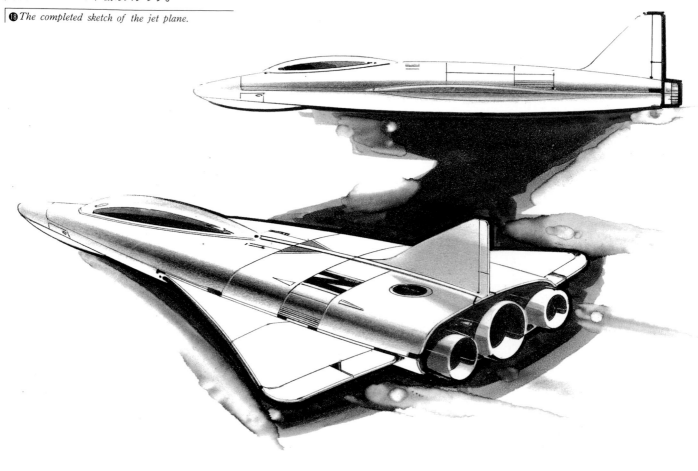

ダークグレイ細描きマーカーの両面（紙の表面，裏面）描きで，微妙なハーフトーンを描出する

Express the delicate half-tones by drawing on both sides of the paper with a slender dark grey marker.

白のポスターカラーでハイライトスポットをいれる

Add the highlight spot with white poster color.

黒のパステルで，ジェット機ボディーの稜線に沿って線を引く，線上に残ったパステルの粉を指でなぞって稜線のぼかしをする

Draw a black pastel line along the ridge of the jet plane's body and use a finger to shade off the line by smearing the powder to the left of the pastel line.

2つのジェット機をバックグラウンドでジョイントさせることで，スケッチ構図がアトラクティブになる

Join the background to make a most attractive construction attractive sketch.

バックグラウンドはクールグレイマーカーNo.7と黒マーカーを塗って表現する

Use cool grey marker No.7 and a black marker to express the background.

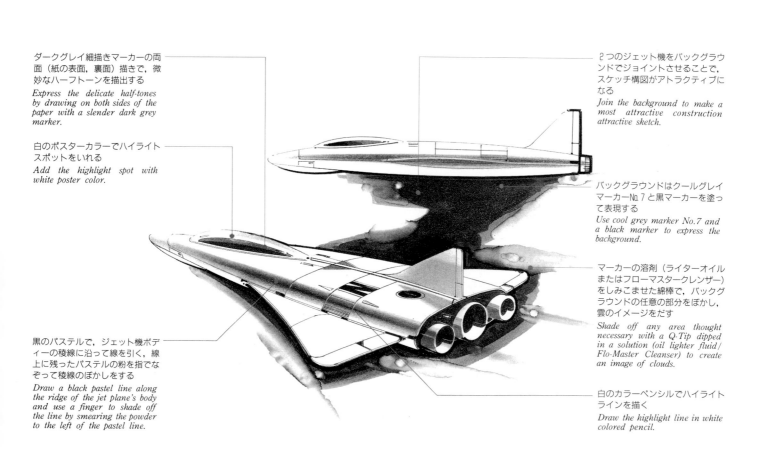

マーカーの溶剤（ライターオイルまたはフローマスタークレンザー）をしみこませた綿棒で，バックグラウンドの任意の部分をぼかし，雲のイメージをだす

Shade off any area thought necessary with a Q-Tip dipped in a solution (oil lighter fluid/ Flo-Master Cleanser) to create an image of clouds.

白のカラーペンシルでハイライトラインを描く

Draw the highlight line in white colored pencil.

6. スケッチデモンストレーションで使用した　主な画材，用具
Materials and tools used for the sketch demonstrations.

●マーカー

多種多様なマーカーが市販されているが，通常われわれが使っている代表的なものを取りあげた。

○スピードライマーカー
油性で細い線，中くらいの線，太い線等，一本で自由な描写ができる。
単品（全151色）

○スピードライマーカーピンポイント（細描き用）
油性で細描き専用。
ラインドローイング，ディテールなどを描くのに適している。
単品（全70色）

○コピック
太描きと細描きが一本についているツインタイプで，コピーのトナーを溶かさない即乾性マーカー。アルコール系マーカーなので，臭いがソフト。
単品（全142色）

その他，パントンマーカー，berol eaglecolor art marker などがある。

●ベロールフローマスタークレンザー（マーカー溶剤）

油性の液体マーカーをうすめたり，定規類に付着した汚れを落とすのに便利。
備考）ライターオイルやテレピンなども溶剤として使える。

●液体マーカー

ティッシュペーパーやコットンパッドで，幅広い面積を塗ったりするのに便利。

○コピックバリオスインク
アルコール系，混色は自由でコピーのトナーを溶かさない。

○ホルベインマーカーインク
油性で混色は自由。

● **Markers**
Many kinds of markers are available on the market, but amongst them the most popular have been used here.
○ *Speed-dry marker*
An oil-based marker for drawing various types of lines ranging from slender lines to thick lines. Sold seperately (151 colors).
○ *Speed-dry marker pinpoint (for slender drawing)*
An oil-based marker for slender drawing use. Suitable for line and detail drawing. Sold seperately (70 colors).
○ *Copic*
A twin-type marker combining functions for two styles of drawing ; thick and slender, as well as a quick-dry marker which does not dissolve copy toners. Sold seperately (142 colors).

○ *There are also Pantone markers and Berol Eaglecolor Art Markers available on the market.*
● *Liquid markers*
Liquid markers are convenient when painting wide areas using tissue paper or cotton.
○ *Copic Various Ink* *An alcohol-based marker which can be blended with various colors, but will not dissolve copy toner.*
○ *Holbein Marker Ink*
Oil-based ink which allows colors to be freely mixed.

● *Berol Flo-Master Cleanser (marker solution)*
This is a handy solution for thinning oil-based liquid markers and removing stains from rulers.
NB : Lighter or Terapin oil can also be used as a solution.

BLAIR マーカースプレーフィキサチーフ

マーカーのテカリや塗りムラ防止スプレーフィキサチーフ。
カラーペンシルのノリも比較的よい。

ニューパステル

粒子がこまかくてよくのび，混色も自由にできる。角型のステックになっているが，プロダクトスケッチを描く場合は，パステルを粉状にして使う。
（12色セット～96色セット）

白ネル

ソフトな布地で，パステルの塗りこみに欠かせない。
備考）ティッシュペーパーもパステルの塗りこみに適している。

イージークリーナー（練りゴム）

スケッチ画面のパステルをふきとったり，ハイライト部分を消して描出したりするのに便利。

鉛筆型消しゴム

ディテールやハイライトライン，デザインラインなどを消して描出するのに適している。

●スケッチ用紙

○トレーシングペーパー

透写しやすいので，スケッチの下描きなどには欠かせない。
また，パステルを粉にするベースとしたり，マスキングに使うなど用途は広い。

○ PM パッドホワイト

マーカー，パステル用に開発されたレイアウトペーパーで，適度の粗さ，硬さがあるためにマーカー，パステルのノリがよい。（B
2～B5サイズまで）

○ヴェラム紙（VRパッド）

ヴェラム紙は透明度がすぐれているので透写がしやすい。また，マーカー等の裏面処理で微妙なハーフトーンの表現も簡単にできる。（B2～B4サイズまで）

○パントンカラーペーパー

上質紙に刷られたもので，色ムラがなく，ハイライトスケッチには最適の用紙といえる。
（全743色）

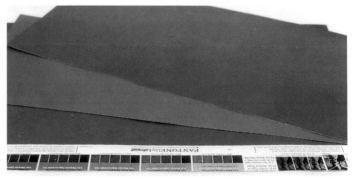

Blair Marker Spray Fixative

A spray to prevent gloss and uneven marker coats.
The colors of colored pencil can be spread quite well.

Nupastel

Spreads and blends well as it is composed of fine particles.
Comes in cube-shape sticks, but is used as a powder to draw product designs. (One set ranges from 12 to 96 colors).

White Flannel

A soft cloth which is indispensable for pastel coloring.
NB : Tissue paper can also be used for pastel coloring.

● **Easy-cleaner (kneaded rubber)**

A handy tool to wipe out pastel on sketches or express highlights by erasing them.

● **Pencil Eraser**

This is suitable for expressing details, highlights and design lines.

● **Sketch Pads**

○ *Tracing Paper*
An indispensible tool for drawing rough sketches as objects can be traced well.
It also has a wide range of applications such as being used as a base to powder pastel or masking.

○ *White PM Pad*
Having been especially developed for marker and pastel use, this layout paper has a certain roughness and hardness in quality which makes
markers and pastels spread well.
(Sizes from B2 to B5 are available).

○ *Vellum Paper (VR Pad)*
Having an excellent transparent quality, Vellum is ideal for tracing. Delicate half-tones can easily be expressed by using both sides of the paper for marker work.
(Sizes from B2 to B4 are available).

○ *Pantone Color Paper*
No uneven marks will be left on this top quality paper which is most suitable for highlight sketches. (743 colors).

●アクリル直定規

下描き，ラインドローイング，溝引きをする時に使う。（長さ40セ
ンチ，アクリル製，溝付き）

●楕円定規

透明塩化ビニール製で，円の透視図表現には欠かせない定規。投
影角15°〜60°まで20枚組が使いやすい。

●レンダリングカーブ定規（いづみやんカーブ定規）

曲線の表現には欠かせない定規。（Ａ型，Ｂ型，Ｃ型それぞれ10
枚組）

●ボールペン（細）

スケッチのラインドローイングに使う。
サインペンより細い線を引くときにはボールペンのほうがよい。

●バニーマスキングテープ

半透明，幅９ミリ〜40ミリまで。

●白ポスターカラー

チューブタイプ，スケッチの最終仕上げ段階で，ハイライトライ
ン，ハイライトスポットなどの描出に使う。

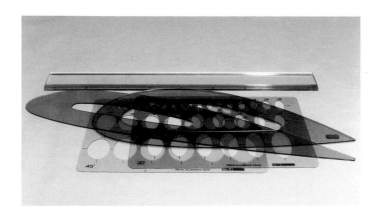

●ベロールイーグルカラーペンシル

芯が柔らかいので，マーカーなどで描いた上からでも色がのり，
スケッチ最終仕上げのタッチアップには欠かせない。（12色セット
〜72色セット）

●水性黒サインペン

スケッチのラインドローイングや下描きに使用する。（0.2ミリか
0.3ミリがラインドローイングには使いやすい）

●筆

面相１号〜３号，スケッチ最終仕上げ段階で，ハイライトライン，
ハイライトスポットなどの描出に使う。

●ティッシュペーパー

パステルの塗りこみ，定規類などの汚れを拭いたり，その用途は
広い。

●ナイフ（NT カッター）

● **Acrylic Straight Ruler**
*This is used for rough sketches, line drawings
and slotted ruler drawings.*

● **Eliptical Template**
*This is a clear polyvinyl-chloride ruler indis-
pensible for expressing circles or perspective
drawings. This example with twenty templates
in a set containing the projection angles from
15° to 60° is recommended.*

● **Rendering Curve Ruler**
*Another indispensible tool for expressing
curves. There are three types - A, B, C - and
one set comes with 10 rulers respectively.*

● **Berol Eaglecolor Pencil**
*Indispensible for those final touches on a
sketch as the lead is soft and they draw well
on top of markers.
(12 colors to 72 colors in one set).*

● **Water-color Black Felt-tip Pen**
*Used in line drawing of sketches and rough
drawing. (0.2mm-0.3mm thickness is suitable
for line drawing).*

● **Ball-point Pen (slender)**
*Used for line drawing in sketches.
Ball-point pens are more suitable for drawing
slender lines than felt-tip pens.*

● **Bunny Masking Tape**
*Semi-transparent, the widths available are
from 9mm to 40mm.*

● **White Poster Color**
*A tube type which is used to express highlight
lines and highlight spots on the final stages
of a sketch.*

● **Brushes**
*Available in sizes ranging from No.1 to No.3
and used to express highlight lines and highlight spots during the final stages of a sketch.*

● **Tissue Paper**
*Tissue paper has a wide range of applications
such as being used for coloring or wiping of
the marker stains stuck onto rulers.*

● **Knife (NT cutter)**

PAPER MODEL MAKING

ペーパーモデル
メーキング

小島 孝
Takashi Kojima

ペーパーモデルメーキングにあたって

デザインプロセスの中でデザイナーは自分のイメージ，アイディアを第三者へ的確に伝える手段が必要となる。その際の手段としてレポート，スケッチ，図面，モデルといった方法がとられる。アイディアの具体化におけるステップとして形状，量感，質感そして色彩など平面的表現から立体的表現に移行してモデリングによるイメージの展開や確認が行われる。大別するとモデルには下記の種類がある。

1. イメージモデル──デザイナー自身のイメージ，アイディアの展開・確認用。
2. ラフモックアップモデル──イメージ，アイディアの具体化や比較・検討，確認用モデル。スタディモデルともいう。
3. プレゼンテーションモデル──提示用モデルで検討，確認，決定への最終デザインモデル。
4. プロトタイプモデル──製品機能を備えた商品同等の試作品でワーキングモデルともいう。

モデルはその性質や段階によって使用される材料や制作の完成度に当然の事ながら差異が生じるため，その時々の目的や条件に合わせた材料の選択，加工方法でのモデル制作が必要となる。
ペーパーモデルはイメージモデル，ラフモックアップモデルに適し仕上げ方によってプレゼンテーションモデルにもなる。また，他のモデル材料に比べ加工性に優れ特殊な設備や工具も不要で，机上で手軽に，早く制作できる。軽いため持ち運びも簡単で場所を選ばず検討確認ができる。
しかしペーパーモデルにおいても不得手なところがあり，クレイモデルでは比較的容易にできる複合 R など三次曲面のモデリングが難しいのである。それを補うためにペーパーモデルの場合，スタイロフォーム EK，発泡ウレタン，発泡アクリルなどと組み合わせることにより三次曲面のモデリングに対応できる。さらにモデリングの際，使用できそうな現品（ツマミ，スイッチ，LED など）はそのまま組み込むとよい。また，組み立てた際に生じるパーツ間のギャップなどにはケント紙，イラストレーションボードなどの紙類の厚みを利用すると便利である。
このように身近にある素材，物品を上手に活用することもモデルワークを速やかに進めるために必要である。
本編においては基礎編と制作編の二部構成になっており制作編は基礎編の応用で，まずは実際に基礎編を何度も練習して身につけることをお勧めする。それにより各自の目的や条件に合ったペーパーモデルメーキングのお役に立てれば幸いである。

モデルボードの性質

発泡スチロールの両面に純白サラシクラフト紙を貼り合わせたボードで，カッターナイフでのカットや紙の剥がし，ヤスリ・サンドペーパーによる削りなどで折り曲げや R が容易に得られ，表面処理もスプレー塗装・刷毛塗りが可能で，別紙はもとよりカッティングシート・スクリーントーンの貼り込み，インスタントレタリングの転写等など仕上げによっては最終モデルにもなりうる。

Making a paper model

In the course of a design process, a designer inevitably need means to convey his image or idea to others in an accurate and precise manner. Such means include reports, sketches, drawings or models.

The step to follow in the embodiment of ideas will start with shapes, volume, qualities, and colors, which should be referred to as undimensional expressions. The next step will be to develop and verify the images by means of a modeling techniques, which should be referred to as a multi-dimensional expression.

Modeling will be summarized under the following categories :

1. Image models——for development and verification of a designer's own images or ideas
2. Rough mock-up models——for visualizing, comparing, studying, or verifying images or ideas
3. Presentation models——models for exhibition purposes which should provide information to finalize studies, confirmation and decision-making
4. Prototype models——they are also called working models, which are made on an experimental basis but equipped full product functions.

The level of perfection of a model varies depending on the features it carries or the materials available at the time of production. It is necessary to use materials and employ processing methods that are best suited for particular objectives or existing conditions.

Paper models can be used as presentation models if processed by adequate finishing methods to create image models or rough mock-up models (study models). In addition, paper models have superior machinability as compared whith other model materials, and do not need any special equipment or tools. Paper models excel any other model materials in the speed and ease of the production. They do not stain your hands. They are so light that they can be carried anywhere with no limitation as to the places where designers can get together and discuss with the models visualized in front of them. Despite all these advantages that paper models can offer, there is one point in which paper models are weak. It is a modeling work of three-dimensional curvature such as a combination of multiple Rs, which can easily be handled by clay modeling, but poses some difficulties to paper modeling. In order to compensate for this deficiency, paper materials are combined with such materials as styrofoam EKs, urethane foam, acrylic foam to make the models equipped with the three-dimensional curvature.

As more hints and tips which will help do your paper modeling work, we recommend the use of actual components such as knobs, switches, LEDs and so forth if their sizes sit well with your model size. If there is any gap between integral parts after assembly, you can make use of the thickness of paper materials such as Kent paper or illustration boards. Using such materials which are readily avaiable around as will facilitate the speed of paper modeling work.

This book is made up of two parts ; Basic Course and Production Course. In the Production Course, the techniques in the Basic Course are expanded to a wider range of applications. I recommend, therefore that you first learn the procedure and make models yourself in the Basic Course. As you learn the basic knowledge and apply the knowledge to a further advanced level of paper modeling, I am sure that paper modeling will be able to meet your purpose and different conditions, and make a powerful tool for you.

Property of model boards

A model board has a kind of laminated structure ; a styrofoam board sandwiched in between top and bottom pieces of pure-white bleached craft paper. It allows cutting with a cutter knife, paper peeling, shaving with a file or a sandpaper, bending, forming of curved surfaces and so on. It also allows surface finishing by spray painting as well as brush painting. It can be used even as a final model if combined with the overlay of cutting sheets, screen tone or instant lettering.

・大きさ　　B1判(800 × 1100ミリ)
　　　　　　B2判(550 × 800ミリ)
　　　　　　B3判(400 × 550ミリ)

・厚さ　　　1,2,3,5,7ミリ

・方向性

Size　　　: B1 size (800 × 1100mm)
　　　　　　　B2 size (550 × 800mm)
　　　　　　　B3 size (400 × 550mm)
Thickness : 1mm, 2mm, 3mm, 5mm, 7mm
Product orientation :

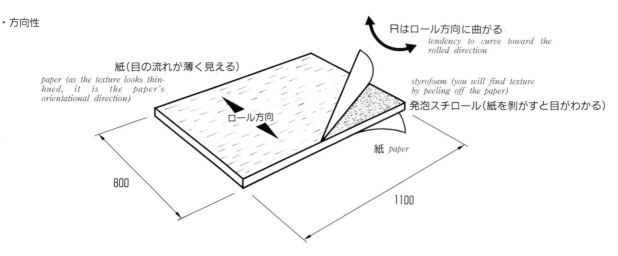

Rはロール方向に曲がる
tendency to curve toward the rolled direction

紙(目の流れが薄く見える)
paper (as the texture looks thin-hued, it is the paper's orientational direction)

ロール方向

styrofoam (you will find texture by peeling off the paper)
発泡スチロール(紙を剥がすと目がわかる)

紙 paper

800

1100

モデルボードの特性

寸法精度	0.5ミリ程度から可能
平面性	問題なし
二次曲面	ほとんど問題なくできる
三次曲面	多少は可能であるが，モデルによっては他の材料との組み合わせが必要である。
R　面	小から大まで可能
球　面	モデルによっては可能
塗　装	水性カラースプレー塗料，アクリル絵具などが可能。ラッカーエナメル塗料の使用は発泡スチロールが溶けるのでジェッソ等の下塗りまたは紙貼りを施すことにより可能であるが使用しないほうが無難である。
仕上げ	スクリーントーン，インスタントレタリングなどの貼り込みが可能

Characteristics of model boards

Dimentional availability : available from the thickness 0.5mm
Flatness : good
Quadric surface : hardly any problem
Cubic surface : possible to a certain degree, but a combination with other materials will become necessary in some cases.
Round surface : possible from mild to steep curvature
Spherical surface : possible depending on the model you make
Painting : possible——water color, acrilic, etc.
Note : When you use laquer enamel paint, underpainting of acrilics or coating of paper over the model becomes necessary because the paint dissolves styrofoam. The use of laquer enamel paint, however, should be avoided.
Finishing : Possible to stick on the model overlay films, instant lettering or lines

1. カット。

❶上紙のみをカットする。

1. Cutting

❶Cutting only paper.

← カッター
a cutter

スチール定規
a steel ruler

↓紙
paper

↑紙
paper

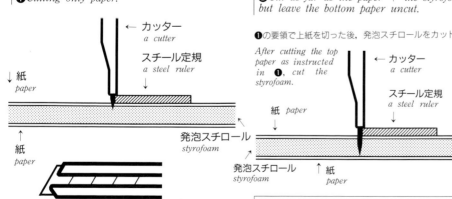

刃は短くしてカッターのこの部分をスチール定規に当ててカットする。
Set short the blade of a cutter. Push it against the ruler for a straight cutting line.

❷上紙 + 発泡スチロールまでカットする。(紙一枚残すこと)

❷Cut as far as the paper + the styrofoam, but leave the bottom paper uncut.

❶の要領で上紙を切った後，発泡スチロールをカットする。
After cutting the top paper as instructed in ❶, cut the styrofoam.

← カッター
a cutter

スチール定規
a steel ruler

紙 paper

発泡スチロール
styrofoam

発泡スチロール
styrofoam

↑紙
paper

注：カッターの刃は親指，人指し指，中指の3本でしっかり固定してカットすること。厚みのあるものをカットする時はカッターを2，3回に分けて引くときれいにできる。

❸切断する。
❷までの要領でカットした後，下紙をカットする。

❸Cutting
After completing the step of ❷, cut the bottom paper.

Note : When holding the blade against the ruler for cutting, do not slant the blade. Hold it firmly with your thumb, forefinger and middle finger. When cutting a material of a larger thickness, cutting the same place two to three times will give you a better cut finish.

❹Rをカットする。
A：モデルボードにRをトレースし、B：直線
のみカットする。C：裏返しにしてRを描き、
カッターで厚みの半分までカットし、D：表に
返してRをカットする。
注：この際カッターの刃先を使用し、数回に分
けてカットする。
他にサークルカッターでRをカットしてから直
線をカットする方法もある。(つくる物により順
序を逆にする)

❹*Cutting a rounded corner*
A. Trace a curve an a model board. B. Cut only straight lines. C. Turn the board with the bottomup, draw the curve on it and cut to half of the board's thickness. D. Again turn the board face up and cut the curve. Note : Use only the edge portion of the blade. In doing so, use a few strokes on the same line for better results. There is another way of doing this process. (The order of doing either the curve or straight line first depends on the model you are going to make.)

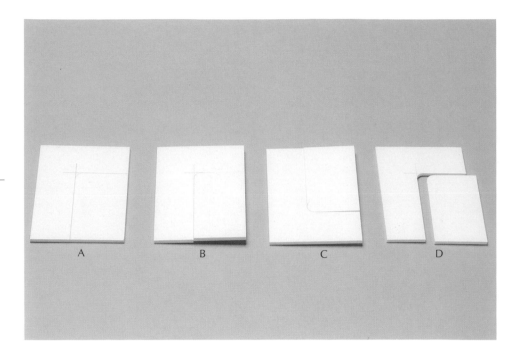

2. 角度をつける。

❶45°。
A：モデルボードに板厚と同じ幅で線を引き、
B：上紙のみをカットして剥がす。C：鉄工ヤ
スリまたはサンドペーパーで発泡スチロールの
部分を削り、D：完成。
馴れるとカッターでも可能。

2. Angle cutting

❶*45°*
A. Draw a line with the width equal to the plate thickness of a model board. B. Cut only the top paper and remove it. C. Scrape the styrofoam portion using an iron-working file or a sandpaper. D. When the styrofoam portion is finished, your work is done. As you get used to this process, you will be able to obtain the same good results using only a cutter.

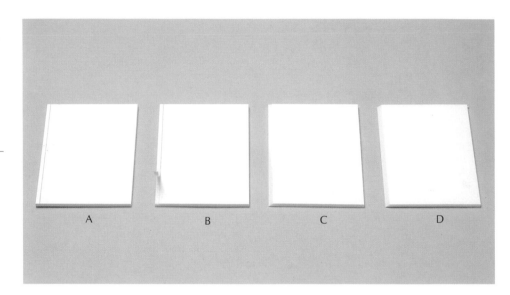

❷2枚合わせ 45°。
A：エッジを直角にカットしたモデルボードを
用意し、B：別の45°のモデルボードの切り口に
両面テープを貼る。C：互いに貼り合わせポリ・
ガンで接着する。
他に、直接スチロール用のり、クリアボンド等
で接着してもよい。

❷*Joining two pieces by 45°*
A. Prepare a model board that has its edges cut in a right angle. B. Stick a double-side tape on the cut face of 45° of the model board, which was prepared separate of the board mentioned in above A. C. Join both model boards and glue them together with a Poli-gun. You can also glue them with a styrofoam glue, Clearbond or other types of glues.

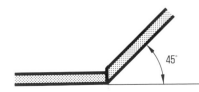

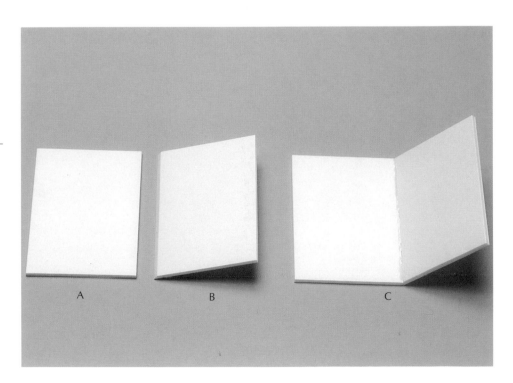

❸1枚Vカット 45°。
Ａ：モデルボードに板厚と同じ幅で線を引き，
Ｂ：一方の線は上紙のみカットし，もう一方の
線は発泡スチロールまでカットして上紙を剥が
す。Ｃ：反対に折り曲げてヤスリで発泡スチ
ロールの部分を削り，Ｄ：できた谷間に接着剤を
塗る。Ｅ：貼り合わせて完成。

❸*Cutting one piece by a 45° V*
A. Draw lines on a model board with the
width equal to the board's plate thickness. **B.**
Cut one line as far as only the top paper and
cut another line as far as the styrofoam.
Then remove the top paper. **C.** *Fold the paper*
to the other side and scrape the styrofoam. **D.**
Coat adhesive on the valley-shaped portion.
E. *Joining the boards will complete this*
process.

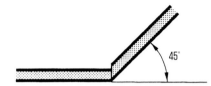

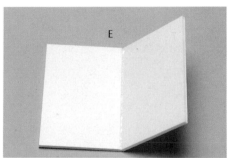

❹1枚Vカット 90°。
Ａ：モデルボードに板厚の2倍の幅とそのセンタ
ーに線を引き，Ｂ：センターの線（折り曲げ位置）
を発泡スチロールまでカットする。Ｃ：両側の
線を上紙のみカットして紙を剥がし，Ｄ：反対
に折り曲げて両側の発泡スチロールの部分を削
る。Ｅ：接着剤を塗り，貼り合わせて完成。

❹*Cutting one piece by a V cut 90°*
A. Draw a line on the center of a model
board with the width double the board's
thickness. **B.** *Cut along the center line (a*
folding line) as far as the styrofoam. **C.** *Cut*
only the top paper by the lines on both sides
and remove the paper. **D.** *Fold the board to*
the other side and scrape the styrofoam on
both sides. **E.** *Coat adhesive and join paper.*

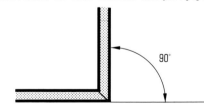

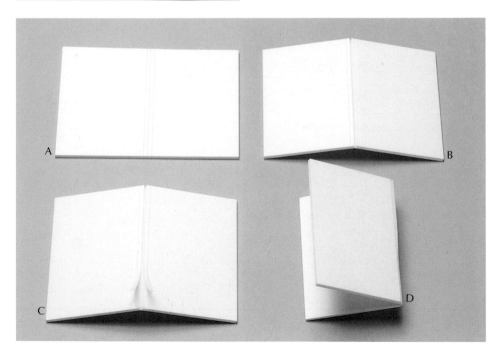

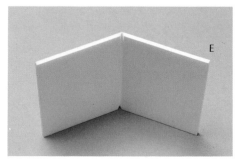

3.Rをつける。

❶小さなR-1（板厚以下）。

3. Forming a rounded corner

❶*A small rounded corner 1 (less than the plate thickness).*

ヤスリでRをつける。 *Form a rounded corner with a file.*

❷小さなR-2（板厚以下）。
A：モデルボードに板厚より小さなRで必要な
Rの線を引き，B：上紙のみをカットして剥が
す。C：サンドペーパーで削ってRをつけ完成。

❷*A small rounded corner 2 (less than the plate thickness).*
A. Draw on the model board a curved line with smaller roundness than the board's plate thickness. B. Cut only the top paper and remove it. C. Scraping the board into a rounded corner will complete this process.

❸簡易R（板厚程度）。
A：Rをつける裏側に切れ目（上紙のみカット）
をいれ，B：折り曲げてポリ・ガンで固定する。

❸*An easy rounded corner (the rounded corner about the plate thickness).*
A. Make a slit on the opposite side to the portion where the rounded corner is to be formed (only the top paper is cut). B. Bend the board and fix it with a Poli-gun.

C：カット線2本の場合（板厚より少し大きめの
R）。

C. In the case of two cut lines (a rounded corner which is a little larger than the plate thickness).

D：カット線1本の場合（板厚程度のR）。

D. In the case of one cut line (a rounded corner which is approximate to the plate thickness).

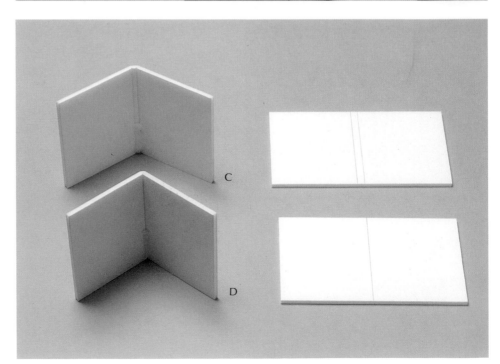

❹板厚程度のR（浅く45°のVカット）。
A：モデルボードに45°（板厚）の線を引き，B：浅くVカットする。C：折り曲げてポリ・ガンで固定する。

❹ *Rounder corner that is approximate to the plate thickness (a shallow V cut of 45°)* A. *Draw a line in a 45° (equal to the plate thickness).* B. *Make a shallow V cut.* C. *Bend the board and fix it with a Poli-gun.*

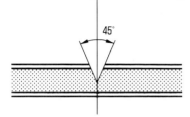

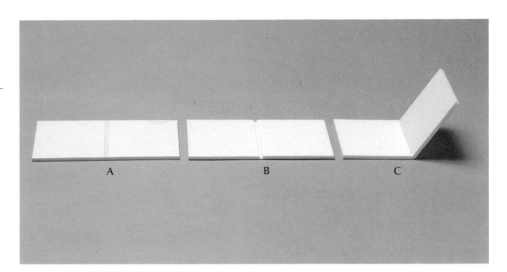

A   B   C

❺板厚程度のR（浅く90°のVカット）。
A：モデルボードに90°（板厚の2倍幅）に線を引き，B：浅くVカットする。C：折り曲げてポリ・ガンで固定する。

❺ *Round corner that is approximate to the plate thickness (a shallow 90° cut).* A. *Draw a line in the 90° (with the width double the plate thickness).* B. *Make a shallow V cut.* C. *Bend the board and fix with a Poli-gun.*

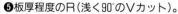

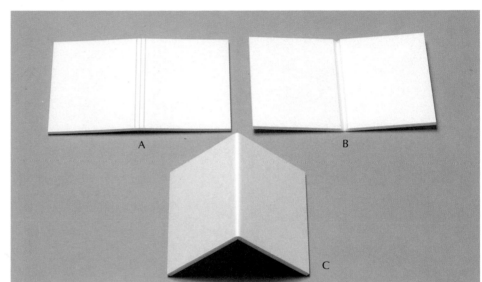

A   B

C

❻R2〜R6程度。
A：モデルボードに必要なRの寸法線を引き，B：センターから切り離して両側の線は上紙のみをカットした後ヤスリで削る。C：ボンドで接着してガラス棒でこすりながらつぶし，サンドペーパーで仕上げる。

❻ *R2〜R6* A. *Draw a line that represents the curvature of the rounded corner.* B. *Cut the board in the center and obtain the piece B. Both sides of piece* **B** *should be scraped with a file after only the top paper is peeled off.* C. *Glue all the cut pieces together with a Bond and crush the corners by scrubbing with a glass rod. Then finish the surface using a sandpaper.*

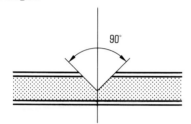

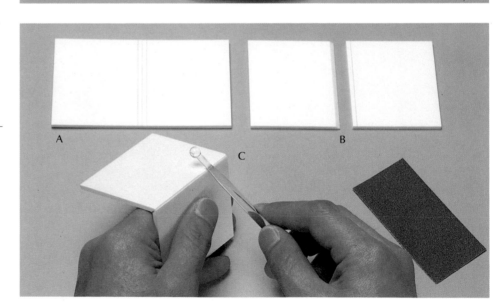

A   B

C

D：途中経過，E：完成。

D. *The rounded corner in process.* **E.** *The rounded corner completed.*

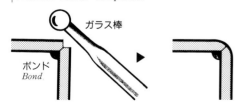

ガラス棒

ボンド
Bond

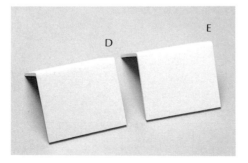

E

D

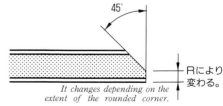

45°

Rにより
変わる。

It changes depending on the extent of the rounded corner.

❼ボードのロール方向にR。
A：モデルボードに必要なRの寸法線を引き上
紙のみをカットし剥がす。B：折り曲げて完成。

❼ *The rounded corner in the direction of the board's rolled direction.*
A. Draw a line that represents the curvature of the intended rounded couner, cut only the top paper and peel it off. B. Bending the board at the portion of the rounded corner will complete this process.

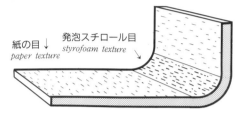

紙の目 ↓　発泡スチロール目
paper texture　*styrofoam texture*

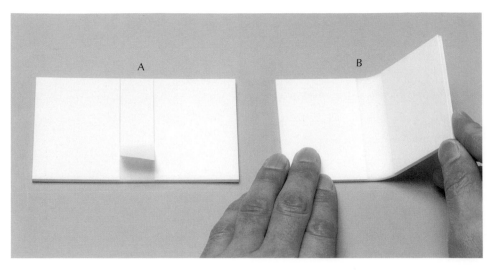

❽ボードのロール方向と逆にR。
A：モデルボードに必要なRの寸法線を引き，
B：発泡スチロールまでカットし上紙を剥がす。
C：発泡スチロールを剥がし，D：同じ幅にカットした目の逆のボードを別に用意して両面紙を剥がす。E：両面テープまたはスチのりで接着し，F：折り曲げて完成。

❽ *The rounded couner reverse to the board's rolled direction.*
A. Draw lines for the intended rounded corner. B. Cut as far as the styrofoam and peel off the top paper. C. Remove the styrofoam. D. Get ready another board that is cut in the same width and has a reverse texture. Peel off both the top and bottom papers of the board. E. Glue both boards with either a double-sided tape or a styrofoam glue. F. Bending as shown in the photo will complete this process.

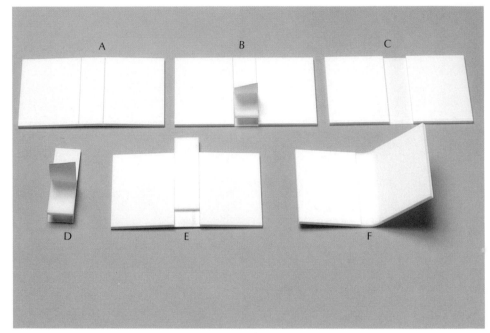

❾ロール方向に大きなR。
A：モデルボードを必要な寸法にカットし，B：裏紙を剥がし，剥がした紙に両面テープを貼る（ケント紙でも可）。

❾ *A large rounded corner in the board's rolled direction.*
A. Cut a model board to the required size. B. Peel off the bottom paper. Then stick a double-sided tape on the bottom paper. (Kent paper can also be used).

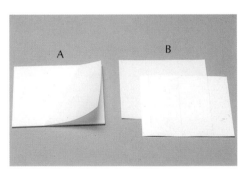

別ピースの発泡スチロール
the styrofoam of another piece

紙の目
paper texture ↓

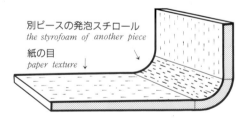

C：必要なRのリブを数本用意し，D：ベースに固定しておく（R治具）。

C. Get ready a few ribs having the required curvature. D. Mount the ribs on a base (R jig).

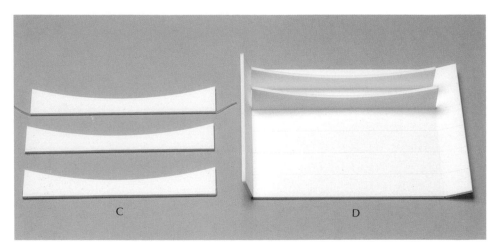

E：R治具にモデルボードの紙を剥がした面を上にして置き，両面テープのついた紙を貼る。

E. Hold the model board with the side facing upward where the paper was peeled off. Then place the board on the R jig and start gluing the paper (with a double-sided tape) on the jig.

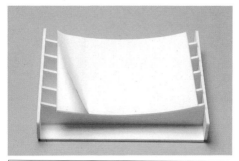

F：Rに沿ってシゴキながら接着する。このとき両面テープは少しずつ剥がしながら貼る。

F. Press the paper along the jig's curvature for adhesion. At this time, adhere the double-sided tape while stripping it little by little off its tape base.

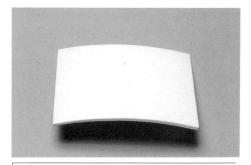

G：余分な所をカットして完成。
注：特に大きなRの場合ボードのソリRでできるものもある。

G. Cutting the extra portion will complete this process.
Note : With the rounded corners that have especially large diameters, you can sometimes make use of the natural warpage of a model board itself.

4.先端にRをつける。

❶通常のR。
A/B：モデルボードを発泡スチロールまでカットし，剥がす。C：両面テープを貼り（ボンドでも可），D：紙を巻き込み接着する。

4. Forming a rounded corner on the tip

❶*Ordinary rounded corners.*
A/B. Cut a model board as far as the styrofoam and remove the styrofoam. C. Adhere a double-sided tape. (It is also OK to use a Bond.) D. Join both pieces while rolling the paper in the joint.

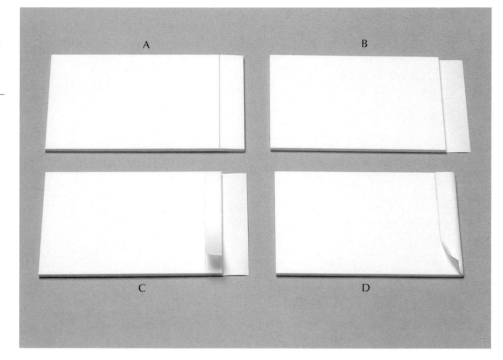

❷小さなR。
A：モデルボードを発泡スチロールまでカットしその内側に紙のみをカットした線を入れる。B：外側は発泡スチロールまで剥がし，内側は紙のみを剥がす。C：発泡スチロールを必要なRまでヤスリで削り，下紙の部分に両面テープを貼る。D：紙を削ったRに沿って巻き込みながら接着。

❷*Small rounded corners*
A. Cut a model board as far as the styrofoam. Then inside the cut, make a cut line only as far as the paper. B. Peel as far as the styrofoam for the outside and peel as far as the paper for the inside. C. Scrape the styrofoam with a file to the required roundness and stick a double-sided tape at around the bottom paper portion. D. Join both pieces while rolling the paper inside the joint portion.

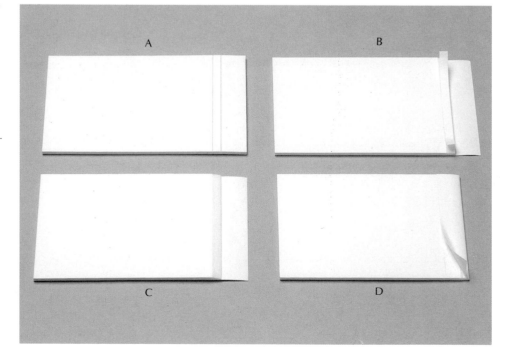

❸板厚より大きなR。
A：モデルボードに板厚の2倍以上の寸法をとり上紙のみカットし、B：紙を剥がし、両面テープまたは接着剤をつける。C：折り曲げて接着。D：大きなRが必要な時には間にボードを挟む。
注：剥がす紙の寸法はRの大きさにより異なる。

❸ *Rounded corners that are larger than the board thickness*
A. Draw a line on a model board by the width that should be more than double the board thickness. Cut along the line only to the top paper. B. Peel off the paper and adhere a double-sided paper or adhesive on the paper. C. Bend and adhere both pieces. D. When a large rounded corner is required, insert a board in between the two pieces. Note: The size of paper to be peeled off depends on the size of roounded corners.

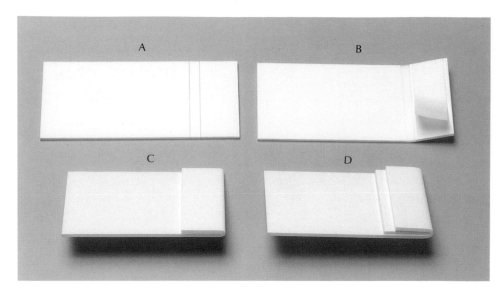

❹大きなR-1。
A：上紙を途中まで剥がし、両面テープを貼る。
B：必要なRにボードを曲げ、剥がした紙をシゴキながら元に戻す。
注：必要に応じてR治具を作成する。

❹ *Large rounded corner 1*
A. Peel off the top paper halfway and adhere a double-sided tape. B. Bend the board to the extent of the intended roundness and put back the peeled paper to its original position while removing any creases.
Note: Prepare an R jig if necessary.

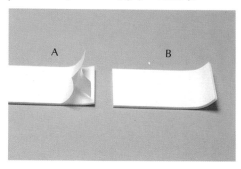

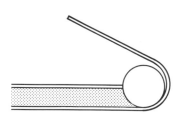

❻ヒンジ等のR。
A：モデルボードの内側は紙のみカット、外側は45°位の角度をつけて（棒の直径で多少変わる）発泡スチロールまでカットする。B：発泡スチロールを剥がし、C：両面テープを貼る。D：丸棒を用意し、E：ボードに当てて両面テープのついた紙をシゴキながら巻き込み接着する。

❻ *Rounded corners for a hinge and others*
A. Cut only the paper for the inside of a model board. Provide an about 45° angle for the outside and cut as the styrofoam. (The angle will vary to some extent depending on the rod's diameter.) B. Remove the styrofoam. C. Adhere a double-sided tape. D. Get ready a round rod. E. Apply the rod against the board and roll in the paper with the double-sided tape while removing its creases.

❺大きなR-2。
A/B：モデルボード内側は紙のみ、外側は発泡スチロールまでカットし、それぞれを剥がす。
C：残った紙に両面テープを貼り発泡スチロール部を曲げ、D：両面テープのついた紙をRに沿ってシゴキながら巻き込み接着する。
注：必要に応じてR治具を作成する。

❺ *Large rounded corner 2*
A/B. Cut a model board only as far as the paper for the inside and as far as the styrofoam for the outside. Remove the paper and styrofoam for each side. C. Adhere a double-sided tape on the remaining paper and bend the styrofoam portion. D. Adhere the paper with the double-sided paper while rolling it along the round shape.
Note: Prepare an R jig if necessary.

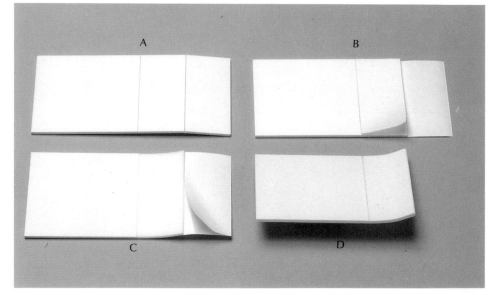

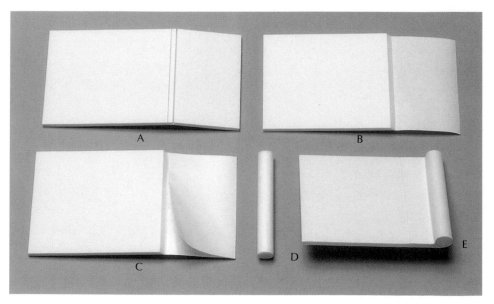

5.溝をつくる。

❶ごく浅い溝-1。
Ａ：必要寸法の幅で上紙のみをカットし，Ｂ：紙を剥がす。Ｃ：上紙の厚みを利用した溝。

5. Making grooves

❶Shallow grooves-1
A. Cut only the top paper to the width according to the required size. B. Peel off the paper. C. This groove was prepared by making use of the thickness of the top paper.

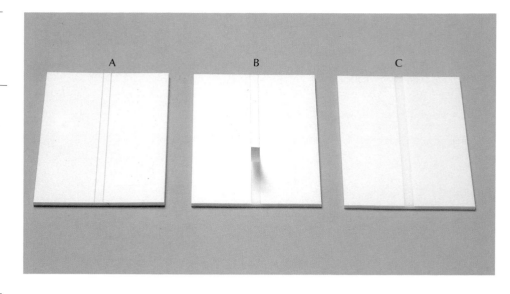

❷ごく浅い溝-2。
Ａ：必要寸法の幅で発泡スチロールまでカットし，Ｂ：上紙を剥がす。Ｃ：溝と同じ幅の物(定規等)で押し潰す。Ｄ：紙を剥がさずに押し潰した溝。

❷Shallow grooves-2
A. Cut as far as the styrofoam by the width that maches the required size. B. Peel off the top paper. C. Crush the styrofoam with a tool (a ruler or something) that has the same width with that of the groove. D. This groove was prepared by crushing without peeling off the paper.

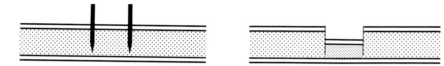

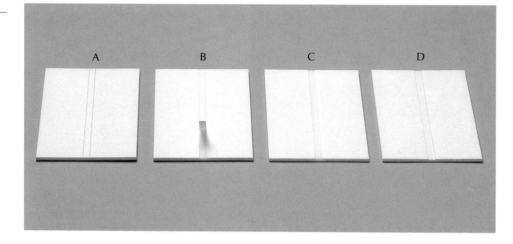

❸ボードの厚みを利用した溝-1。
Ａ：必要寸法の幅で発泡スチロールまでカットし，Ｂ：剥がす。

❸Grooves-1 to be prepared by making use of the board's thickness
A. Cut as far as the styrofoam by the width that matches the required size. B. Remove the styrofoam.

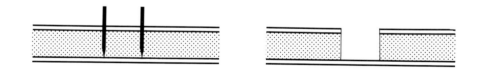

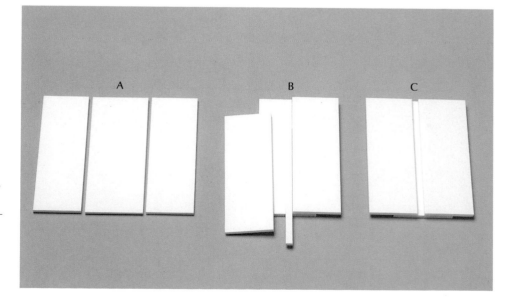

❹ボードの厚みを利用した溝-2。
Ａ：カットしたボード3枚を用意し，Ｂ：一方を接着し必要溝幅のボードを治具としてあてがい，Ｃ：もう一方のボードを接着し治具を抜く。

❹Grooves-2 to be prepared by making use of the board's thickness
A. Get ready 3 pieces of cut boards. B. Adhere two boards and place another board as a jig. C. Adhere another board and extract the jig.

❺V溝。
A：必要寸法の一方を発泡スチロールまで，もう一方を紙のみカットする。B：紙を折り曲げ，発泡スチロールをカッターまたはヤスリで削る。

❺ *V grooves*
A. Cut a width of the desired size with one line cut as far as the styrofoam and the other as far as the paper. ***B.*** *Bend the paper and scrape the styrofoam with either a cutter or a file.*

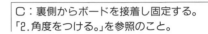

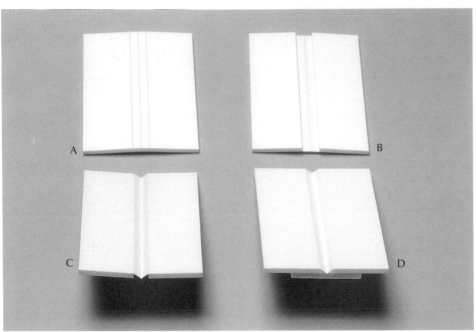

C：裏側からボードを接着し固定する。
「2.角度をつける。」を参照のこと。

C. Adhere another board on the back of the board.
see "2. Angle cutting"

❻V溝（発泡スチロール面を出さない）。
A：発泡スチロールまで必要な角度の出る幅でカットし，B：発泡スチロールを剥がす。C：裏返して谷折りに折り合わせセンターに筋をつけてから開き，両側にも折り目をつける。D：裏側にボードを接着して固定する。

❻ *V grooves (in the case that the styrofoam is not exposed)*
A. Cut the styrofoam to the depth that can give you the desired angle. ***B.*** *Remove the cut styrofoam.* ***C.*** *Turn the board upside down and make a folding line at the bottom paper of the valley, which was formed after the styrofoam was removed. Then open the valley area and make other folding lines on both sides of the center line.* ***D.*** *To the board thus processed, adhere another base support board.*

❼ごく浅いR溝。
A：必要な幅で上紙のみをカットし，B：紙を剥がす（必要であれば剥がさなくてもよい）。C：ガラス棒で押し潰し，またはサンドペーパーで削りR溝をつくる。

❼ *Shallow rounded groove*
A. Cut as far as the top paper by the required width. ***B.*** *Remove the top paper. (In certain cases, you need not remove the top paper.)* ***C.*** *Crush the styrofoam with a glass rod, or scrape with a sandpaper to make a rounded groove.*

❽R溝（発泡スチロール面を出さない）。
A：必要な幅で発泡スチロールまでカットし，B：紙を剥がす。C：発泡スチロールを剥がした後，裏返してカット線に沿って折り目をつけ，D：必要なRに間隔を詰めて裏側からボードを接着して固定する。

❽ *Rounded grooves (in the case that the styrofoam is not exposed)*
A. Cut as far as the styrofoam by the required width. ***B.*** *Peel off the top paper.* ***C.*** *After removing the styrofoam, turn the board upside down and make a folding line along the cut line.* ***D.*** *Squeeze the valley space to the length that can give you the desired roundness. Then adhere another board on the back of this board.*

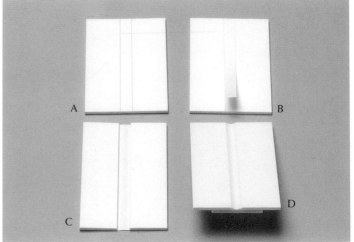

6.段差・穴をつくる。

❶板厚と同じ段差。
Ａ：板厚の幅で発泡スチロールまでカットし，
Ｂ：紙と発泡スチロールを剥がす。Ｃ：カット
線に沿って折り目をつけ，Ｄ：片側に同じ厚み
のボードを裏側から接着し固定する。

6. Making level differences and holes

❶A level difference that is equal to the board thickness
A. Cut as far as the styrofoam by the board thickness. **B.** Remove both the top paper and the styrofoam. **C.** Make a folding line along the cut line. **D.** Adhere another board of the same board thickness on the base of this structure and set all pieces fixed.

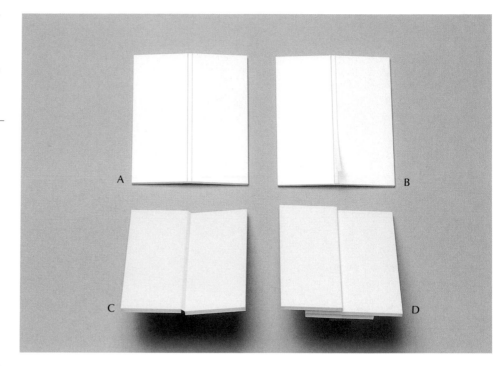

❷板厚より浅い凹面。
Ａ：モデルボードに必要寸法を引き，Ｂ：カッ
ターで切り抜く。

❷Concaves that are shallower than the board thickness
A. Draw lines for the required concave dimensions. **B.** Cut out the portion marked with the lines.

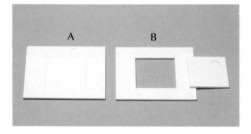

Ｆ：表に返して段差分の仮り止めを外し完成。

F. Turn the board over again and detach the temporary fittings, which will complete this procedure.

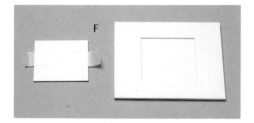

❸風穴・桟。
Ａ：モデルボードに枠線と桟を画き，Ｂ：枠線
を切り抜く。Ｃ：桟の部分を作成し，Ｄ：のり
しろに両面テープを貼る。

❸Wind holes and crosspieces
A. Draw a frame line and crosspieces. **B.** Cut out the frame line. **C.** Make crosspieces. **D.** Stick double-sided tapes on the margin to paste up.

Ｃ：必要な段差分の厚さ（イラストレーションボ
ード等）の物を表から仮り止めする。

C. Prepare a board that has the thickness equal to the required level difference (an illustration board and others), and temporarily set it on the face of the board.

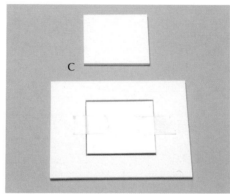

Ｄ：裏返して切り抜いたボードを重ね，Ｅ：ポ
リ・ガンで固定する。

D. Turn the board over. Place the cut board (cut in above **B**) on it. **E.** Fix the cut board with a Poli-gun.

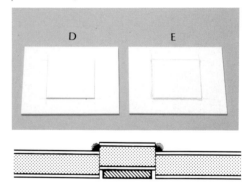

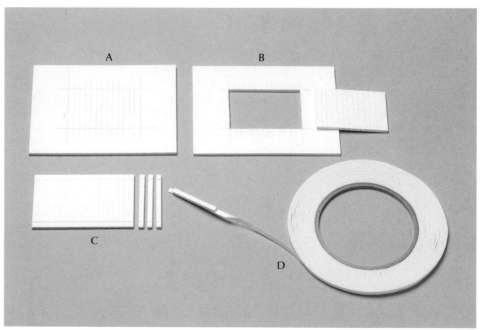

固定方法-1 E：下書きにあわせて桟を貼り，
F：完成。

*Fixing method-1. **E.** Glue each crosspiece
upon the sketch, and **F.** Gluing all crosspieces will complete the crosspiece structure.*

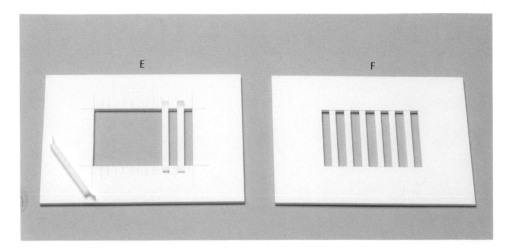

固定方法-2 G：桟を接着する時に穴の治具をつ
くり固定していき，H：完成。

*Fixing method-2. **G.** Fix each crosspiece
using a hole jig which was prepared in
advance. **H.** Setting all crosspieces will complete the crosspiece structure.*

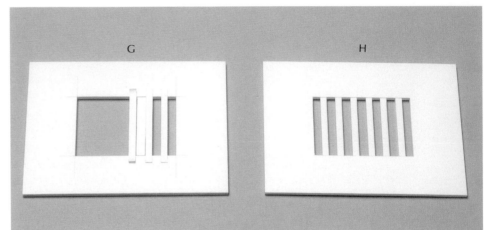

❹段差・穴の凹〜凸

*❹Level differences and holes which are
either depressed or raised.*

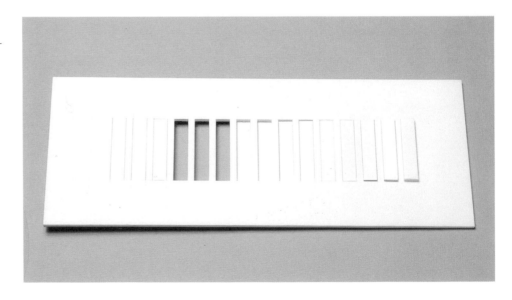

❺角穴の切り方。

❺Cutting corner holes.

1 長辺を上から
　下にカット。

*1. cutting a longer
side from up to down*

2 上下逆にして
　カット。

*2. cutting with the
upside down*

3 長辺カット。
　(裏紙も切る)

*3. cutting a longer
side (also cutting the
bottom paper)*

4 横にして短辺を
　カット。

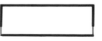

*4. cutting a shorter side
with the board set laterally
(like sticking with a blade
tip)*

5 上下逆にして
　カット。

*5. cutting with the
upside down*

6 短辺カット（裏紙は
　少しだけ切る）。

*6. cutting a shorter side
(cutting into the bottom
paper a bit, not wholly)*

7 裏返しにして
　刃先で刺す感
　じでカット。

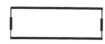

*7. turning the board upside
down and cutting like pricking
with a blade tip*

8 上下逆にして
　カット完成。

*8. setting the board position
upside down will complete this
procedure*

注：一度で切ると切り過ぎることがある。穴の大きさに合わせてカッターを変える。

*Note : If you try to cut through at one time, you may cut the portion that should not have
been cut. Please change a type of cutters, which should be more appropriate for the hole sizes.*

❻小判穴の切り方。

❻ *Cutting oval-shaped holes*

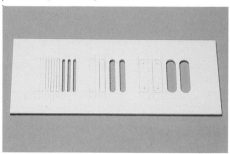

直線をカット。　Rをカット。厚みの半分切る感じ。　上下逆にしてRをカット。　裏返してRをカット。

サークルカッターでカットし針で裏紙に穴を空ける。　円に合わせて直線をカット。　裏返して同様の作業。

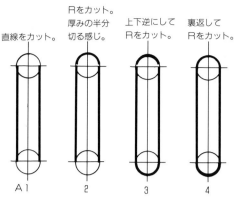

A 1　　2　　3　　4　　　B 1　　2　　3

A. 1. *cut a straight line*
2. *cut a rounded corner*
3. *set the board upside down and cut a rounded corner*
4. *turn over the board and cut a rounded corner*

B. 1. *cut with a circle cutter and make holes on the bottom paper with a needle*
2. *cut a straight line that matches the circle*
3. *turn over the board and repeat the same procedure*

7.球面を作る。

❶発泡スチロール。
Ａ：モデルボードをサークルカッターで円に切り抜き，Ｂ：表裏両面の紙を剥がす。Ｃ：指でシゴキながら球面にする。

7. *Making spherical surfaces*

❶ *Styrofoam*
A. Cut out the model board into a circle with a circle cutter. B. Peel off both top and bottom papers. C. Press the styrofoam with your fingers to form into a spherical surface.

❷大きな球面(テレビ画面等)。
Ａ：モデルボードに加工図を画く。

❷ *Large spherical surface (as a TV screen)*
A. Prepare drawings of each part on the model board.

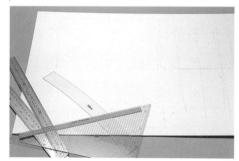

Ｂ：加工図に従い各パーツを作成する。

B. Make each part based on the drawings.

Ｃ：組み立てて，接着固定する。

C. Assemble each part and fix its structure using glue.

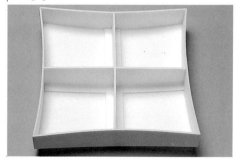

重ねた後，4ケ所にポリ・ガンをつける。

Assemble each part into a unit and apply adhesive on four points with a Poli-gun.

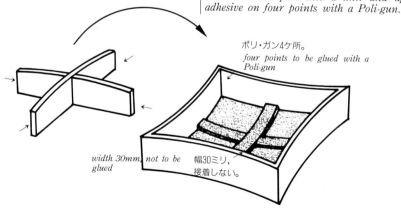

ポリ・ガン4ケ所。
four points to be glued with a Poli-gun

width 30mm, not to be glued　幅30ミリ，接着しない。

Ｄ：完成。

D. Assembly completed.

❸スタイロフォーム EK。(三次曲面)
Ａ：モデルボードでRのついた箱を作成し，Ｂ：角にスタイロフォーム EK を大きめにカットして裏面から接着。Ｃ：サンドペーパーでRに合わせて削る。

❸ *Styrofoam EK*
A. Prepare a box with rounded corners using a model board. B. Cut large pieces of styrofoam EKs and adhere them on the corners from the back. C. Shave the corners with a sandpaper to the roundness of the box.

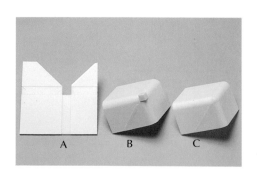

A　　B　　C

8.円筒をつくる。

ツマミ等。
A：モデルボードに加工図を画き，B：上面 サークルカッターで切り抜き，エッジを45°にカットする。C：底面 サークルカッターで切り抜き，D：側面 巻いた時に上になる側の長辺を内側に向かって45°にカットし内側の紙を剥がす。片側は適当な幅で発泡スチロールまで剥がし，のりしろをつくり両面テープを貼る。E：組み立て D を指で丸め接着し，D と B の45°カット部を合わせ接着する。最後に D の底部に C を入れて完成。

8. Making a cylinder

Knob and others
A. Make a drawing for each part. B. Cut out the styrofoam at its bottom portion with a circle cutter and cut the edge to 45°. C. Cut out the styrofoam at its top portion with a circle cutter. D. As for the barrel of a cylinder, note the side of the styrofoam which is to make the outside surface of the cylinder barrel, and cut one end af its longer side by 45° toward the inside of the cylinder body. Then peel off the inside paper of the styrofoam. Also peel the paper on the outside barrel to make a paste margin and adhere a double-sided tape there. E. Assemble the parts. Round the board with fingers, which is to make the barrel body and adhere it to upper and lower covers. Then join the 45° cut portion of D and B and glue them together. Setting the C into the base of the D will complete this procedure.

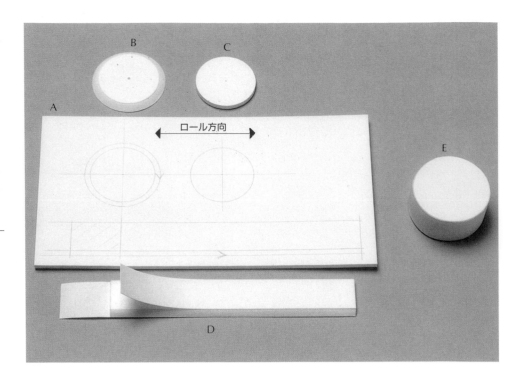

9.円錐形をつくる。

ゴム足・コップ等。
A：モデルボードに加工図を画き，B：側面 サークルカッターで切り抜き底部を55°にカットし内側になる方の紙を剥がす。のりしろの分を発泡スチロールまで剥がし，両面テープを貼る。C：底面（内）サークルカッターで切り抜く。D：底面（外）サークルカッターで切り抜きエッジを55°にカットする。E：組み立て B を指で丸めながら接着し D のカット面と合わせ固定する。補強材として C を内側から押し込んで完成。

9. Making conical shapes

Rubber stem, glasses and others
A. Draw a sketch of each part. B. Side : Cut out with a circle cutter and cut the base portion to 55°. Then peel off the paper which is to make the inside of the glass. Make a margin for paste by peeling the paper and adhere a double-sided paper there. C. Base (inside) : Cut out the base with a circle cutter. D. Base (outside) : Cut out the base with a circle cutter and cut the edge to 45°. E. Round the B with fingers, match it with the D's cut surface and fix these parts in place. Pushing the C into the inside of this structure as a reinforcing material will complete this procedure.

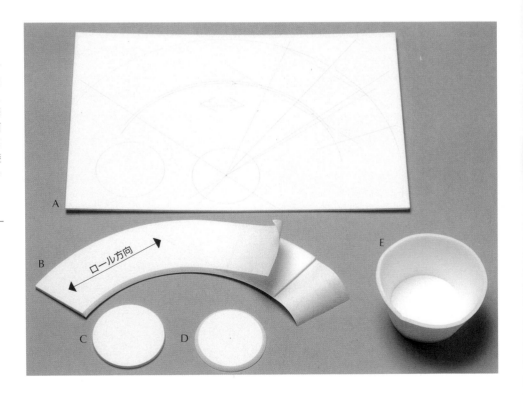

概略イメージの場合モデルボードを切る，曲げる，貼るといった作業自体はラフでよいのである。手早い作業が必要とされるため，接着においてもテープや虫ピンで止めたりしてデザイナー自身が造形確認やイメージの展開，方向づけの理解ができる程度でよい。ペーパーモデルメーキングでは展開図が重要な要素となる。展開図でモデルの性格が決定づけられるため，作業にかかる前にモデルの使用目的や制作工程などを明確にしてから展開図の作成にとりかからなければならない。

展開図作成の注意点
1.モデルの大きさの把握。
2.モデルボード板厚の選択。
3.ロール方向の確認。
4.継ぎ合わせ，貼り合わせ位置の設定。
5.展開図の確認。
6.展開図上に加工表示を記入。

この制作編は基礎編の応用なので，例えば同じ箱をつくるにしても何種類かの方法があり，接着においても，接着しやすい手順，精度が出る手順などさまざまな要素が加わってくる。ここで紹介してあるものは制作作業の種類，手順，方法の一例であることを含み学んでほしい。
モデリングには必ずこうしなければならないといった事はないので，その場の状況によってモデルに合った材料，加工手順・方法など参考例を基に各自のモデルメーキングを希望する次第である。

With the work of through image modeling, cutting, bending or pasting of the model boards should not necessarily be precise. The objective of this kind of rough modeling is speed rather than accuracy. What counts most at this level of modeling will be the facilities that allow designers to confirm their images, develop their ideas and understand the direction they are following. And this key function can be achieved simply by taping and pinning.

In the case of paper model making, an exploded drawing becomes an important factor. Since an exploded drawing determines the characteristics of one model, it is necessary to have a clear picture of the production production process as well as of the objectives for which the model is intended prior to starting the modeling work.

Notes and hints on making an exploded drawing

1. Grasping the size of a model
2. Selecting the thickness of a model board
3. Confirming the rolled direction
4. Establishing the positions of joints or pasted joints
5. Confirming the exploded drawing
6. Describing working directives on the exploded drawing

Here in this Production Course, the knowledge and techniques are further developed based on those of the Basic Course. Accordingly, a variety of other methods are mentioned for making the same simple box which appeared in the Basic Course. Likewise, simple pasting is here elaborated in more details with reference to such as may help your pasting work become more efficient and improve in the level of pasting accuracy. What we describe here may represent only part of the types of modeling, working procedures and modeling methods. We hope you enphance your familiarity with paper modeling and develop the modeling possibilities other than those I mentioned here.

Modeling does not have any definite rule you have to obey. We hope you will flexibly use materials, working techniques that you judge best fit for your specific models.

1. 組み合わせ家具をつくる(1/10スケール)
Making combination furniture items (by a scale of 1/10)

オープンボックス（小）。　Open boxes (small)

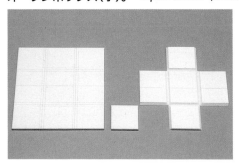

❶モデルボードに展開図を画き，Ｖカットなどの加工をする。

❶Draw an exploded drawing on a model board and do such processing as V cuts.

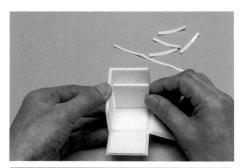

❷両面テープ，ボンドなどで接着し途中で棚板をつける。

❷Adhere the parts with a double-sided tape or Bond and furnish self boards in the course of assembly.

❸完成。扉をつける場合は棚板を板厚分短くとり，扉は内寸法にのりしろをつける。ツマミはスチロール丸棒をカットしてつける。

❸Completed. If you need a door to be also assembled, shorten the shelf boards by the length equal to the board thickness and provide margins for paste at the inside portions of the door. Kobs can be made by cutting a round styrofoam rod.

オープンボックス（大）。

❶ モデルボードに展開図を画きVカットなどの加工をする。

Open boxes (large)

❶ *Draw an exploded drawing on a model board and do such processing as V cuts.*

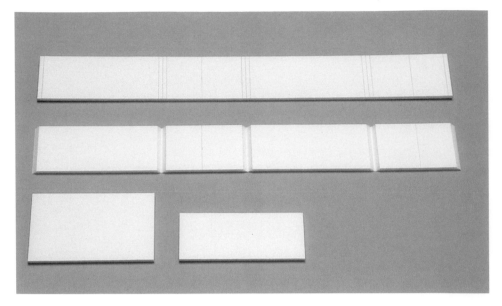

❷ 両面テープ, ボンドなどで接着し途中で背板・棚板をつける。

❷ *Put together the parts with a double-sided tape or Bond and furnish backboards and shelf boards.*

❸ 完成。

❸ *Completed.*

❹ スモーク扉をつける場合。板厚より少し広い紙に両面テープを貼り蝶板とし, 塩ビ板スモーク（t=0.5ミリ）とボード端面に貼る。

❹ *In the case of providing a smoke-finished board. Use sheets of paper having a size a little larger than the board thickness. Adhere double-sided tape on them to make hinged doors and stick them on both the smoke-finished vinyl chloride plates (t=0.5mm) and the board's edge.*

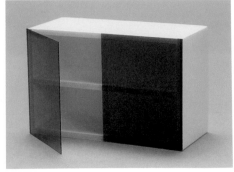

デスクユニット

❶モデルボードに展開図を画きVカットなどの加工をする。

Desk units

❶Draw an exploded view of a desk and do processing such as V cuts.

❷引き出し。
底板をつけ周囲を接着した後，手前の板を接着する。

❷Drawers
After providing a base plate and putting the enclosure parts together, adhere the front plate of the desk.

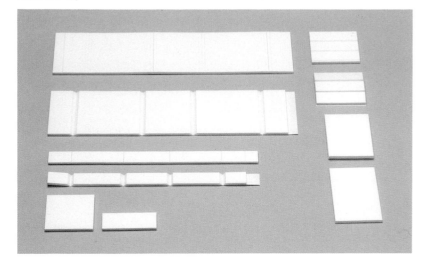

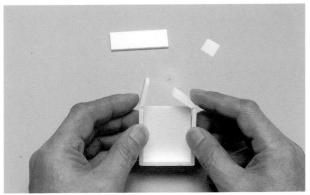

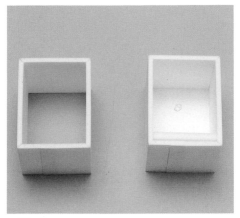

❸キャビネット。
周囲を折り曲げ底面で接着し，台座（補強材）をつけ背板を接着する。

❸Cabinets
Bend the parts forming the cabinet enclosure and joint them at the base. Then set a base platform (a reinforcing material) and adhere the backboard.

❹引き出しの上3段はダミーでそれぞれの間を1ミリ幅で発泡スチロールまで剥がす。ツマミは直径3ミリのスチロール丸棒をカットして最後に接着する。

❹The upper three drawers are gummies. A space of 1mm between each drawer can be made by removing the portion as far as the styrofoam. Knobs can be made by cutting a round styrofoam rod of 3mm diameter. Please adhere these knobs at the last step of this procedure.

❺扉の蝶板は発泡スチロールまで剥がし両面テープで接着する。

❺In order to make hinge plates for doors, peel the board as far as the styrofoam and adhere using a double-sided tape.

❻完成。

❻Completed.

ベッド。

Bed

❶ベッド台の展開図を画きVカットする。

❶ *Draw an exploded drawing of a bed base and provide V cuts.*

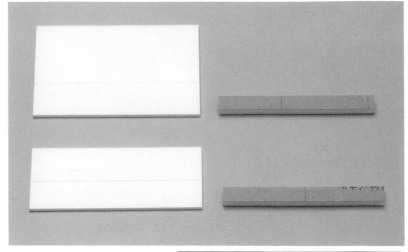

❷ベッドの上下板とベッド台差し込みストッパーのパーツ。（接着剤付パネル板 t=7ミリ）

❷ *Upper and lower plates of a bed and parts for an insertion stopper of a bed base (a panel plate t = 7mm with adhesive).*

❸ベッド下引き出しの制作はオープンボックス（小）と同じ。マットはスタイロフォーム EK。

❸ *The drawing to be installed underneath a bed can be made in the same manner as in the case for open boxes (small). A mat can be made using the styrofoam EK.*

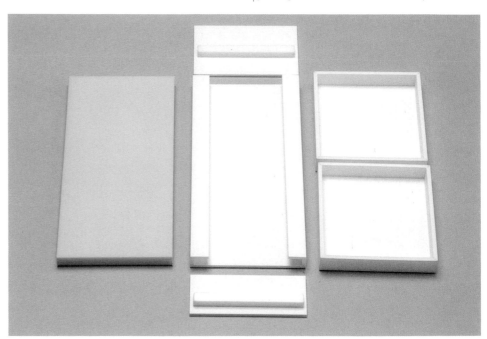

❹完成。

❹ *Completed.*

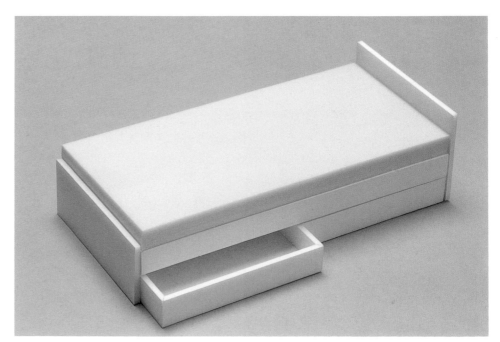

ダイニングボード。

❶ キャビネットの展開図を画きVカットする。

Dining board

❶ *Draw an exploded drawing of a cabinet and provide V cuts.*

❷ ガラス扉を加工図に沿って切り抜き，周囲をCカットする。

❷ *Cut out glass windows according to the drawing and C-cut the window outline.*

❸ 引き出しはダミー。下扉は蝶板用ののりしろを残す。棚板4枚。ガラスの代用は塩ビ板スモーク（t＝0.5ミリ）を裏側から両面テープで接着する。ツマミはスチロール丸棒をカット。仕切り板1枚をそれぞれ接着し組み立てる。

❸ *Drawers are dummies. Please leave a paste margin for hinge plates with the lower doors. The number of shelf boards is 4. To imitate glass, adhere a smoke-finished vinyl chloride plate (t=0.5mm) from the back using a double-sided tape. Knobs can be made by cutting a round styrofoam rod. Assemble the dining board by gluing one partition plate for each board.*

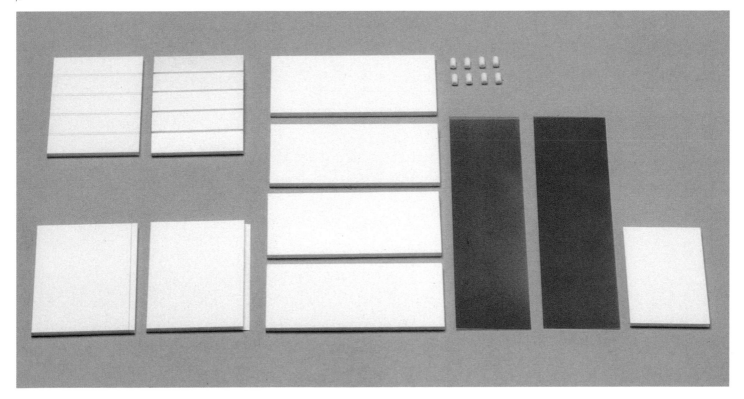

❹完成。

❹*Completed.*

❶ディスプレイ上ケース(接着剤付パネル板 t=7ミリ)Aとディスプレイ下ケース(モデルボード t=5ミリ)Bにそれぞれ加工寸法図を画く。

❶*Draw a sketch of a digital telephone with specific dimensions on both the upper display case (a panel plate with adhesive t=7mm) and the lower display case (a model board t=1.5mm).*

❷受話口の桟にカッターで切れ目をいれておく。

❷*Make slits on the crosspieces of an ear piece.*

❸カッターやサークルカッターを使い外形を切り抜く。

❸*Cut out the contour using a cutter or a circle cutter.*

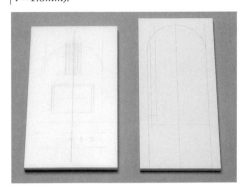

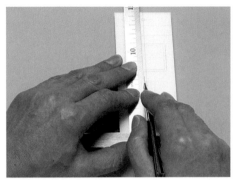

❹ディスプレイ窓を切り抜き周囲をCカットし,モデルボード t=5ミリを窓と同じサイズにカットしておく。

❹*Cut the display window and C-cut the same portion. Get ready the model board 5mm and cut it in the same size as with the window.*

❺ディスプレイ上・下ケースの内側にアンテナ用の溝をカッターや丸ヤスリで削る。

❺*Make a groove for an antenna inside both the upper and lower display cases with a cutter or a round file.*

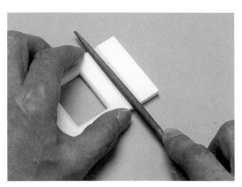

❻電源ボタン部の凹Rをヤスリで削る。

❻*Scrape the power button portion into a depressed rounded shape with a file.*

❾周囲Rをサンドペーパーで作成する。

❾*Streamline all the rounded corners with a sandpaper.*

❽ディスプレイ上・下ケースを合わせてディスプレイ窓と同じサイズのモデルボードを埋め込み接着する。

❽*Match the upper and lower display cases. Put a model board with the same size as the cut-out window into the portion. Then glue them all.*

❿ヒンジパイプ用の窪みをつける。

❿*Making a depression for a hinge pipe.*

❼上部Rをサンドペーパーで作成する。

❼*Form the upper portion of the power button into a rounded shape with a sandpaper.*

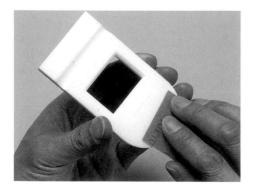

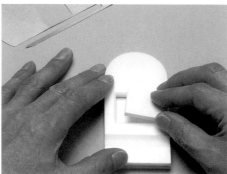

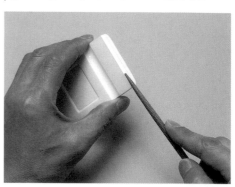

❸貼り合わせて余分な紙はカットする。

❸*Stick both together and cut off any extra paper.*

❹ヒンジ受け部分（ダイヤルボタンベースのヒンジ）の紙をカットする。

❹*Cut the paper at the portion where the hinge rests. (In the case of a push button type telephone.)*

❶固定用紙に両面テープを貼り，表側の凹Rから指でシゴキながら接着する。
ヒンジ固定用紙材料：モデルボード剥がし紙。
ヒンジ材料：直径3ミリの真鍮パイプ。

❶*Adhere a double-sided tape on the fixed paper and paste it starting with the depressed rounded portion of the front side while pressing the tape for removing the creases. Paper material to be used for fixing a hinge : paper peeled from the model board. Material to be used as a hinge : a brass pipe of 3mm diameter.*

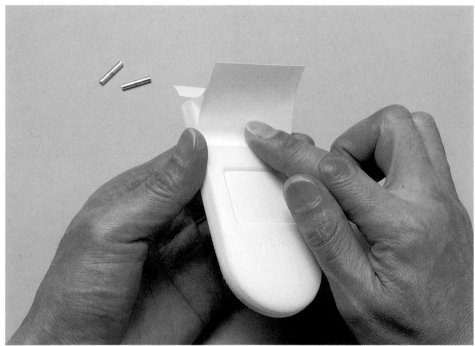

❷裏返しにしてヒンジパイプを窪みに固定し，両面テープのついている紙を指でシゴキながらパイプに沿って接着する。

❷*Turn over the board and fix a hinge pipe in the depressed portion. Adhere the paper with a double-sided paper along the pipe while pressing the tape for removing creases.*

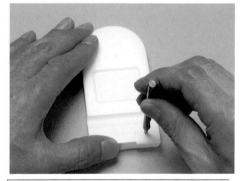

❸表側の操作ボタン用穴を革ポンチであける。

❸*Make the holes for operation buttons on the surface with a leather punch.*

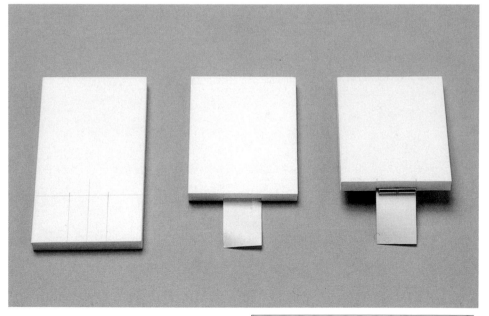

❹ヒンジ巻き込み部分を残してカットし，両面テープでヒンジをつける。
ダイヤルボタンベース材料：モデルボード t＝7ミリ。
ヒンジ：直径3ミリの真鍮パイプ。

❹*Cut the area except the portion where the hinge is installed and then mount the hinge with a double-sided tape. Base materials for dialing buttons : a model board t＝7mm. Hinge : a brass pipe of 3mm diameter.*

⓱ヒンジの丸みに沿って紙をしっかり接着する。

⓱*Adhere the paper firmly along the hinge's roundness.*

⓲ディスプレイケース側ヒンジの余分をカットする。

⓲*Cut the extra portion of the hinge on the display case side.*

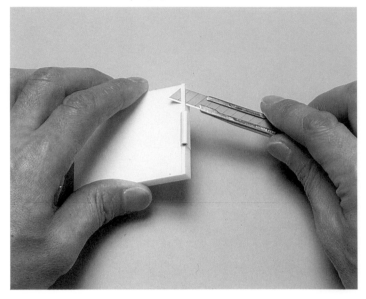

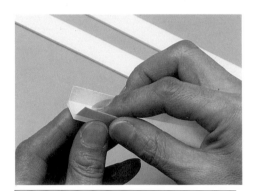

㉑カッターで両側のR作成ガイドを切る。

㉑*Cut the rounded corner guide lines on both sides with a cutter.*

㉒上質紙でダイヤルボタン用の巻き込み紙をつくり，紙の全面に両面テープを貼り，凹Rに合わせて指でシゴキながら接着する。

㉒*Prepare wrapping paper for dial buttons using quality paper. Adhere a double-sided tape on the entire area of the paper. Roll the paper into a stick form while pressing with fingers for removing creases.*

㉓できたボタンの棒を必要寸法にカットする。

㉓*Cut the stick into each individual button size.*

⓲ダイヤルボタンベース飾りをカットして革用ポンチで凹穴をあける。
材料：イラストレーションボード　t＝1ミリ。

⓲*Cut the button accessories and make depressed holes with a leather punch. Materials : an illustration board t＝1mm.*

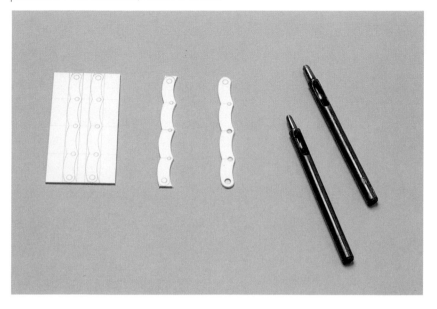

⓴ダイヤルボタンは大きめのボードに必要寸法の幅で発泡スチロールまでカットし，上紙を剥がしヤスリで凹Rをつける。
材料：モデルボード　t＝3ミリ。

⓴*In order to make buttons, cut a larger board as far as the styrofoam by the required width and peel off the top paper. Then form rounded corners with a file. Materials : a model board t＝3mm.*

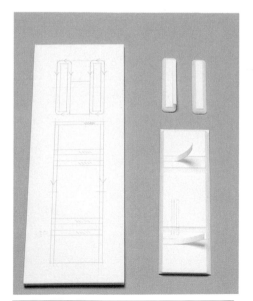

㉔送話ケースを加工図に従い外形を45°にカットし必要な部分の上紙や発泡スチロールを剥がす。
材料：モデルボード　t＝3ミリ（ロール方向の目を長辺にとる）。

㉔*Cut the board with the outside contour cut in 45° to make a telephone case. Peel off the top paper and remove the styrofoam. Materials : a model board t＝3mm (the texture in the rolling direction should be a longer side of the handset).*

㉕送話口の桟（角穴）を表・裏両面から切り抜く。

㉕*Cut out the crosspieces (corner holes) of the mouth piece from both the top and bottom surfaces.*

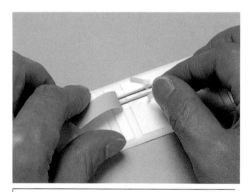

㉖送話口角穴に裏側からグレーのカラーペーパーを貼る。

㉖*Adhere a piece of grey-colored paper on the corner holes of the mouth piece rom the back.*

㉗のりしろに接着剤をつけ，裏側に両面テープで補強材を貼り固定する。

㉗Put adhesive on the margin and set reinforcing materials on the back of the margin with a double-sided tape.

㉘送話ケースの充電用穴をつくる。サークルカッターでボードの厚みの半分程度までカットする。

㉘Prepare a hole for charging the telephone case. Cut as far as about half the depth of the board with a circle cutter.

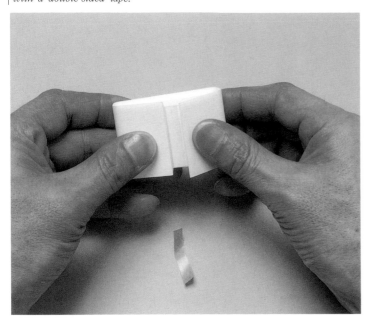

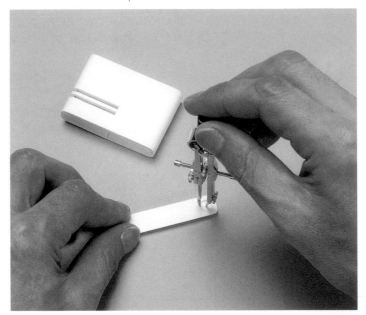

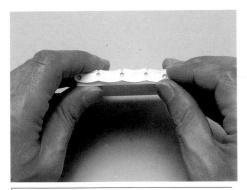

㉜ボタンベースの両側にベース飾りを接着する。

㉜Adhere base accessories on both sides of the button base.

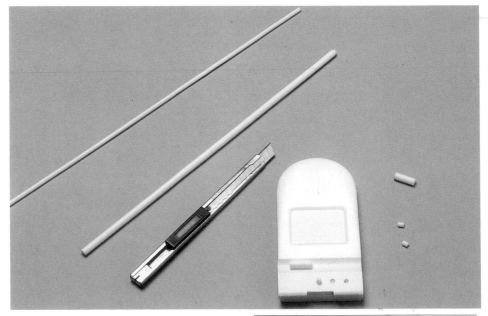

㉝ダイヤルボタンベースと送話ケースを接着する。

㉝Adhere the dial button base to the telephone case.

㉞電源ボタン（スチロール丸棒直径5ミリ）と操作ボタン（直径3ミリ）をそれぞれ接着する。この時接着剤がはみ出ないよう注意。操作ボタンは棒の先端をサンドペーパーで丸くしてカットする。

㉞Glue together a power button (cut from a round styrofoam rod of 5mm diameter) and operation buttons (cut from a rod of 3mm diameter). At this time, take caution not to let the adhesive protrude. Round the point of the rod with a sandpaper and then cut to a piece to make an operation button.

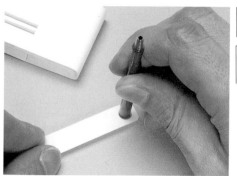

㉙カットした直径と同じ位の大きさの物で押し潰し凹にする。

㉙Crush the hole using a tool as large as the diameter of the cut hole and make it a collapsed depression hole.

㉛ボタンが曲がらず，間隔が一定になるよう注意してダイヤルボタンベースにダイヤルボタンを接着する。

㉛Adhere dial buttons on the dial button base so that each button is set straight at an equal interval.

㉚上・下とも接着して周囲に軽くサンドペーパーをかけて送話ケース完成。

㉚Join the upper and lower boards and apply light shaving on the body to complete the construction of the telephone.

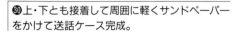

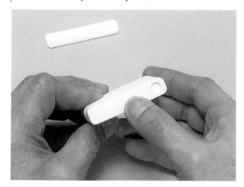

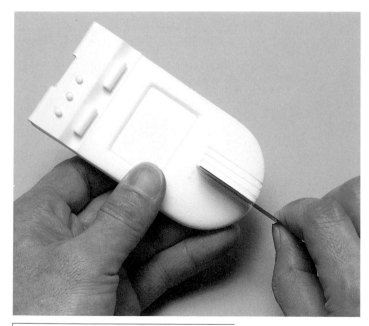

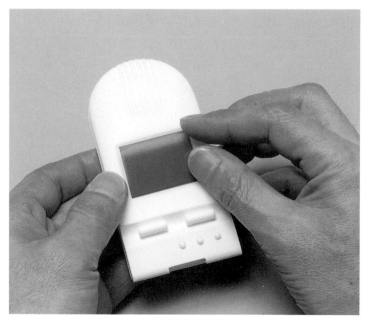

㉟受話口桟の溝をスチール定規の厚み(0.5ミリ)を利用して深さが均一になるよう押し潰し作成する。

㉟Level off the grooves for uniform depth by crushing the ear piece's grooves with a steel scale of thickness 0.5mm.

㊱ディスプレイパネルを窓と同じサイズにカットして接着する。
材料：塩ビ板 t＝0.5ミリ，パントンオーバーレイ。

㊱Cut out a display panel in the same size as with the window, and paste it.
Materials : a vinyl chloride plate t＝0.5mm, Pantone overlay.

㊲スチロール丸棒（直径5ミリ）の先端をヤスリで丸くして必要寸法にカットし，アンテナをつくる。

㊲Round the top of the round styrofoam (5mm diameter) with a file and cut into a required size for making an antenna.

㊳パントンオーバーレイを適当にカットしアンテナ上部に貼りラインをいれ，ディスプレイケースに差し込む。長短にスライドするよう接着はしない。

㊳Cut Panton overlays in a proper size and attach them on the upper part of the antenna. Draw lines and insert the antenna into the display case. The antenna is, in this case, not made to expand or contract.

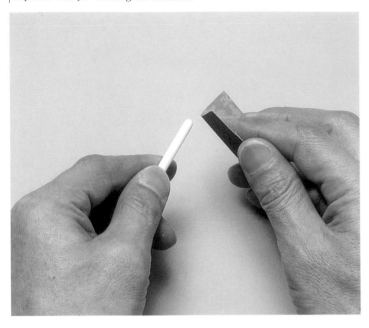

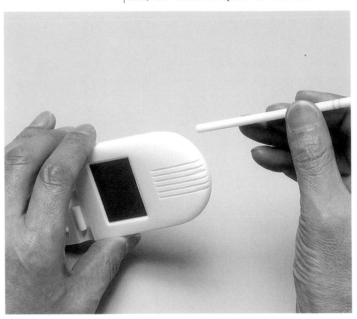

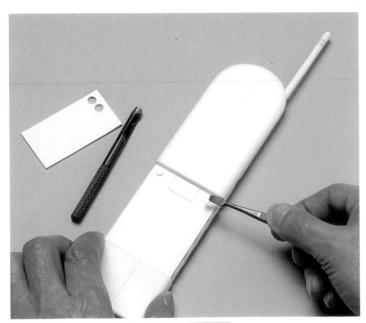

㊷ダイヤルボタンベース背面にポンチで抜いたスペーサー（モデルボード t＝2ミリ）を接着する。

㊷Adhere a spacer cut with a punch on the back of the dial button base.

㊸完成。

㊸Completed.

❸❾ディスプレイケースとダイヤルボタンベースのヒンジ部を合わせ，芯になる竹ヒゴ（直径2ミリ）を差し込む。

❸❾*Match the display case with the hinge portion of the dial button base, and insert a bamboo splinter (2mm diameter).*

❹⓿ヒンジパイプを隠すため，ケント紙をポンチで抜き接着剤をつけピンセットなどで両面に貼る。

❹⓿*In order to hide the hinge pipe, cut out Kent paper into a small piece, apply adhesive on it and adhere it on both sides with a pair of tweezers.*

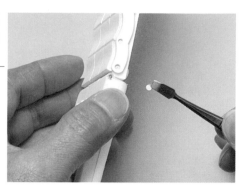

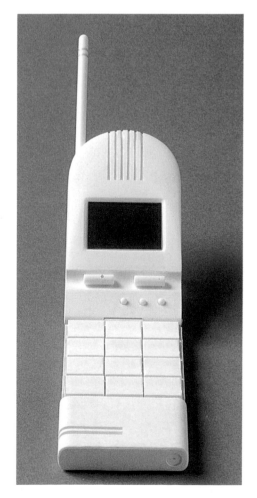

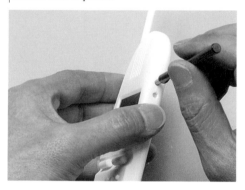

❹①音量調節穴をポンチであける。

❹①*Make a hole for the volume adjusting button with a punch.*

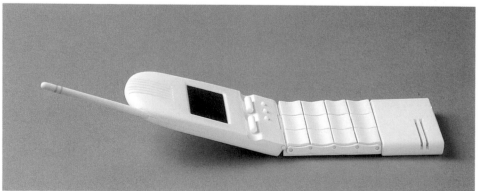

❶キャビネット。
A：モデルボードに展開図を画き，B：Vカット加工をし，発泡スチロールまで剝がす。C：折り曲げて接着する。

❶*Cabinet*
A. Draw an exploded drawing on a model board. B. Make V cuts and as far as the styrofoam. C. Bend the board and adhere ends.

❷D〜F：キャビネット寸法不足分をA〜Cと同様に作成する。G〜I：補強材。

❷*D〜F: Other portions to make up the cabinet should be made in the manner as instructed in C. G〜I: Reinforcing materials.*

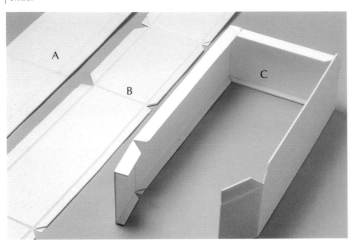

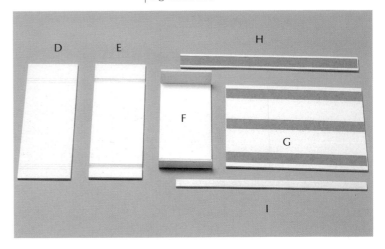

❺フロントヘッド。
A：モデルボードに展開図を画き，B：Vカット加工，紙剝がしをする。C：長手方向から接着し，D：両サイドのRを接着する。E：マスキング塗装。
注：R部は最後に接着すると誤差が少なくなる。

❺*Front head*
A. Draw an exploded drawing on a model board. B. Make V cuts and peel off the top paper. C. Start gluing from the longer side. D. Glue rounded corners on both sides. E. Mask the surface and paint.
Note : Gluing the rounded portions at the final step of this procedure will increase the dimensional tolerance during the assembly.

❻フロントケース。
A：モデルボードに展開図を画き，B：Vカット加工，R部紙のみカット。C：上・下，左・右の直線を接着し次に上紙を剝がす(ロール方向短辺)。D：R部を曲げ接着し，E：缶取り出し口ケースの逃げ穴をカットする。F：ボカシ塗装。
注：Rのついた物は接着後穴加工するとよい。

❻*Front case*
A. Draw an exploded drawing on a model board. B. Make V cuts and peel off the top paper. C. Start gluing from the longer side. D. Glue rounded corners on both sides. E. Mask the surface and paint.
Note : Cutting the corners into a rounded shape after gluing the parts will increase the dimensional tolerance during the assembly.

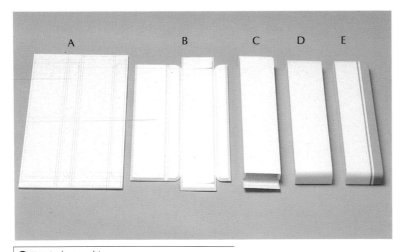

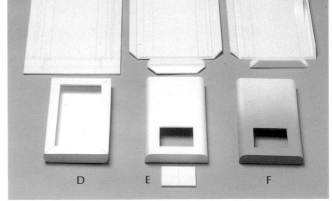

❹各パーツを組み立て，接着固定する。

❹*Assemble the parts and adhere them with glue.*

❸J〜L：センター補強材。M：スペーサー。
釣銭口ケースの逃げ穴をカットしておく。

❸*J〜L: Center reinforcing materials. M: spacer.*
Make a prepared hole for a coin return case in advance.

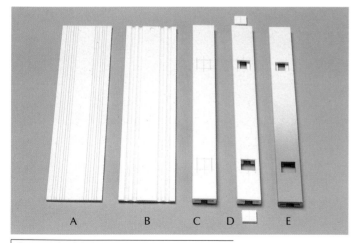

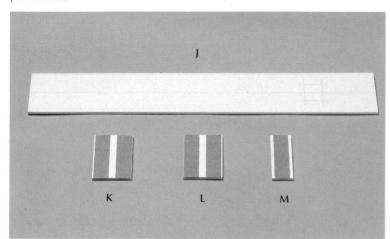

❼フロントパネル。
A：モデルボードに展開図を画き，B：Vカット加工する。C：折り曲げて接着し，D：札口・釣銭口，ケースの逃げ穴をカットする。E：ボカシ塗装。
注：切り抜き穴と折り曲げ位置が狭いときは接着固定後穴加工する。

❼*Front panel*
A. Draw an exploded drawing on a model board. B. Make V cuts. C. Bend and adhere ends. D. Cut prepared holes for a money intake case and a coin return case. E. Provide shaded painting.
Note: When the holes are too small or the space for bending is too tight, first complete the assembly of each part and then make holes.

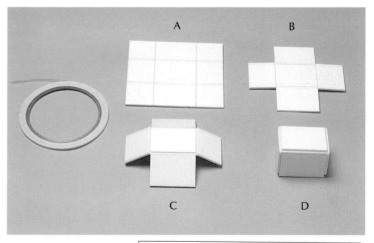

❽缶取り出し口ケース。
A：モデルボード（t＝2ミリ）に展開図を画き，B：発泡スチロールまでカットする。C：折り曲げて，D：接着。

❽*Can receiving case*
A. Draw an exploded drawing on a model board (t=2mm). B. Cut the board as far as the styrofoam. C. Bend the board. D. Adhere ends.

❾缶取り出し口フレーム。
Ａ：モデルボード(t＝5ミリ)に加工図を画き，削り線を側面にもいれる。Ｂ：裏紙を剥がし，Ｃ：ヤスリで削る。Ｄ：フレームをカットする。

❾*Frame of the can receiving case*
A. Draw a sketch on a model board (t = 5mm) and also provide lines alongside the thickness portion of the board for later cutting. B. Peel off the bottom paper. C. Scrape the styrofoam with a file. D. Cut the board into the frame shape.

❿フレームをケースに接着して塗装する。カバーは塩ビ板スモーク(t＝0.5ミリ)をカットし折り曲げる。

❿*Adhere the frame onto the case and provide painting on it. Make a case cover using a smoke-finished vinyl chloride plate (t = 0.5mm). Bend the plate to make it look like a cover.*

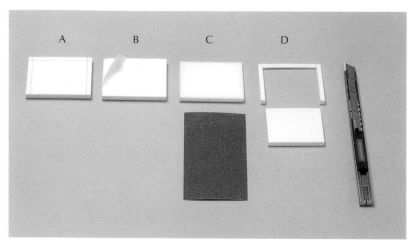

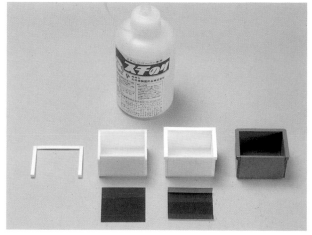

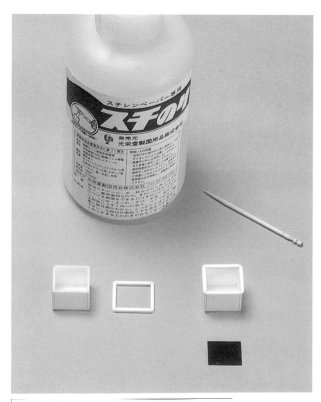

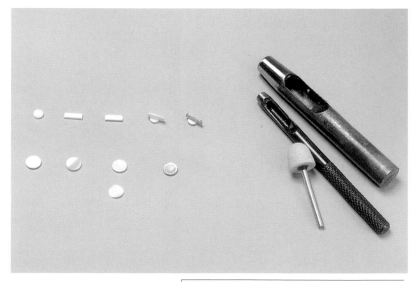

⓭フレームをケースに接着して塗装する。カバーは塩ビ板スモーク(t＝0.5ミリ)。

⓭*Adhere the frame onto the case and paint the frame. Use a smoke-finished vinyl chloride plate (t = 0.5mm) for the cover.*

⓮返却レバー・コイン投入口。
モデルボード(t＝1ミリ)をポンチで抜き，凹部・レバーをつけて塗装する。

⓮*Coin return lever and coin intake*
Cut a model board (t = 1mm) to make a coin return and a coin intake with a punch. Then provide depressed portions and psinting.

⓫札入れ口。
A：モデルボード(t=1ミリ)に加工図を画き,
B：ヤスリで4ケ所角Rをつくる。C：発泡スチ
ロールまでカットし, D：折り曲げて接着。E：
塗装。F：カバーは塩ビ板スモーク(t=0.5ミ
リ)。
注：細かいものの接着は楊枝などを使うと便利。

⓫*Money intake*
*A. Draw a sketch on a model board (t=
1mm). B. Make four rounded corners with a
file. C. Cut the board as far as the styrofoam.
D. Bend and adhere the ends. E. Provide
painting. F. Use a smoke-finished vinyl chloride plate (t=0.5mm) for the cover.
Note : When adhering the materials of a
tiny size, toothpicks will make a convenient
tool.*

⓬釣銭口ケース。
A：モデルボード(t=1ミリ)に展開図を画き,
B：発泡スチロールまでカット。C：折り曲げ
て接着。D：フレーム加工図を画き, E：ヤス
リで4ケ所角Rをつくり, F：切り抜き。

⓬*Coin return case*
*A. Draw an exploded drawing on a model
board (t=1mm). B. Cut the board as far as
the styrofoam. C. Bend and adhere the ends.
D. Draw a frame sketch. E. Make four
rounded corners with a file. F. Cut out.*

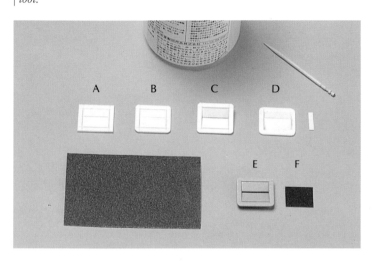

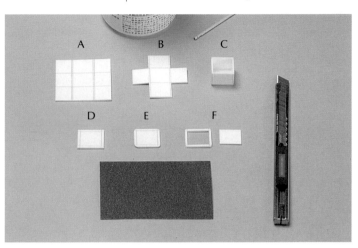

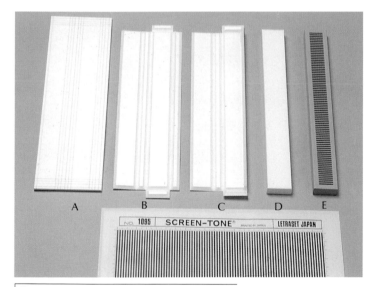

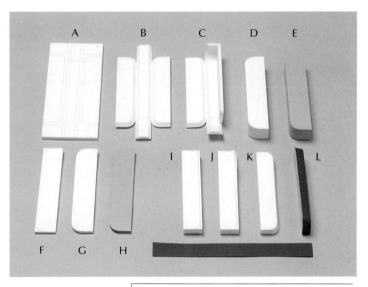

⓯通風孔。
A：モデルボードに展開図を画き, B：Vカッ
ト加工する。C：長手方向から接着する。D：
接着完了。E：塗装後スクリーントーンのスト
ライプを貼る。

⓯*Wind holes*
*A. Draw an exploded drawing on a model
board. B. Make V cuts. C. Start adhering
from a longer side. D. Adhering completed.
E. After painting, stick a stripe pattern of
overlay.*

⓰ディスプレイケース。
A～E：フロントパネルと同様に作成する。F
～H：カットして塗装する。I～K：カットして
上紙を剥がし, サンドペーパーでテーパーをつ
ける。L：パントンカラーペーパーを接着して,
はみ出した部分はカットする。

⓰*Display case*
*A～E. Make a display case in the same
manner as with the front panel. F～H. Cut
and paint. I～K. Cut and peel off the top
paper. Provide a tapered finish over the
board's tip with a sandpaper. L. Adhere a
piece of Panton color paper and cut the
protruded portions.*

71

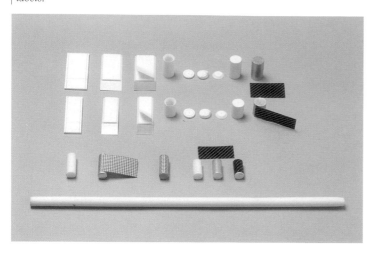

⓱缶。
制作は「8.円筒」を参照のこと。細缶は直径10ミ
リのスチロール丸棒をカットして塗装する。ラ
ベルは包装紙を使う。

⓱Cans
Please refer to "8. Making a cylinder" to make cans. For slim-type cans, cut a round styrofoam rod of 10mm diameter into cans and paint them. Use wrapping papers for the labels.

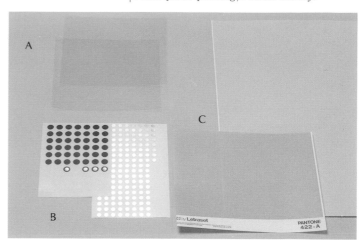

⓲Ａ：ディスプレイケースカバー/塩ビ板透明
（t＝0.2ミリ）。Ｂ：セレクトボタン/タックラベ
ル 黒-直径8ミリ，銀-直径5ミリ。Ｃ：フロント
パネル印刷/パントンオーバーレイ。

⓲A. *Display case cover/a transparent vinyl chloride plate (t＝0.2mm).* **B.** *Selection buttons/black tucking labels (8mm diameter), silver tucking labels (5mm diameter).* **C.** *Front panel printing/Panton overlay.*

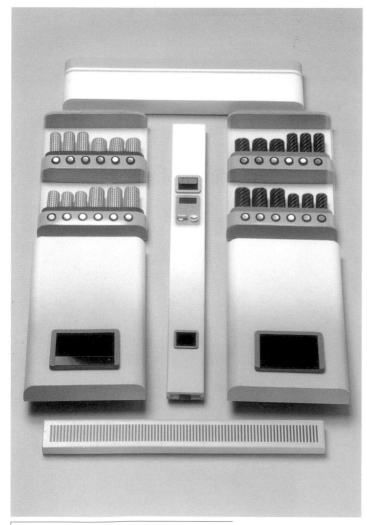

⓳各部品を接着，組み立てる。

⓳*Adhere each part and assemble.*

⓴完成。

⓴*Completed.*

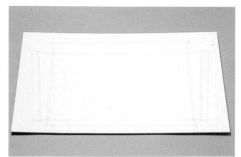

❶アンダーケース。
モデルボード(t=3ミリ)に展開図を画く。

❶*Under case*
Draw an exploded view on a model board (t = 3mm).

❸発泡スチロールを剝がし，折り曲げて接着する。

❸*Peel off the styrofoam. Bend and adhere the ends.*

❷Vカットなどの加工をする。

❷*Make V cuts and other preparations.*

❹ポリ・ガンによる接着。

❹*Adhere the parts with a Poli-gun.*

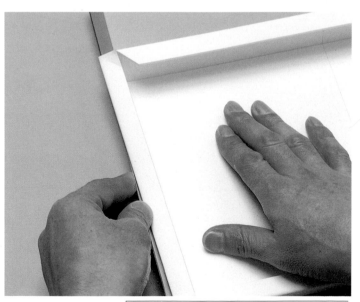

❺長い部分はスチール定規などをあてて折り曲げる。

❺*When bending a longer side, use a steel ruler for a straight bending line.*

❻アッパーケース。
モデルボード（t＝3ミリ）に展開図を画きVカット
などの加工をする。

❻*Upper case.*
Draw an exploded view on a model board
(t＝3mm) and make V cuts.

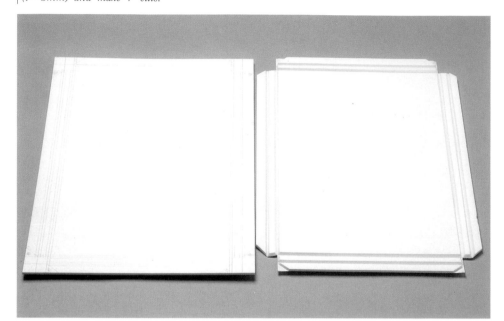

❼折り曲げ・接着の際には角材を使うと便利。

❼*When bending or adhering, a square bar*
will make a useful tool.

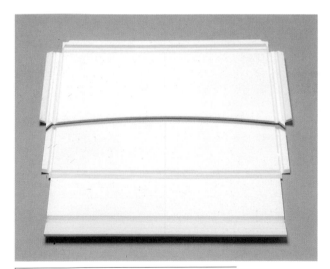

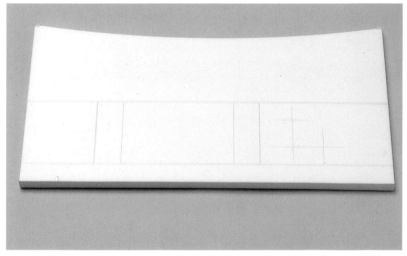

⓫Vカットなどの加工をする。

⓫*Make V cuts.*

⓬フロントケースA。
表に鉛筆で薄く線を引き，カッターで上紙のみ
をカットする。

⓬*Front case A*
Draw a thin line on the surface and cut
along the line as far as the top paper.

❾スペーサー。
モデルボード(t=3ミリ)に❶でつくるフロント
ケースBのスタンド用穴を，角度をつけてあけ
る。

❾*Spacer*
A hole for a stand of a front case B (to be made by ❶) should be made with a certain angle.

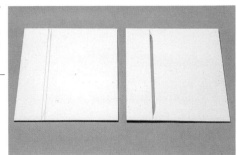

❽接着固定した後，ハンドセットフックの逃げ
穴などをあける。

❽*After gluing and fixing the parts, make prepared holes for a handset and others.*

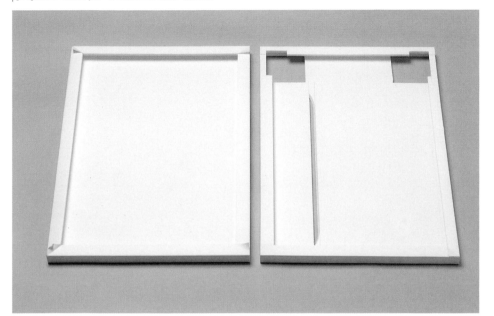

❿フロントケースA・B。
モデルボード(t=3ミリ)に展開図を画く。

❿*Front case A + B*
Draw an exploded view on a model board (t = 3mm).

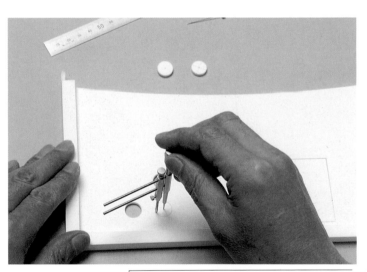

⓭サークルカッターでプッシュボタンの穴と周
囲凹の外周を厚みの半分ぐらいカットした後，
虫ピンでセンターの穴を裏まで通す。

⓭*First cut to about half the board thickness with a circle cutter to make the holes for push buttons as well as for the peripheral areas around the holes. Then pierce a pin through to the bottom of the board.*

⓮裏返して虫ピンの穴をセンターにサークルカ
ッターで穴を抜き，抜いた円はプッシュボタン
として使用する。

⓮*Turn the board over. Align the center of a circle cutter with the hole made with the pin and cut out a hole. The cut-out circle should be used as a push button.*

❻フロントケースB。
折り曲げて接着する。ソリ防止のため補強としてデザイン形状に支障のない範囲で巻き込み接着する。

❻*Front case B*
Bend the board and adhere the ends. In order to prevent warpage, bend and tuck in the extra board portion for reinforcement to the extent that such will not impair the original design form.

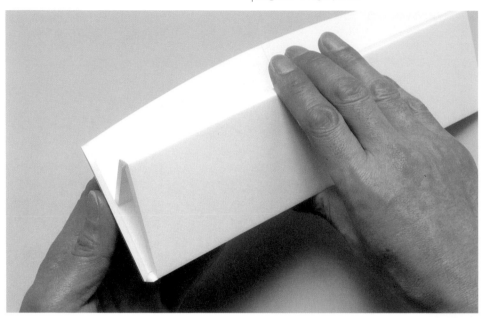

❺ダイヤルボタン位置の角穴をカットし，プッシュボタン周囲の凹をスタイラスで押し潰す。

❺*Cut the corner holes at the dial button position and crush the depressions around the push buttons with a stylus.*

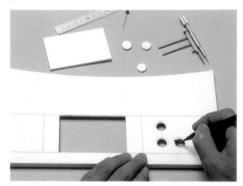

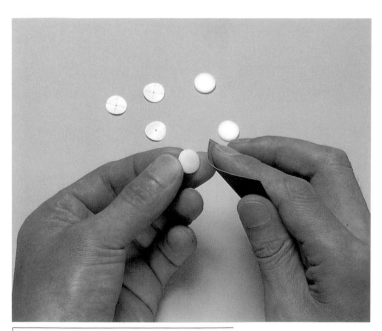

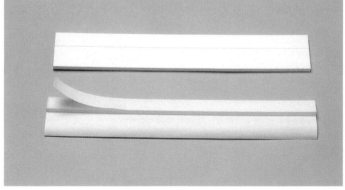

⓴ダイヤルボタン。
モデルボード(t＝5ミリ)をボタンの幅寸法で発泡スチロールまでカットして上紙を剝がす。巻き込み接着用，のりしろは発泡スチロールまで剝がす。

⓴*Dial buttons*
Cut a model board (t＝5mm) to the styrofoam by the width equal to that of buttons and peel off the top paper. Peel as far as the styrofoam for the board portions which are to used as a reinforcing board or as a paste margin.

⓳プッシュボタン。
⓮で切り抜いた円の紙を剝がしサンドペーパーで凸Rにする。

⓳*Push buttons*
Peel off the paper of the circle which was cut in the step ⓮ and shave the cut circle to make protruded curvature with a sandpaper.

⓱表に鉛筆で細い線と太い線を薄く引き分け，細い方はスチール定規15センチ，太い方はスチール定規30センチの厚みを利用して押し潰し凹溝を作成する。

⓱Draw both thin and thick lines on the surface with a pencil. Use the thin lines for a steel ruler 15cm and the thick lines for a steel ruler 30cm, both of which will make use of their own ruler thickness and crush the styrofoam for making depressed grooves.

⓲フロントケースA・Bの裏側。ソリ防止のため，折り曲げて補強してある。

⓲The back side of front cases A and B. The board is bent for reinforcement in order to prevent warpage.

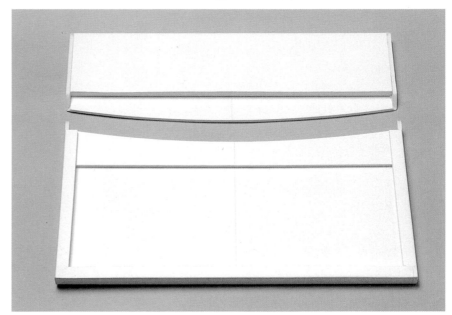

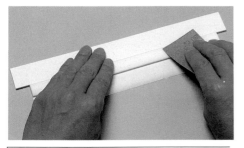

㉑モデルボード(t=3ミリ)を当てサンドペーパーのガイドとして凸Rを作成する。

㉑Apply a model board (t=3mm) and make protruded curvature as a guide for a sandpaper.

㉓カットしたダイヤルボタンを貼り合わせる。

㉓Adhere the dial buttons which were cut.

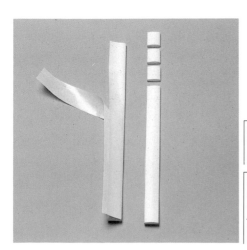

㉒のりしろ全面に両面テープをつけ形状に沿って指でシゴキながら巻き込み接着する。できたボタンの棒を一定の寸法でカットする。

㉒Adhere a double-sided tape on the entire portion of a paste margin and roll in the tape while pressing the tape along the shape for removing tape creases. The bar thus made should be cut to a certain size to make each button.

❷フロントケースＡに裏側からダイヤルボタン，プッシュボタンそしてフロントケースＢの受け台を接着し，表の凹溝をスチール定規で作成する。

❷Dial buttons, push buttons and the cradle for the front case B should be adhered onto the case A from the rear side. Then the depressed grooves should be made on the surface using a steel ruler.

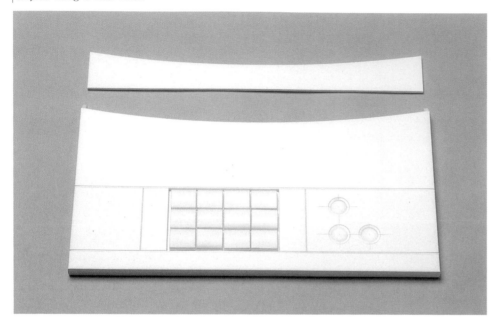

❷ハンドセット。
ロール方向を長辺にとったモデルボード(t=5ミリ)を展開図に基づき，曲げ・形状の確認をする。

*❷Handset
On the basis of the exploded drawing, confirm the bending and form of the model board (t = 5mm), which was made using a longer side in the rolled direction.*

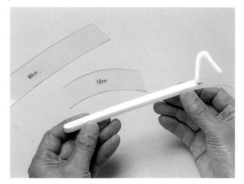

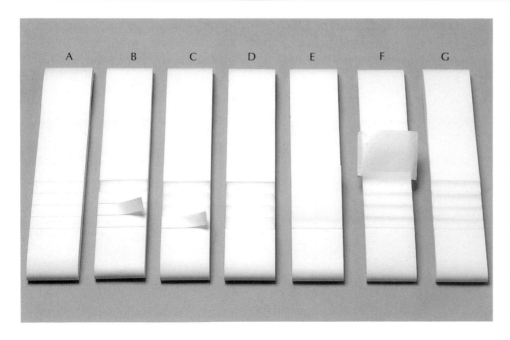

❷ハンドセット凹Ｒの作成。
Ａ：表からＲ幅の線を引き，両方の側面に円定規で凹Ｒを画き，上紙のみカットする。Ｂ〜Ｄ：上紙を剝がしヤスリで凹Ｒを作成する(写真❶参照)。ヤスリは一段おきに削り，両側の紙をガイドにするとよい。Ｅ：剝がした紙に両面テープを貼り，凹Ｒに合わせて指でシゴキながら接着する(写真❷参照)。Ｆ：凹Ｒの最後は両面テープの紙をあててカットする。Ｇ：完成。

*❷Making depressed roundness of a handset
A. Draw lines from the surface by the interval equal to the corresponding curvature, draw depressed curves on both sides with a round ruler and cut only the top paper. B ~ D. Peel the top paper and form the depressed curvature with a file (see photo ❶). Apply the file every other line. The paper on both sides will become a good guide. E. Stick a double-sided tape on the paper that was peeled off and adhere it while pressing the tape along the depressed curved shape with fingers (see Photo ❷). F. Cut the portion of the tape at the end of the depressed curvature by attaching the base paper of the double-sided tape. G. Completed.*

㉖カットして上紙を剥がし，折り曲げ線，カット線を画き発泡スチロールを剥がして両面テープを貼る。

㉖*Cut the board, peel off the top paper and draw bending lines as well as cutting lines. Then remove the styrofoam and adhere a double-sided tape.*

㉗送話側を折り曲げてR定規に合わせて接着する。

㉗*Bend the mouth piece portion and adhere it so as to be fixed at a position designated by an R ruler.*

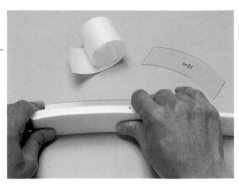

㉘受話側も同様に接着し，形状に合わせて送話側の紙を受話側に接着し固定する。

㉘*Adhere an ear piece portion in the same way. Join the paper of the mouth piece portion with the ear piece portion and fix both to form the designated handset design.*

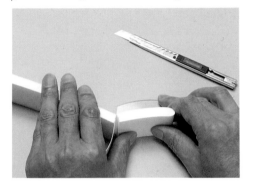

❶

❷
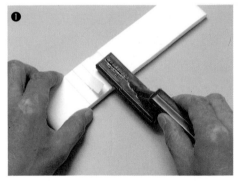

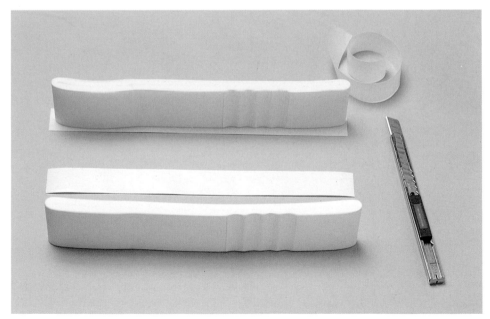

㉚剥がした紙に両面テープを貼りハンドセット側面に接着し余った部分は形状に合わせてカットする。

㉚*Adhere a double-sided tape on the paper that was peeled off. Cut off any extra portions off the contour*

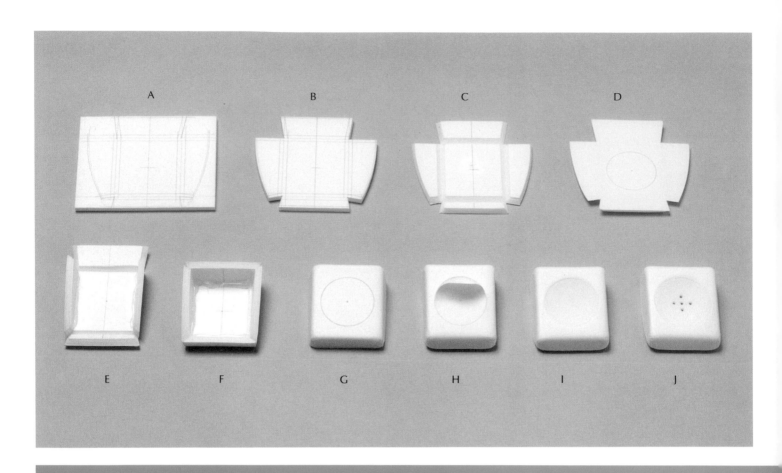

㉜送話口。
モデルボード(t＝3ミリ)で受話口同様に作成する。

㉜*Mouth piece*
Make a mouth piece using a model board (t＝3mm) in the same way as with the ear piece.

㉝受話口，送話口を接着してハンドセット完成。

㉝*Adhering the ear piece and the mouth piece will complete a handset.*

㉛受話口。
A：モデルボード(t＝3ミリ)に展開図を画き，B：外形を切り抜く。C：Vカットして，D：表からサークルカッターで上紙のみをカットする。E：折り曲げ接着。F：接着完了。G：ガラス棒やサンドペーパーで全体のRを作成する(写真❸参照)。H：円の上紙を剥がし，I：サンドペーパーで凹Rを作成(写真❹参照)。J：千枚通しで穴をあけて完成(写真❺参照)。

㉛*Ear piece*
A. Draw an exploded view on a model board (t = 3mm). B. Cut out the external shape of an ear piece. C. Make V cuts. D. Cut only the top paper from the surface with a circle cutter. E. Bend and adhere the ends. F. Gluing completed. G. Form the overall round surface with a glass rod or a sandpaper (see Photo ❸). H. Peel off the top paper of the circle. I. Form a depressed curvature with a sandpaper (see Photo ❹). J. Making holes with an awl will complete this procedure (see Photo ❺).

❹
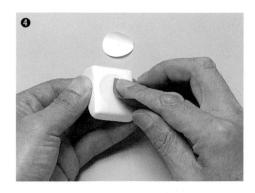

❸
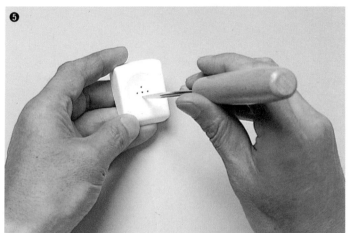

❺

㉞ハンドセットフックベース。
A：モデルボード(t＝3ミリ)に加工図を画き，B：裏返して紙を剥がす。C：ヤスリ，サンドペーパーで削り凸Rを作成する。D：表のストライプを紙のみカットしスチール定規で押し潰して凹溝を作成し，フック部を切り抜く。E：裏返して切り抜いた穴の周囲をCカットする。

㉞*Hook base of a handset*
A. Draw a sketch on a model board (t = 3mm). B. Turn over the board and peel off the paper. C. Form a projected curvature by scraping with a file and a sandpaper. D. Cut the only to the paper, crush with a steel ruler to make depressed grooves and cut out the hook portion. E. Turn over the board and C-cut the surrounding area of the cut-out hole.

㉟ハンドセットフック。
モデルボード(t＝3ミリ)に展開図を画き，カット・折り曲げてポリ・ガンで接着する。

㉟*Handset hook*
Draw an exploded drawing on a modelboard (t = 3mm), cut out the shape, bend and fix by adhering with a Poli-gun.

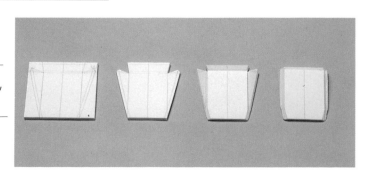

㊱裏からベースにフックを接着して，表からフック周囲をヤスリでRをつける。

㊱Adhere the hook on the base from the rear and then form rounded corners around the hook from the surface with a file.

㊲各部品を接着して完成。

㊲Adhering each part will complete this procedure.

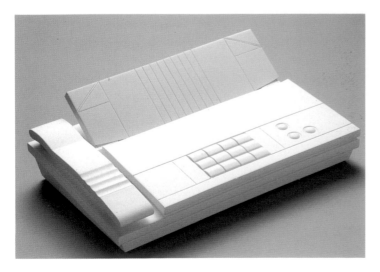

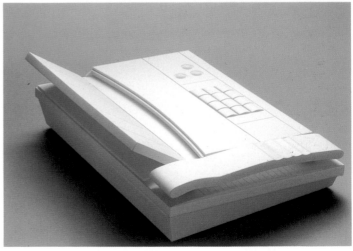

CONCEPTS AND DEVELOPMENT THROUGH STUDY MODELS

スタディモデルによる
発想と展開

田野雅三 *Masazo Tano*

デザイン領域の拡大にともないデザインプロセスの分業化が進み，情報機器の発展も手伝ってデザインワークは大きく変化してきている。何をデザインするにしてもまずコンセプトが創られ，その"ことば"にどれだけ生産の形を与えられるかがデザイナーに要求される。それは"ことば"への創造を3次元の具体的な形として導き，量産の形へと移すことでもある。

イメージをスケッチにおこし，さらにデザイン図に，あるいはコンピューターによるシュミレーションと，直に形に触れ，手を汚さなくても読んだり，見るだけでデザインの展開はできる。しかし，形態の持つ奥行き，量感や動作の把握にはスケッチ，図面，CDなどの2次元のツールで十分だろうか。

モデリングでの時々刻々の変化は試行錯誤の機会を与えてくれ，時には発想の転換をも求められるが，この直にモノに触れるスタディモデル（study model）による展開は，発想をより豊かで確かなものにしてくれる。

コンセンサスを得る目的で外観を本物そっくりに仕上げるプレゼンテーションモデル（presentation model）や性能，動作，生産性の最終検討のためのプロトタイプモデル（prototype model）などに比べスタディモデルはアイディアの発想展開に及ぼす役割が大きく，特に人が手にするモノは，立体で発想，有機的な展開とシュミレーションを繰り返し，デザインの可能性を広げるべきである。また，スタディモデルを効果的に進めるには，その形が生産されるであろう加工法，プラスチックの成形あるいは，鋳物のように3次曲面による構成の可能な場合は，それに合ったモデリング材料，粘土（油土，インダストリアルクレイ　アルファクレイ），発泡材（アクリル，ウレタン，スチレンのフォーム材）や石膏を使用する。主として2次曲面の構成による場合は，シート材（紙類，スチレンボード，バルサ，プラスチック板，金属板）を，フレーム構成による場合は，バー材（プラスチック，金属の丸・角棒，パイプ）とその予想される生産法に類似した素材を選ぶことでより具体的な検討ができる。

これら以外に身近な材料をできるだけ合理的かつ経済的に活用，迅速に組み立てることも限られたデザインプロセスにおいて大切なことであることを付け加えておきたい。

With the advancement of the specialization that is occuring in design processes, in accordance with the expansion of the whole field of design and the aid of development of communication machinery and tools, design work is experiencing a metamorphosis. The creation of concepts is essential for any type of design, and it is required of designers to express their ideas into productive forms. It is the work of transforming words and ideas into definite three-dimensional forms and then onto the mass-production form.

It is possible to develop designs by simply reading or viewing the image sketches, design plans or computer simulation so one does not need to dirty one's hands. However, are two-dimensional tools such as sketches, plans and CDs good enough to provide one with enough detail on depth, volume and movement of a shape?

The opportunity of 'trial and error' is provided during the process of modelling which means the shape can change from one minute to the next, leading to important conceptional amendments.

A study model helps one to directly feel the development which leads to a more wealthy and convincing concept.

In a comparison between the presentation model, which should provide the exact image of the object in order to achieve its necessary consensus, and the prototype model, which expresses the capacity and movement for a final examination in productivity, the study model plays a large role in the development of a concept. Especially for objects upon which we place our hands, we should be able to conceive the object as three-dimensional and repeat its organic development and simulation to extend the possibilities of the design. In order to proceed with the work of a study model effectively, one has to use the same processing method as is used on finishing the actual product and the correct materials. If the construction will use a third-degree surface, such as plastic or casting, it is advisable to use the most appropriate modelling material such as clay (oil-based clay, industrial clay, Alpha clay), foam materials (acryle, urethane or foam polystyrol), and plaster. Should the construction use a two-degree surface, a concrete examination can be made using sheet materials (paper, polystyrol, balsa, plastic sheets and metal sheets). For frame construction, it is advisable to use bar materials (plastic, rounded metal, square bars and pipes), and similar materials which will be used for the conceptional product.

Apart from using the above materials, it is also important to use materials which are rationally and economically easy to come by during the limited design stage.

プライウッドチェア
Plywood chair

ペーパーモデル

紙類，スチレンボード，バルサ；プラスチック板，金属板，それに金網などの薄手のシート材は，手で曲げ癖をつける，曲げたものを何枚か重ね貼り合わせる，ハーフカットを入れ曲げる，熱を加え型に押しつけるなどして形をつくることができる。
ここでスチレンペーパーとケント紙を使いプライウッド（成形合板）チェアをデザインしてみる。スチレンペーパーの表裏に数条のハーフカットを入れ曲げる，成形合板は単板を積層，接着剤，加圧，加熱によって成形される，どちらも２次曲面が原則であるが，工夫によって浅い３次曲面もつくれる類似性がある。
Ｓ＝1/5のペーパーモデルで部材取り，構造さらにスタッキング（積み重ねて収納）とイメージについてスタディしてみる。

Paper model

For thin materials, such as paper, styrene board, balsa, plastic sheets, metal sheets and wire netting, one can produce the required shapes by bending them with the hands, plastering already formed pieces together or inserting half-cuts to make the bend and then adding heat.
Here I will explain how to design a plywood chair with the use of styrene paper and Kent paper. Insert many half-cuts on the back of the paper. Plywood is constructed by piling many layers of single plates up with the aid of a bonding agent and then adding pressure and heat. As a rule, both types of paper are used for expressing the two-degree surface, but it is possible to create a three-degree effect with the use of a little mental application. Here we will study the image of how to cut out, stack and structure the materials on a 1/5 scale paper model.

プライウッドチェア

木のもつ温かさにプライウッド（成形合板）の曲面性と強さを生かしたチェアデザインのメモスケッチ

Plywood chair

This is a memo sketch of the chair design, emphasizing the warmth of the wood, the curved wood and the steady appearence of the plywood.

モデリング段取図
Modeling design plan

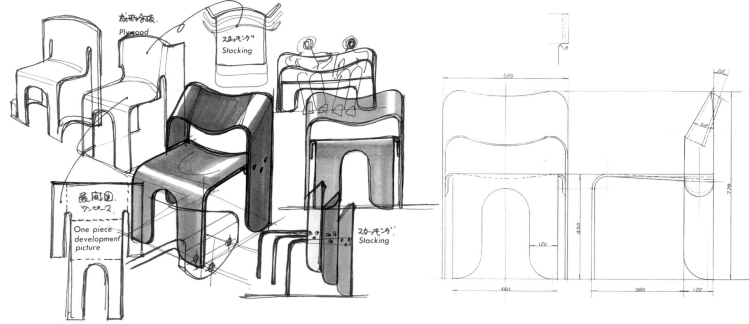

❶スタイロフォームＥＫブロックから座と前脚，背と後脚の外形をカットし，座，背のカーブづけをする。

❶*Cut out the external shape of the seat, front legs, chair back and back legs from the styrofoam EK block.*

❷スタイロフォームの座部，背部のカーブにトレーシングペーパーをあて，形状を写し取る。

❷*Place a piece of tracing paper on the curved lines of the styrofoam seat and back to trace the shapes.*

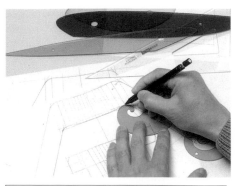

❸形状を平面に移し，板厚を考慮しながら展開図をつくる。

❸*Copy the shapes onto a plane surface and draw the unfolded plan whilst considering the thickness of the board.*

❺t3mmのスチレンペーパーに展開型紙をのせ、外形線，曲げ位置を写す。

❺*Place the pattern on a 3mm thick piece of styrene paper and copy the external shape lines and bending positions.*

❹展開図を少し厚目の紙に写し型紙をつくる。

❹*Copy the unfolded plan onto a slightly thick piece of paper to make the pattern.*

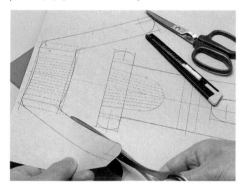

❻内曲げ，外曲げによってスチレンペーパーの表裏にそれぞれハーフカットを入れる。曲げR（アール）によってピッチに粗密をつける。ハーフカット作業後外形をカットする。

❻*Insert half cut-lines on the front and back of the styrene paper depending on whether the bend is to go inwards or outwards. Add density to the pitch with the use of an R-curve. Cut out the external shape having completed the halfcuts.*

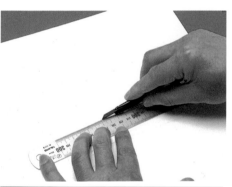

❼カットしたスチレンペーパーの座部，背部をスタイロフォーム型にあて，曲げ癖をつける。

❼*Place the cut out styrene paper seat and back parts of the chair on the styrofoam pattern and bend them to the correct shapes.*

❽スタイロフォーム型に固定されたスチレンペーパーの座部，背部の表面に両面テープを貼り，型からはずし同様に内側にも両面テープを貼る。はみだしたテープはカットする。

❽*Stick double-sided adhesive tape on the front of the styrene paper seat and back parts of the chair which are fixed to the styrofoam pattern. Stick the tape from the inside as well, and cut off any excess pieces.*

❾展開型紙を参考に少し大きめに薄口ケント紙をそれぞれ2枚ずつ切り取る。

❾*Using the unfolded pattern as a reference, cut out two pieces of thin Kent paper to a slightly larger size than the pattern.*

❿内曲げRの小さいところは接着剤（スチノリ）で補強，戻りをおさえる。

❿*Strengthen the small inner R-curved section with an adhesive glue to prevent unfolding.*

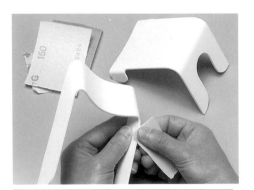

⓮スチレンペーパー，薄口ケント紙のこばをサンドペーパー（#240）で軽く仕上げる。

⓮*Use a piece of sandpaper (#240) to give a light finishing touch to the edges of the styrene paper and Kent paper.*

⓯仕上った座部と背部を組付け完了，同形モデルを2脚つくりスタッキングの検討を行う。

⓯*Put the finished seat and back parts of the chair together to complete. Make two of the same shapes of the model and consider the necessity of stacking.*

⓫座部，背部とも内側に薄口ケント紙を貼る。

⓫*Stick the thin pieces of Kent paper onto the inner sides of the seat and back parts of the chair.*

⓬薄口ケント紙のはみだした部分をカットする。

⓬*Cut the excess paper away.*

⓭座部，背部の表面に薄口ケント紙を貼り，はみだした部分をカットする。

⓭*Stick the thin pieces of Kent paper onto the front surface of the seat and back parts of the chair and cut away any excess pieces.*

⓰着色（ガッシュ）し従来の木目以外のカラーイメージを試す。

⓰*Color them in, but try to think of a different color image from conventional wood grain.*

⓱スタッキングの動作を検討する。

⓱*Study for the condition of stacking.*

2. フォールディングチェア
Folding Chair

フレームモデル

公園の遊具，ストリートファニチャーからベッド，テーブル，イス，照明などのインテリアエレメントまで，フレーム構造の美しさ，特性を上手く生かしたデザインをみることができる。なかでもバー材やパイプ材がよく用いられるフォールディング（折りたたみ収納）チェアをデザインしてみる。

ヒューマンサイズと構造的な安定性，フォールディングの動作とおさまりを細い銅パイプのS＝1/5フレームモデルでスタディする。

パイプの曲げ限界，接合法，部材の合理的な取り方から全体のイメージなどをシュミレーションする。

Frame model

The beautiful framework and designs skillfully expressed by making the best use of the special characteristics of such products ranging from amusement facilities in parks and streetchairs, to interior elements including beds, tables, chairs and light fitments can easily be viewed. Above all, here I will demonstrate how to design a folding chair, a product which is usually constructed from bars and pipe material.

We will utilize a 1/5 scale narrow copper pipe frame mode and study the human size, the constructual stability, the folding action and the fold-up form.

The demonstration will be shown from the limits of the bending ability of pipe, the joint method and the rational way in which to cut out partial materials ; right up to the entire image including simulation.

フォールディングチェア
Folding chair

モデリング段取図
Modelling arrangement plan

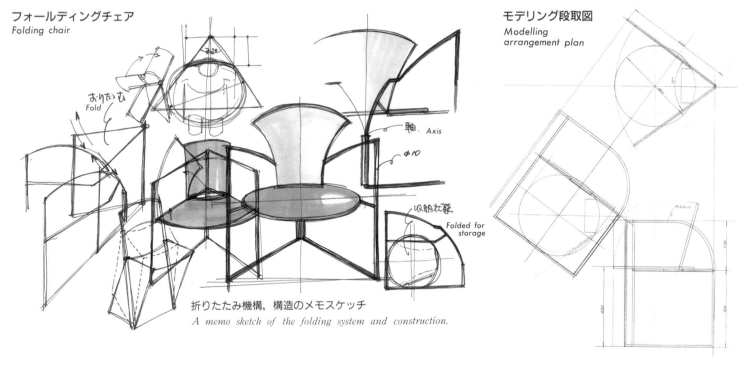

折りたたみ機構，構造のメモスケッチ
A memo sketch of the folding system and construction.

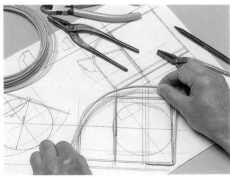

❶アイディアから簡単なS＝1/5図をつくる縮尺にあった太さのカラー針金でイスフレームをつくる。

❶Draw a brief 1/5th scale plan from the idea. Use the correct thickness of color wire for the reduced scale to make the chair frame.

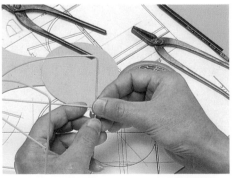

❷同じ形状のフレームは針金を2本束ね同時に曲げる。部材はセロファンテープで固定する。

❷Put the two wires together for the same shaped frames, and bend them together.
Use adhesive tape to fix the partial materials.

❸座，背は片面白ボール紙を切りぬき，フレームとセロファンテープで固定ラフモデルを仕上げる。折りたたみの構造，動き，収納等十分検討してディテールをつめる。

❸Cut out the seat and the back-rest of the chair from the one-sided white board and fix the frame to it to complete the rough model. Fill in the details after fully considering the construction, movement and folding ability of the chair.

❹修正を加えた図をもとに，より具体的な加工
のできる銅パイプ（φ2mm）をフレーム材とし，
必要長さに切断，2本束ね，曲げ位置をだす。

❹*Based on the altered plan, cut out the core of
the more definite processable copper pipe (2mm
diameter) into the necessary lengths for the
frame material, and place them together. Work
out the bending positions.*

❺2本束ねた銅パイプを小さなベンダーやヤッ
トコを使って曲げる。

❺*Use a small bender or flat pliers to bend the
two copper pipes together.*

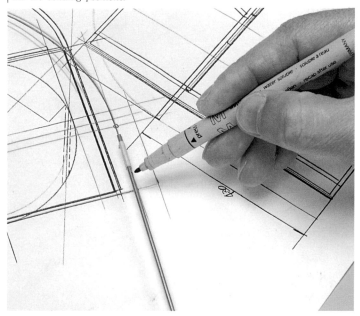

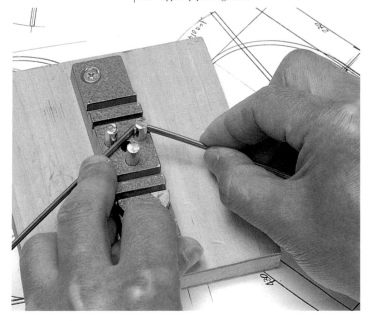

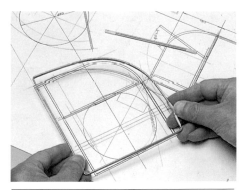

❻図に合せ曲げ具合，ねじれの調整をする。

❻*Correct the bends and twists to the plan.*

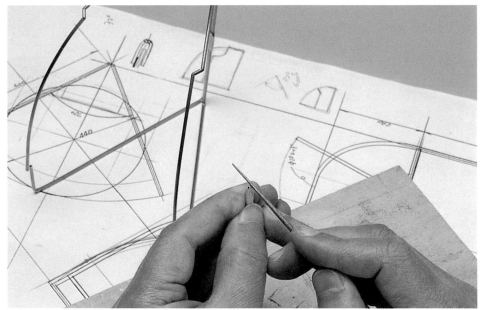

❽左右フレームに座受け，横部材を取り付ける。

❽*Fit the left and right frames with a horizontal
piece of the partial material to catch the seat.*

❼左右フレームに背を受ける段差をつけるため，
銅パイプにヤスリでVカットを入れる。

❼*Use a file to insert the V cuts onto the copper
pipes in order to offer a difference in level to the
left and right frames for catching the back-rest
of the chair.*

❿ハンダ付けをする。

❿Carry out the soldering.

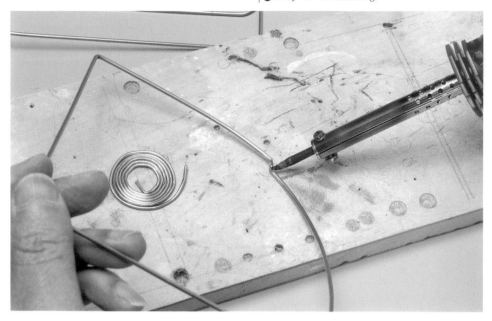

❾切断，曲げを終えたパイプ部材のハンダ付け
箇所を研磨する。

*❾Polish the section of the pipe which has been
cut and bent and requires soldering.*

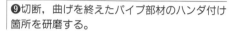

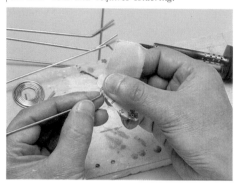

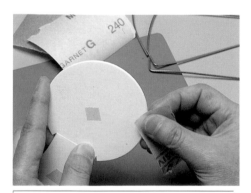

⓭突き出たスチロールのこばにサンドペーパー
（#240）で丸味をつける。

*⓭ Round off the projecting styrene shingle with
sandpaper（#240）.*

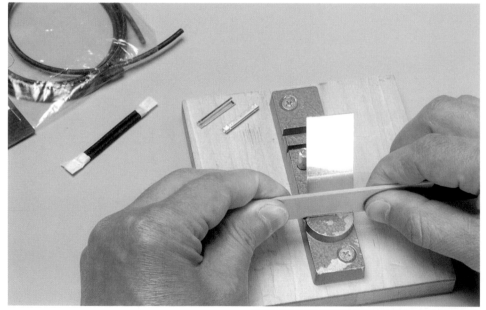

⓯身近の小物部品，金属板を利用して左右フレ
ームの回転軸や座受け金具をつくる。

*⓯Make the shaft and the metal fitting for the
seat catch for the left and right frames with the
use of the familiar small parts or metal sheet.*

⓮ジェッソを塗り，こば，表面を整える。

*⓮Put a coat of Jesso onto the surface to treat the
shingle.*

❶余分なハンダをヤスリで仕上げる。

❶*Rub off any excess solder with a file to complete.*

❷スチレンボードに座と背の形状を描き，カットする。こばに丸味をつけるためスチレンボードの表，裏紙を芯のスチロールと切り分ける。

❷*Draw the shape of the seat and back-rest on the styrene board and cut them out.*
In order to round the edges, cut and divide the front and back pieces of styrene board from the styrene for interfacing.

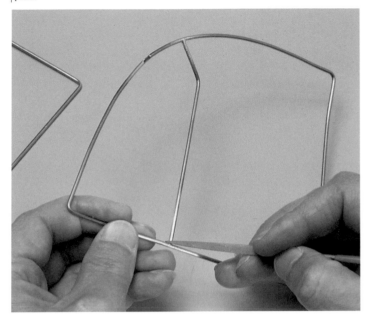

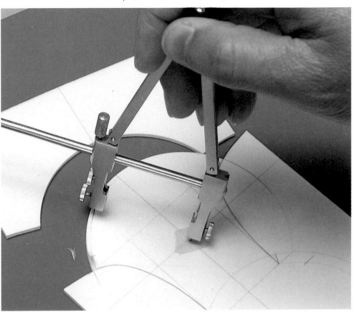

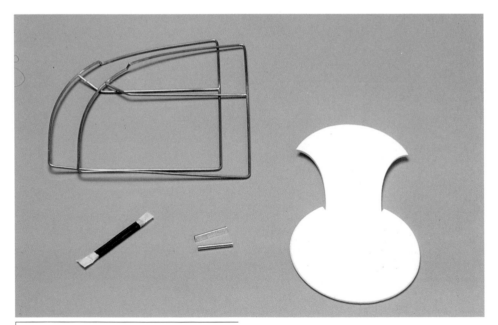

❶左右フレーム，回転軸，座と背，座受け金具のパーツ加工を終える。

❶*Finish off the process of the left and right frames, the shaft and the metal fittings for the seat and back-rest.*

❷左右フレームにプライマーをスプレーし，下地を整える。

❷*Spray on a coat of primer to the left and right frames to correct the groundwork.*

❸座受け金具を接着剤（エポキシ系）で固定する。

❸*Use an adhesive (epoxy resin) to fix on the metal fittings of the seat catch.*

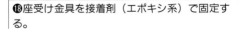

⑳座，背をフレームにのせてみる。

⑳*Place the seat and back-rest on the frame.*

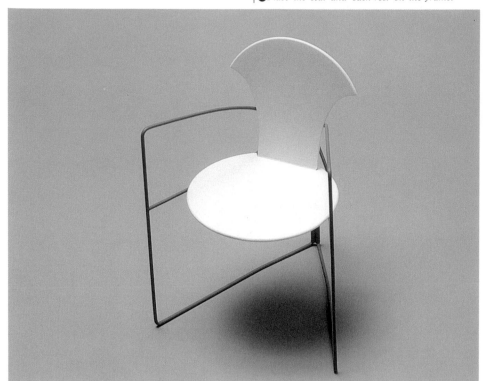

⑲左右のフレームに回転軸を通す。

⑲*Thread the shaft through the left and right frames.*

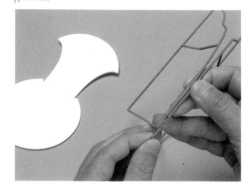

㉓座と背がフレーム間にコンパクトに折りたたまれる。

㉓*The seat and back-rest can be completely folded between the frames.*

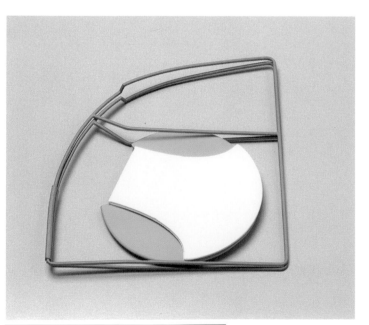

完成。

Complete.

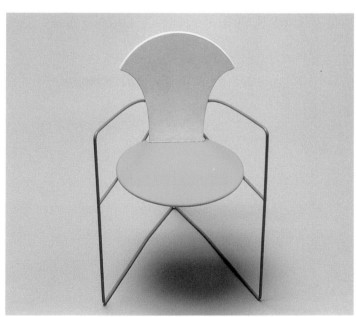

㉑それぞれのパーツに着色（ガッシュ）する。

㉑*Color in the individual parts.*

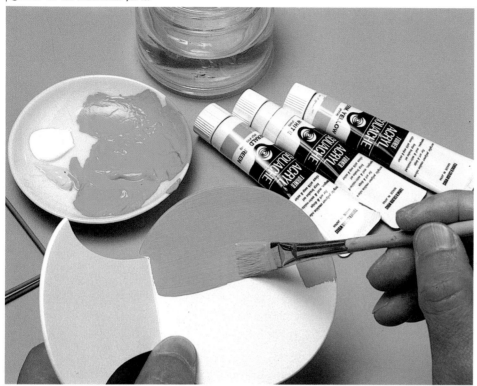

㉒座受け金具をフレームにかしめる。

㉒*Caulk the metal fittings of the seat catch to the frame.*

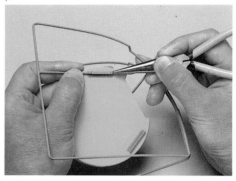

完成。

Complete.

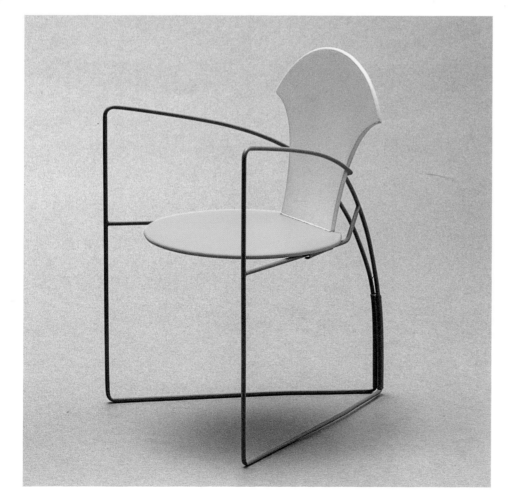

3. テーブルランプ
Table lamp

プラスチックフォームモデル

イメージを立体に移すとき，それが主に３次曲面で構成されている場合，クレイ（粘土）のようなやわらかい物を積み重ねるか，木や石膏のブロックを彫り込んでいくかのどちらかの方法で形をつくる。

プラスチック（スタイロフォーム＝発泡スチロール）は後者で材質が均一で軽量，熱切断ができ，サンドペーパーで簡単に削れる。特に凸形の３次曲面には最適である。ただ複雑な凹形曲面や，削りすぎたとき，クレイのように盛りつけることができない。また，塗料によっては母材が侵される場合があるので，塗料，発泡プラスチックの選択に注意すること。

ここで軽合金のキャスト（鋳物）か，プラスチック成形品としてテーブルランプをスタディしてみる。

Plastic form model

When an image is transfered into a solid body and is especially constructed for a three-degree surface, there are two methods available. One is the method of using some kind of soft material like clay to form the shape through repeated piling. The other is the method of carving out the image from a block of wood or stone. Plastic belongs to the later method. It is light and has a uniform quality. It is also easily shaped with sandpaper and can be cut with heat. This is an especially suitable medium for creating three-degree convex surfaces. However, one cannot cover up mistakes when working on concave surfaces or when the surface has been over curved as is possible with the clay medium.

One must also be careful in choosing coatings as foam plastic, if used as a basic material, is easily damaged by certain kinds of coatings. Here we are going to study a light alloy cast and a plastic table lamp.

テーブルランプ

西瓜からテーブルランプへ。アイデアのメタモルフォーゼ　メモスケッチ

Table lamp

From a watermelon to a table lamp
A memo sketch of a metamorphosis idea.

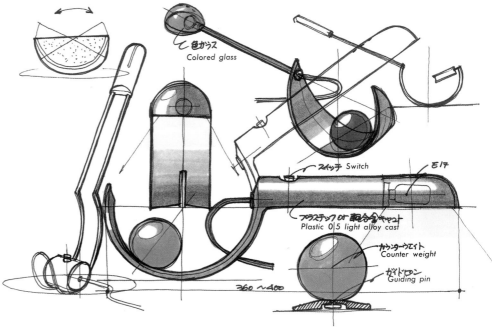

色ガラス
Colored glass

スイッチ Switch

E 17

プラスチック or 軽合金キャスト
Plastic 0.5 light alloy cast

カウンターウエイト
Counter weight

ガイドピン
Guiding pin

360〜400

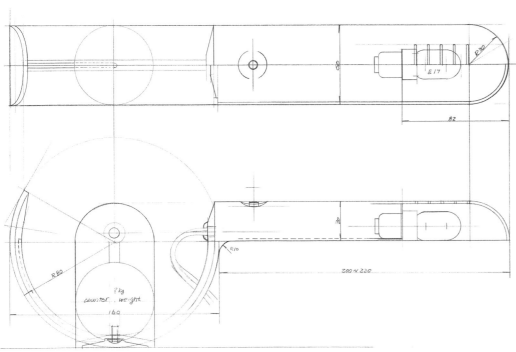

モデリング段取図
Modeling arrangement plan

94

❶スタイロフォームEKをカットし仕上げるための型紙を片面白ボール紙でつくる。

❶*Make patterns on the half-sided white cardboard for the styrofoam EK cut finish.*

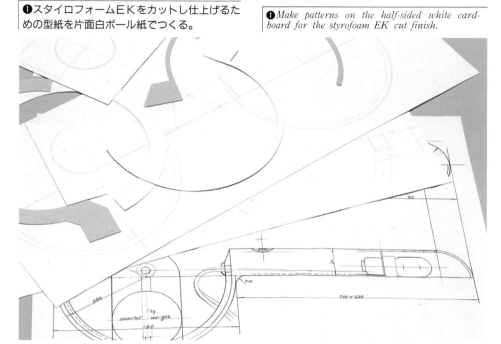

❷両面テープで型紙をスタイロフォームに固定，ガイドにしてスタイロフォームをヒートカッターで切断する。

❷*Stick them onto the styrofoam with adhesive tape and cut the styrofoam along the pattern using a heat cutter.*

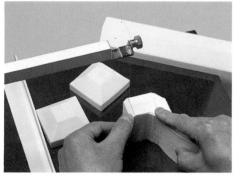

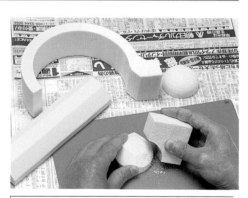

❹1/4円を切り取ったスタイロフォームの当（あて）凹面にサンドペーパー荒目を両面テープで固定，それで円筒にカットしたスタイロフォームに球面をつける。

❹*Fix a piece of rough grain sandpaper onto the concave side of the styrofoam pad after the quarter-circle has been cut out with double-sided adhesive tape. Use it to add the spherical surface to the cylindrical shaped styrofoam.*

❸スタイロフォームで半球をつくる。半球はそれを内接する直方体をつくり半球接線にそって45°の面取りを行い，さらに円筒にカットする。

❸*Make the shape of a hemisphere with the styrofoam. Create the shape of a hexahedron, which is inscribed within the hemisphere and draw a 45° angle along the tangent line of the hemisphere. Then cut it out to the cylindrical shape.*

❺それぞれのスタイロフォーム部材に型紙を固定，当をしたサンドペーパーで削り込む。

❺*Fix the patterns onto each partial material and shave them with the padded sandpaper.*

❻ランプハウスを彫り込みサンドペーパーで仕上げる。

❻*Shave the lamp housing to the correct shape with the sandpaper.*

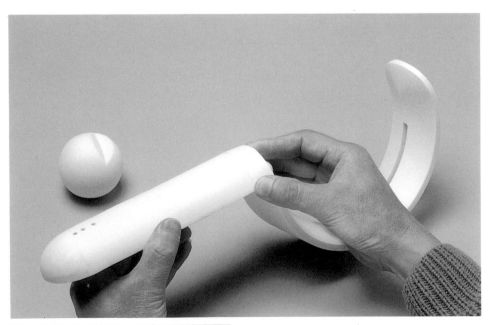

❿接合部の面合せを行い表面を仕上げる。

❿*Smooth out the joint sections.*

❾部材を組付け両面テープ，スチノリ（スチロール用接着剤）で貼り合せる。

❾*Assemble the partial materials with the use of double-sided adhesive tape adhesive bond.*

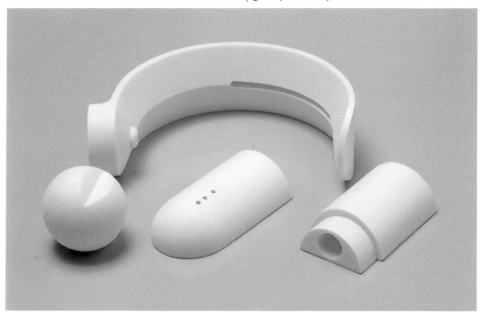

❼カウンターウェイトはそれぞれ半球内側を彫り込み鉛を入れ，貼り合せ球体にする。

❼*Shave off the inner sides of each hemisphere for the location of the lead counter weight and stick them together to create the spherical shape.*

⓫スタイロフォームの表面の目止めと安定のため，ジェッソ（リキテックス）を塗る。

⓫*Paint on a layer of Jesso (Liquitex) to prevent the grain of the styrofoam from dislodging.*

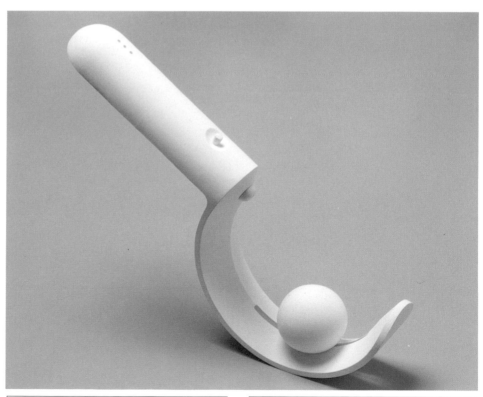

⓬球体のカウンターウェイトをのせ，白地モデルの完成。

⓬*Place the spherical shaped counter weight to complete the white ground model.*

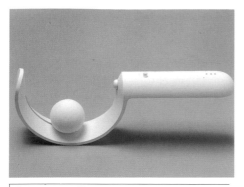

⓭ウェイトの位置をかえ，動作の検討をする。

⓭*Study the movement by changing the position of the weight.*

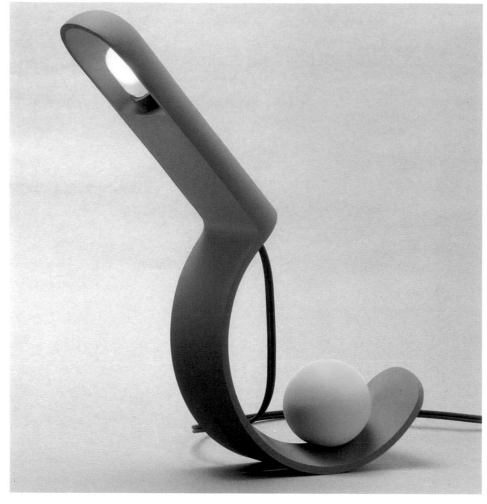

⓮色彩の検討を加えさらに光源を取り付け，照明の具合いをみる。

⓮*Think of the color and bathe it in light to check that the lighting is acceptable.*

⓯完成。

⓯*Complete.*

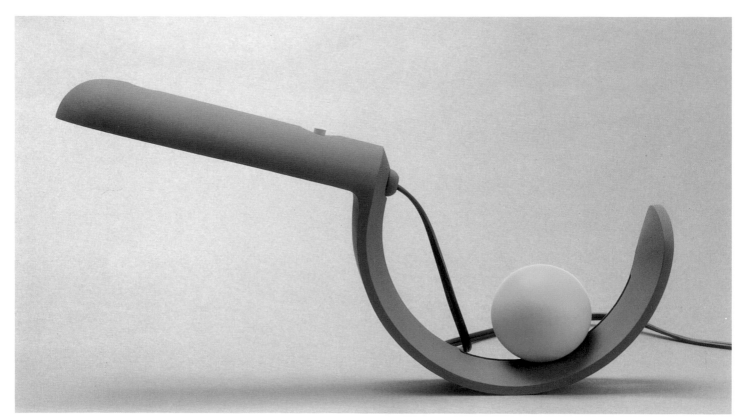

4. ウオーターピッチャー
Water pitcher

石膏ロクロ→プラスターモデル

回転体の形をその中心断面図で検討されることが多いが，立体にしてみるとずいぶん平面でのイメージと違うことに気付く。やはり，まず立体でイメージすることが大切である。石膏ロクロはあらかじめ円筒形に流し込まれた石膏をロクロ鉋で全体のバランスをみながら，思う形に削り込む。中心断面を薄い金属版に写し，箱に固定，中心に軸を置き，軸に石膏泥漿をかけながら形を成長させる，トリメ箱によっても石膏の回転体はできるが，途中での試行錯誤はできない。

製品生産においても金属の絞り型，プラスチックの成形型の加工の基本は回転体であり，石膏ロクロによる造形は，このことにも通じる。

ステンレスのウォーターピッチャーのデザインを石膏ロクロのモデルでスタディしてみる。

Plaster potter's wheel→Plaster model

The shape of a revolving body is often cut in half and studied as a cutaway view, but there are cases where one will find a great difference in image when it is transformed from the plane into a cubic body. Therefore, it is important to create an image with a cubic body from the beginning. This plaster potter's wheel is made into shape by pouring plaster into a cylindrical mold which has been shaved on a plaster lathe whilst considering the entire balance. Copy the center cut surface onto a thin metal sheet and fix it to a box. Place a shaft in the center and pour plaster into the shaft to build up the shape.

The basic process for a metal squeezed mold and a plastic mold during the production is the revolving body. The creation of the cast lathe has something to do with this.

Here we are going to study the design of a stainless-steel water pitcher through the cast lathe method.

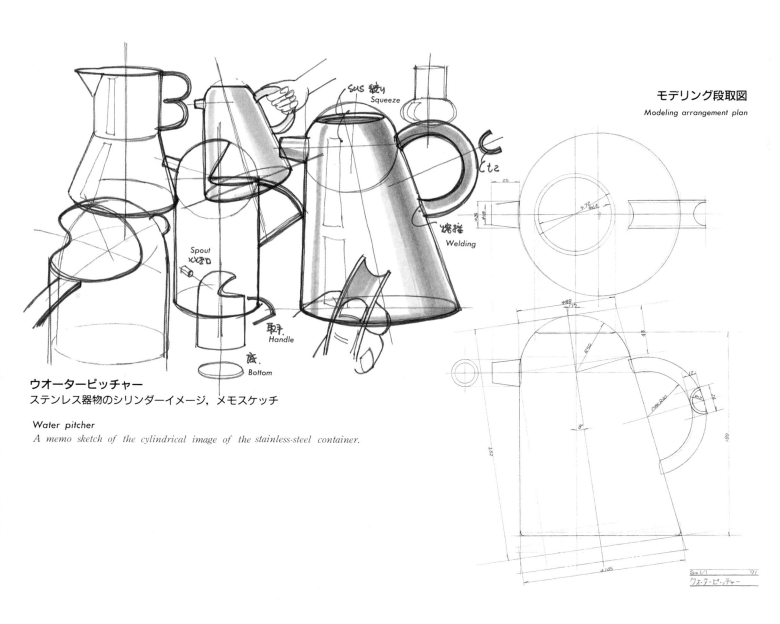

モデリング段取図
Modeling arrangement plan

ウオーターピッチャー
ステンレス器物のシリンダーイメージ，メモスケッチ

Water pitcher
A memo sketch of the cylindrical image of the stainless-steel container.

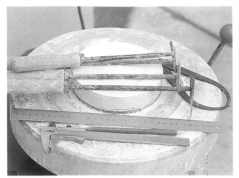

❶ロクロ鉋（かんな），スケール，ノギス，外パスなど石膏ロクロ用ツール。

❶*Tools for the cast lathe ; lathe plane, scale, slide calipers outside calipers etc.*

❸必要な石膏のサイズより少し大きめの円筒形を塩ビ板（t0.5mm）でつくり，石膏回転テーブルに固定する。

❸*Make a cylinder which is slightly larger than the size required for the cast model in vinyl chloride sheeting (0.5mm thick) and fix it to the potter's wheel.*

❷新しい石膏がつきやすくするため石膏回転テーブル上に刻みを入れる。

❷*Indent the rotary potter's wheel in order to make it easy for the new cast to stick.*

❻少し振動を与え，混入した空気をにがし石膏の沈殿するのを待つ。

❻*Give the container a gentle shake to release the air and wait until the cast settles.*

❼分離した上澄み液をすてる。

❼*Dispose of the clear water seperated from the cast.*

❽気泡を抱きこまないよう，少し粘性がでるまで撹拌する。

❽*Stir it gently, without making bubbles, until the consistency takes on a slightly sticky feel.*

❾できた石膏泥漿を回転テーブル上の円筒に流し込む。

❾*Pour the cast slip into the cylinder on the potter's wheel.*

❹石膏の必要高さを決める。

❹*Decide the level to fill with the necessary amount of cast.*

❺石膏泥漿（混水石膏）をつくる
必要な石膏泥漿と同容量の水を容器に取り。気泡球をつくらぬようメッシュを通し美術工芸用Ａ級焼石膏を，少し上に水を残すまで静かに入れる。

❺*Make the cast mold.*
Pour the necessary amount of cast slip and the same amount of water into a container through a mesh without creating air bubbles, and add A-class cast, used for artistic handicraft, gradually until a small amount of water is left on top.

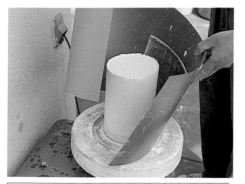

❿発熱し硬化がはじまったころ塩ビ板円筒をはずす。

❿*Remove the cylindrical vinyl chloride sheeting once it has started to generate heat and become hard.*

⓫肩からロクロ向い側の壁に支持棒を渡しロクロ鉋の握り手を固定し回転テーブル上の石膏円柱に刃をあてる。

⓫*Place a support bar across the shoulders to the opposite side and fix the handle of the lathe to it. The blade should be facing towards the cast cylinder on the potter's wheel.*

⓬石膏が硬化する前に荒削りを行い円柱の芯だしをする。

⓬*Before the cast hardens, take a rough shaving to remove the core of the cylinder.*

❸まず，イメージしたウオーターピッチャーが
おさまる円錐台を削る。高さ，上底，下底を決
め罫がく。

❸*First of all carve out the truncated cone to fit
the image of the water pitcher. Fix the height, top
and bottom bases and draw in ruled lines.*

❹側面を削る。

❹*Shave the sides.*

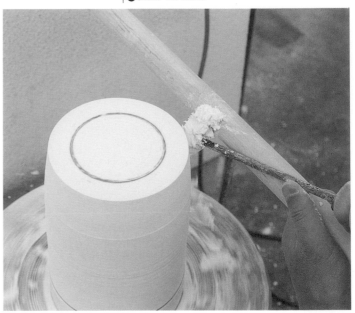

❼形を確かめながら慎重に削り込む。

❼*Shaving around the shape with great care while
continually confirming the shape.*

❽全体のバランスをみながら下底切断位置を決
める。

❽*Decide on the cutting position on the bottom
base while considering the entire balance.*

❾表面に軽くサンドペーパー（#240）をかけ仕
上げる。

❾*Give the surface a light rub with a piece of
sandpaper (#240) to finish off.*

⓯全体のバランスをみながら必要寸法のチェックをする。

⓯While studying the entire balance, check the required measurements.

⓰上部R（アール）づけ位置を罫がく。

⓰Draw a ruled line for the R-shaped position on the upper section.

⓴下底，切り込み位置を粗目鋸で切断。

⓴Use a rough bladed saw to cut off at the base cutting position.

㉑注ぎ口をつくる，芯だしされた石膏円筒に寸法を罫がく。

㉑Create the spout. Draw the measurements with a ruler on the revealed cast core.

㉒感じをみながら外形を削り込む。

㉒*Shave around the external shape while occasionally confirming the shape.*

㉓中剖（ぐ）り
注ぎ口端面の厚さをだす。

㉓*The boring.*
Produce the thickness of the spout edge.

㉗凹型に削り込むための型紙を準備する。

㉗*Prepare a pattern to shave out the concave shape.*

㉖取手をつくる。まずU字断面のドーナツ形をつくる。芯出しされた石膏円筒に取手断面の1/2外形を凹型（雌型）として削り込むため寸法取りをする。

㉖*Make the handle. Firstly, make it in a doughnut shape with a U-shaped cross-section.*
Take the measurements of the revealed core on the cast cylinder in order to carve the concave shape as a half-size of the external shape for the cross-section of the handle.

㉔下底部に切り込みを入れ鉋先で突切る。

㉔*Insert the cutting line on the bottom base section and use the edge blade of a plane to cut through.*

㉕石膏ロクロより注ぎ口を切り取る。

㉕*Cut out the spout from the cast on the potter's wheel.*

㉘型紙で確認しながらロクロ鉋で凹形に削り込む。

㉘*Use a lathe to shave out the concave shape while continuously confirming the pattern.*

㉙離型剤（カリ石けん）をパレットナイフで容器に移し取り，それに湯を加え，石けん液をつくる。

㉙*Transfer some potash soap into a container with a knife and add some water to make liquid soap.*

㉚表面を仕上げ凹部のみ離型剤のカリ石けん液を均一に塗る。

㉚*Complete the surface and apply even coats of the potash soap only to the concave section.*

㉛余分な石けん液を水を含んだスポンジでふき取る。2〜3回繰り返す。

㉛*Wipe off the excess liquid soap with a damp sponge. Repeat this process two or three times.*

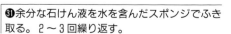

㉜取手中心面になる位置にマーキングをする。

㉜*Mark the position that will become the center surface of the handle.*

㉝外周を雌型に削り込んだ石膏を囲うように塩ビ板（t0.5mm）で円筒をつくり，石膏泥漿を流し込む。

㉝*Make a cylinder with a vinyl chloride sheet (0.5mm thick) to enclose the cast, of which the external roundness has been shaved into a concave shape, and pour some cast slip into it.*

㊱ドーナツ形の内径を罫がく。

㊱*Draw a doughnut shape inside diameter.*

㊲内径部をその中心（マーキングした位置）に向って削り下げる。

㊲*Shave down the inner diameter towards the center (marked position).*

㉞新たに流し込まれた石膏の境界線から上方に取手幅寸法を罫がく。

㉞*Draw in measurement lines for the width of the handle on the section above the boundary line of the newly poured cast.*

㉟取手幅まで円筒を削り下げ，その側面をU字形に削り込む。

㉟*Shave down the cylinder to the width of the handle and shave out the sides into a U-shape.*

㊴表面に軽くサンドペーパー（#240）をかける。厚さ約2㎜，U字断面ドーナツ形の仕上がり。

㊴*Lightly rub the surface with sandpaper (#240). Complete the doughnut shape U-shape cross-cut with a thickness of about 2mm.*

㊳凹型（雌型）でつけた丸みと同形の凸形丸味を内側につける。

㊳*Give a convex shape roundness to the inner part which is the same as the roundness given to the concave shapes.*

⓴本体石膏の芯だしをする。

⓴*Remove the core from the main cast.*

⓪軽くもち上げるとU字断面ドーナツ形が下の
石膏雌型からはずれる。

⓪*The U-shaped cross-cut doughnut shape will
come off from the lower concave cast by lifting
gently.*

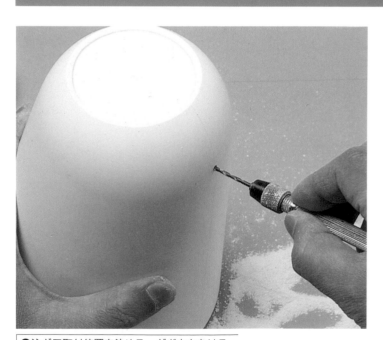

⓯注ぎ口取付位置を決める。ダボ穴をあける。

⓯*Fix the position for the spout. Drill a hole with
a joggle.*

⓰エポキン系接着剤で注ぎ口を固定する。

⓰*Fix the spout to the body with an epoxy resin
adhesive.*

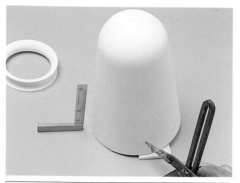

㊷本体に傾斜をつける。

㊷*Add a slope to the main body.*

㊸底部を斜めに切断する。

㊸*Cut the bottom base diagonally.*

㊹頭部に開口部を彫り込む。

㊹*Cut an opening at the top.*

㊺注ぎ口に座をつくり本体とすり合せる。

㊺*Make a platform on the spout and shave it to fit the body.*

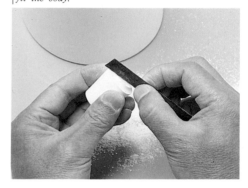

㊽U字断面ドーナツ形から取手の大きさを決める。

㊽*Fix the size of the handle from the U-shaped cross-cut doughnut shape.*

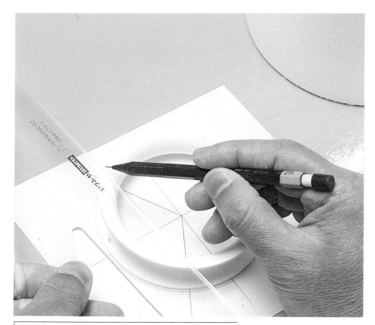

㊾鋸刃で切断。

㊾*Cut with a saw.*

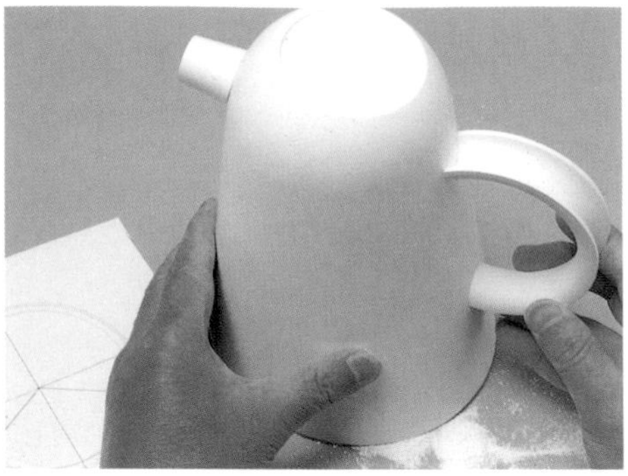

(50)本体とすり合せをして注ぎ口と同様接着固定する。

(50)Shave it to fit the body and fix it with an adhesive in the same style as the spout.

(51)完成。

(51)Completion.

(52)完成。

(52)Completion.

5. カトラリー
Cutlery

クレイモデル→プラスターモデル

カトラリーの柄，ドアの取手，鍋の握り，自転車ハンドルのグリップ等は，実際に手に触れてみてはじめて納得のいく形が得られる。おおまかなボリュームをクレイで手の中でつくり上げる，微妙な形の変化や硬さは，石膏におきかえて検討する。

スプーン，フォーク，ナイフの頭部も柄と同様，石膏でつくることができるが非常に繊細で壊れやすいのでシリコン雌型から石膏荒形を複数準備し，微妙な検討にあてるとよい。

Clay model→Plaster model

It is impossible to become satisfied with shapes with regards to the handles of cutlery, doors, saucepans and bicycle grips until they are actually felt with the hands and tried out.
The rough volume will be created to shape with the use of clay and the hands. The delicate change and hardness of the shapes will be studied in place of the plaster.
The top parts of spoons, forks and knives can be made with plaster in the same way as the handles, but it is advisable to prepare many different types from concave silicone shapes to rough plaster shapes in order to apply a delicate study of these fragile objects.

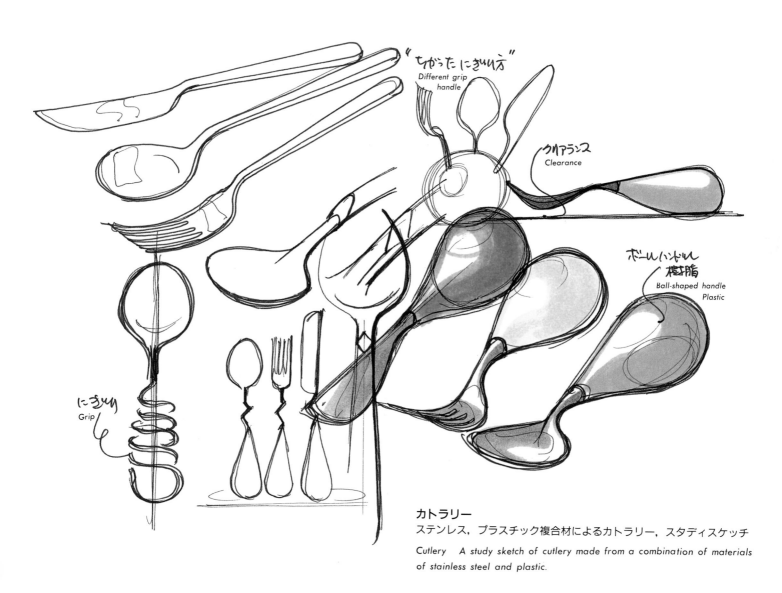

"ちからたにぎり方"
Different grip handle

クリアランス
Clearance

ボールハンドル 樹脂
Ball-shaped handle Plastic

にぎり
Grip

カトラリー

ステンレス，プラスチック複合材によるカトラリー，スタディスケッチ

Cutlery   A study sketch of cutlery made from a combination of materials of stainless steel and plastic.

❶ちがった握り方のできる柄，手にフィットする大きさ，形をクレイでスタディする。

❶*Use clay to study the size and shape which will fit the different grip handles.*

❷厚紙にスプーン，フォーク，ナイフの形を描く。

❷*Draw the shape of the spoon, fork and knife on thick paper.*

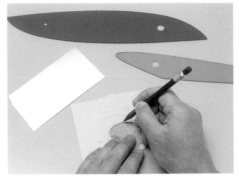

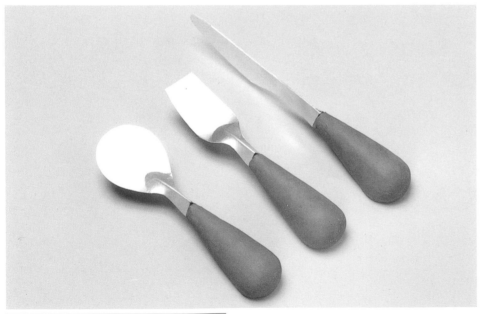

❺テーブル上での安定した置き方の工夫を柄に加える。

❺*Add some work to the handles to make them stable when they are placed on the table.*

❻さらに手に取り，使い勝手，全体のバランスを検討する。

❻*Give a further study to the entire balance by holding them in the hands.*

❼スプーン，フォーク，ナイフの外形及び主断面型紙をつくる。

❼*Make the patterns for the external shapes of the spoon, fork and knife and their chief cross cut patterns.*

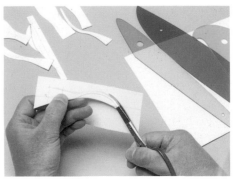

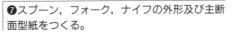

❸それらを切り取り，折り曲げおおまかなイメージを創る。

❸*Cut them out and fold them to make rough images.*

❹クレイの柄に厚紙のスプーン，フォーク，ナイフをつけてみる。

❹*Attach the spoon, fork and knife, made of thick paper, to the clay handles.*

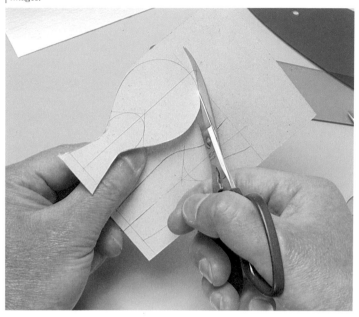

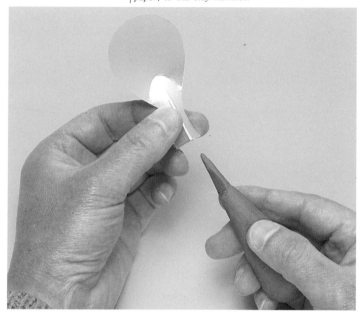

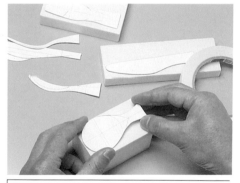

❽荒取りされたスタイロフォームEKに型紙を両面テープで軽く固定する。

❽*Lightly fix the patterns onto the roughly cut-out styrofoam EK with double-sided adhesive tape.*

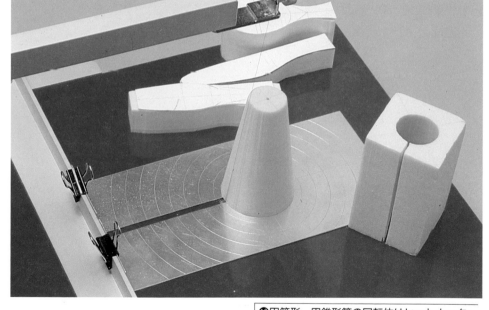

❿円筒形，円錐形等の回転体はヒートカッターのニクロム線角度の変化とテーブル上に回転軸を工夫することで荒取りができる。

❿*Rough shapes of the body revolution, cylindrical or cone shapes, can be achieved by changing the angles of the nichrome wire of the heat cutter and placing a rotary shaft on the table.*

❾型紙にそってスタイロフォームをヒートカッター（プロフォームカッター）で切り取る。

❾*Use a heat-cutter (Proform cutter) to cut the styrofoam along the patterns.*

❶クレイ柄を参考にスタイロフォーム荒取りに
丸味をつける。

❶*Round the roughly cut styrofoam while using
the clay handle as a reference.*

❷スプーンのスタイロフォーム荒取りにヒート
カッター（ヒートニードル型）で凹面をつける。

❷*Give a concave surface to the roughly cut out
styrofoam spoon with the heat cutter (heat needle
type).*

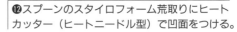

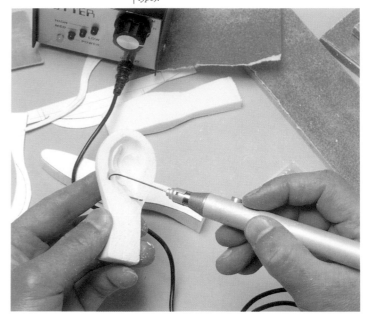

❶シリコン硬化後（触媒と室温によって硬化時
間は異なる）スタイロフォーム荒形を取り出し
シリコン雌型表面を中性洗剤で洗う。

❶*Take out the rough styrofoam shapes from the
frames after the silicone has hardened (The time
required for hardening will differ in accordance
with the catalytic agent used and the room temperature) and wash the concave silicone mold with a
neutral washing powder.*

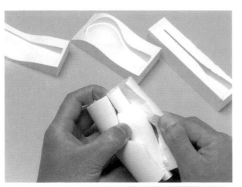

❶流し込んだ石膏泥漿が少し硬化しはじめたころ、
ヘラで余分な石膏を取り除き表面を整えておく。

❶*Remove the excess cast with a spatula used to
treat surfaces when the cast slip begins to harden.*

❶シリコン雌型に石膏泥漿（作り方は№.4 参照）
を流し込む。

❶*Pour the cast slip (See No.4 for directions on
making) into the concave silicone molds.*

⓭スプーン，フォーク，ナイフと柄，各部のスタイロフォーム，荒形にジェッソ（リキテックス）を塗り，表面を整える。

⓭*Add some coats of Jesso (Liquitex) to each rough styrofoam spoon, fork and knife including the handles to treat the surfaces.*

⓮スタイロフォーム荒形から石膏荒形を複数得るためスタイロフォームを型にシリコン雌型をつくる。型取り用シリコン液に触媒を添加（取扱い説明書を参考）撹拌する。

⓮*Create a concave silicone pattern, using the styrofoam as a pattern, in order to produce plural number of rough cast shapes from the styrofoam shapes.*
Add a catalytic agent to the silicone solution to make the molds (read the instructions) and stir.

⓯スタイロフォーム荒形に注型枠を設け，シリコン液を注ぐ。

⓯*Prepare the pour-on mold frames for the rough styrofoam shapes and pour in the silicone solution.*

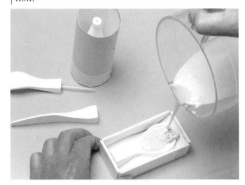

⓳発熱硬化後，シリコン雌型から柄，スプーン，フォーク，ナイフの石膏荒形を脱型する。

⓳*Take out the rough cast shapes of the spoon, fork and knife after they begin to generate heat and become hard.*

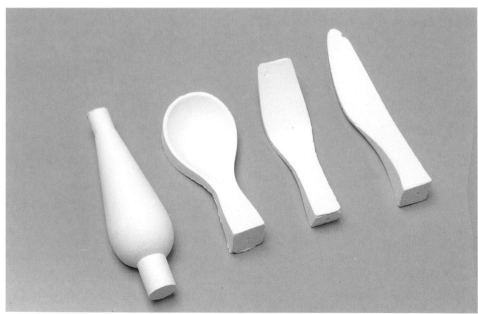

⓴削り込み形状バリエーションをえるため，シリコン雌型から複数の石膏荒形をおこしておく。

⓴*Make several rough cast shapes in the silicone molds in order to get various shavings.*

㉑それぞれの石膏荒形の不要な部分を鋸刃（金属用荒目）で落す。

㉑Cut away the unnecessary parts on each rough cast with a saw (rough blade for metalwork use).

㉒形状をみながら鋸刃で削り込んでいく。

㉒Shave them into shape, using the saw blade, whilst continuously confirming the shapes.

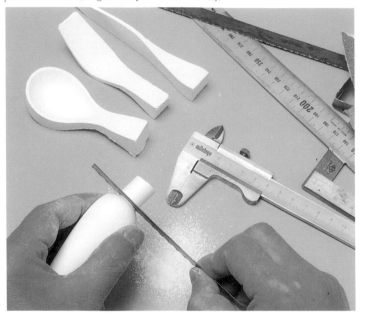

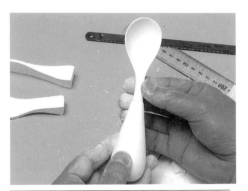

㉕柄石膏荒形も同様に検討を加え，仕上げる。

㉕Use the same process on the rough cast handle to complete.

㉖接合用のダボ穴（φ2㎜）をあける。

㉖Use a ioggle to drill a hole (2mm diameter) for the jointing.

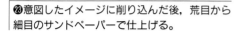

㉓意図したイメージに削り込んだ後，荒目から
細目のサンドペーパーで仕上げる。

㉓*Use a range of sandpaper from rough to fine
grain to complete after they have been shaved
into the image shapes.*

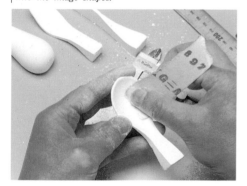

㉔スプーンの仕上り。

㉔*The completed spoon.*

㉗スプーン，フォーク，ナイフの頭部と柄部を
接着剤（エポキシ系）で固定する。

㉗*Fix the head parts of the spoon, fork and knife
to the handle parts with an adhesive agent (epoxy
resin).*

㉘スプーン，フォーク，ナイフそれぞれの頭部
が直にテーブルに接触しないよう柄部下面カッ
トの調整をする。

㉘*Add small adjustments to the surfaces of the
handles facing downwards when they are on the
table to prevent the head parts of the spoon, fork
and knife from directly coming into contact with
the table.*

㉙手に取りその握り具合，使い勝手を試してみる。

㉙*Hold them to see if they are comfortable to grip and use.*

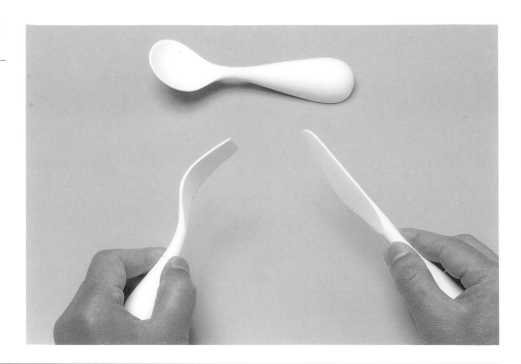

㉚柄部に着色，頭部との異素材感を検討する。

㉚*Color the handles and study the material differences from the head parts.*

6. バスタブ
Bath tub

プラスチックフォームモデル→プラスターモデル

浴槽には，木，ホーロー，ステンレス，FRP と色々な材料が使われている。

ここでは，最近よく用いられる人造大理石浴槽のデザインをしてみる。

型にプラスチックを注型して生産される浴槽でプラスチックを石膏におきかえればモデリングも生産と類似し，量産の制約もあらかじめ予測できる。

S=1/5モデルでは，浴槽の凹部を凸型でスタディ，それに石膏をかけ，できた荒形浴槽を検討しながら削り込む。

Plastic foam model→Plaster model

Many different materials such as wood, enamel, stainless steel and F. R.P. are used for bath tubs.

Here I will demonstrate how to design an artificial marble bath tub which is the latest fashion.

This tub is produced by pouring plastic into a mold. If the plastic is replaced with a plaster cast, the model will be similar to the production model. Therefore, the restrictions of massproduction can be anticipated beforehand.

We will study the concave part of the bath tub made in a convex mold on a scale of 1/5, and then pour cast into it and shave the rough shape of the bath.

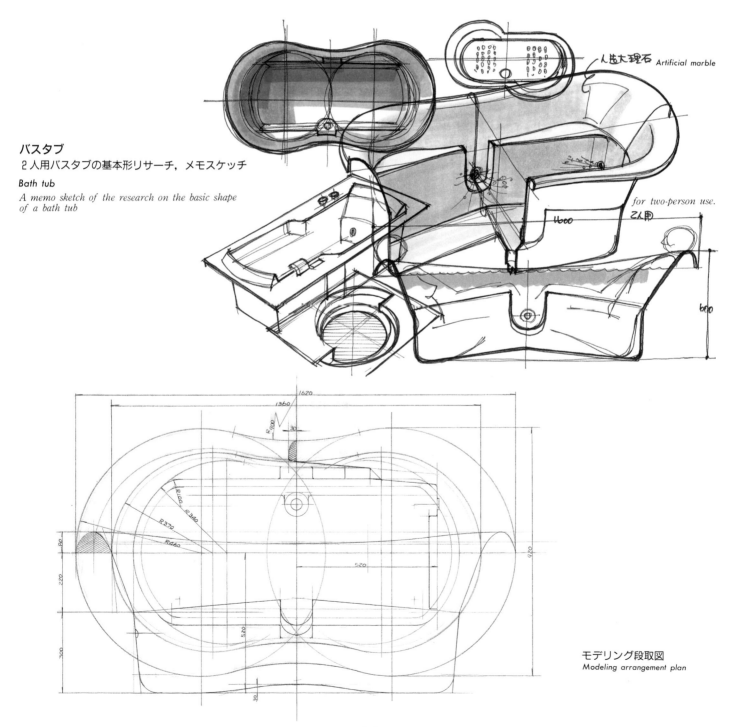

バスタブ
２人用バスタブの基本形リサーチ，メモスケッチ

Bath tub
A memo sketch of the research on the basic shape of a bath tub

人造大理石 Artificial marble

for two-person use.

モデリング段取図
Modeling arrangement plan

❶人体寸法から浴槽のＳ＝1/5基本寸法図をおこす。槽部の凹形状の彫り込みが困難なため，逆に凸形で槽部のイメージ検討を行う。図を型紙にスタイロフォームＥＫの荒取りをする。

❶*Work out the basic measurements on a 1/5 scale for the bath tub by measuring a person to draw the plan.*
We will study the image of the tub part from the convex shape in which the reverse concave shape of the bath tub will become as the carving of a concave shape will prove too difficult.
With the plan as a pattern, cut out a rough piece of styrofoam EK.

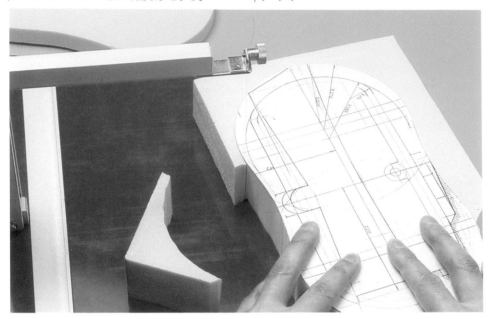

❷生産に際し無視できない条件，ヌキテーパー，コーナＲ（アール）など考慮しながら彫り込みイメージを形にしていく。

❷*Whilst considering basic conditions that cannot be ignored, such as the taper and R-shape areas, fashion a shape into the shaving image.*

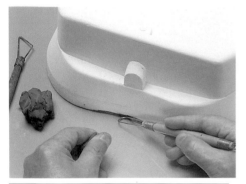

❻石膏をかけた時，型下に石膏が潜り込まないようクレイで隙間をうめる。

❻*Block the open edges at the bottom of the mold with clay to prevent penetration of the cast when it is poured.*

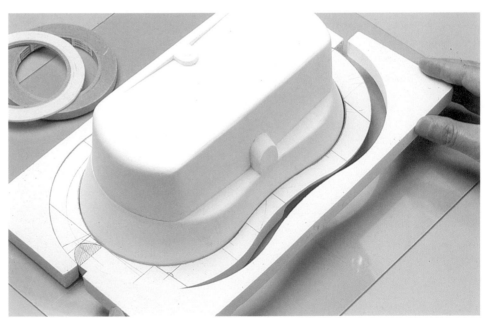

❼浴槽フランジ部分の厚さと形状を得るため外周に注型枠を設ける。

❼*Build up a pour-on mold frame around the mold to get the thickness and shape of the fringe part of the bath tub.*

❸部品加工したものを組みつける。

❸Attach the processed parts to the tub.

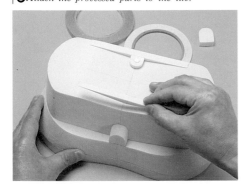

❹接合部，コーナーRの仕上げをする。

❹Add a final touch to the joints and the corner R-shape.

❺スタイロフォームの表面を整え脱型をよくするためジェッソを塗る。

❺Treat the surface of the styrofoam and give it a few coats of Jesso to ensure the mold will come off easily.

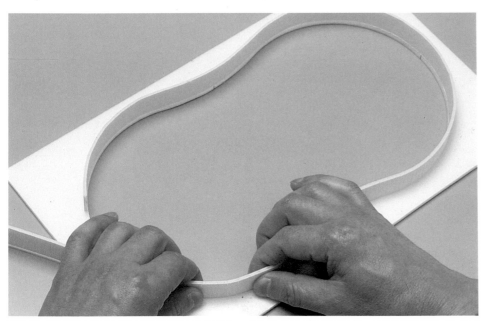

❽スチレンボードで石膏泥漿用の枠をつくる。

❽Make a frame for the cast slip with a styrene board.

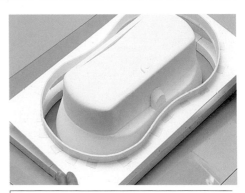

❾浴槽部の凸型から石膏泥漿の流れ込むフランジ部凹型のでき上り。

❾The cast slip is poured into the fringe part through the convex shaped bath tub to complete a concave mold.

⑩離型剤（カリ石けん液）を表面に塗りスポンジでふきとる。これを2～3回繰り返す。

⑩ *Wipe the surface clean with a sponge soaked in potash liquid soap. Repeat this process two or three times.*

⑪石膏泥漿を作り流動性のある泥漿をまず型表面に一通りかける。

⑪ *Make some cast slip and pour it over the surface of the mold at first.*

⑫少し硬くなりはじめた石膏泥漿を型に盛り上げる。

⑫ *Build up the cast slip which has started to harden on the mold.*

⑮S＝1/5石膏の荒形浴槽のでき上がり。

⑮ *The 1/5 scale rough cast of the bath tub is now complete.*

⑯フランジ部分のイメージをスタイロフォームでスタディ，浴槽に合わせて検討する。

⑯ *Study the image of the fringe part made of styrofoam to check that it matches the bath tub.*

⓭石膏泥漿が発熱硬化後，型枠類をはずし脱型する。

⓭*After the cast slip has begun to generate heat and harden, remove it from the frame.*

⓱最もマッチするフランジ部イメージを石膏浴槽フランジにうつし込む。

⓱*Copy the suitable fringe part image onto the cast bath tub.*

⓲荒取りをする。

⓲*Give it a rough shave.*

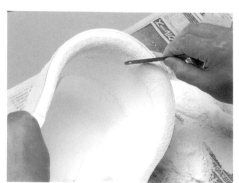

⑲丸味をつけ彫り込む。

⑲*Shave off the roundness.*

⑳荒目から細目のサンドペーパーで細部，表面
の仕上げを行う。

⑳*Use sandpaper ranging from rough grain to
fine grain to complete the details and surface.*

㉑S=1/5石膏浴槽の仕上がり。

㉑*The 1/5 scale cast bath tub is now complete.*

㉒実際使用される状態に浴槽を取りつけてみる。

㉒*Fit the bath tub into similar conditions as a
real one to see if it is viable.*

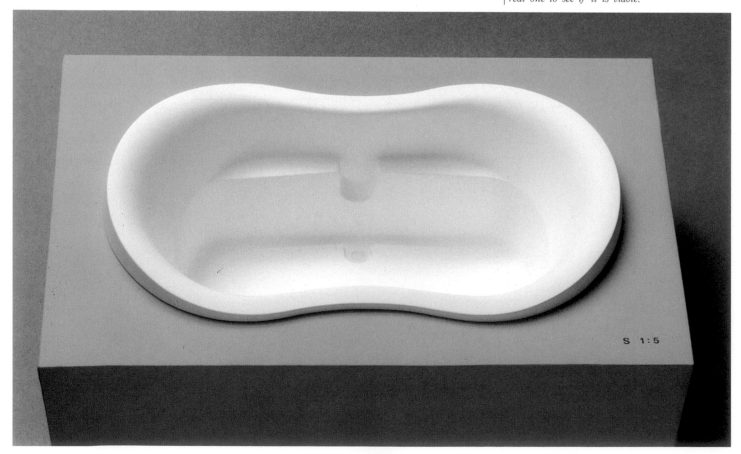

S 1:5

クレイモデル→プラスターモデル

オイルクレイ（油土）を盛りつけたり，削り取ったりしながら，思いのままの形に変化させていく，2次曲面，3次曲面などの自由曲面の造形にクレイは，すばらしいモデリング材料である。デザイン造形用クレイとして硬めのインダストリアルクレイもあり，オーブンで温め，盛り上げ，仕上げた後表面処理もできる。ここではごく普通のオイルクレイを使って丸型軒樋用のじょうごをデザインしてみる。

十分検討を加えたクレイ原形から石膏の雌型を起こし，さら雌型に石膏泥漿を流し込みクレイ原型を石膏におきかえる。

この石膏モデルで色彩，成形金型の検討や，真空成形用の型としての活用もできる。

Clay model→plaster model

Clay is a wonderful material for modeling any two-degree or three-degree surfaces as sunken areas can be refilled with oil-base clay, and shaving into any desired shape is possible.

For design modeling, a hard type of industrial clay is available on the market. This clay can be heated in an oven to make it rise and will easily take surface treatment after the model is complete.

Here I am going to design a round-shaped eave gutter using ordinary oil-based clay.

Make a concave cast mold from the well-studied original clay pattern and pour cast slip into it to replace the original clay pattern with cast.

With this cast model one can study color, plastic ingot molds and also the use of the mold for vacuum foaming.

軒樋じょうご
丸型軒樋用じょうごイメージ，メモスケッチ

Eave gutter
Image sketches of a rounded eave gutter.

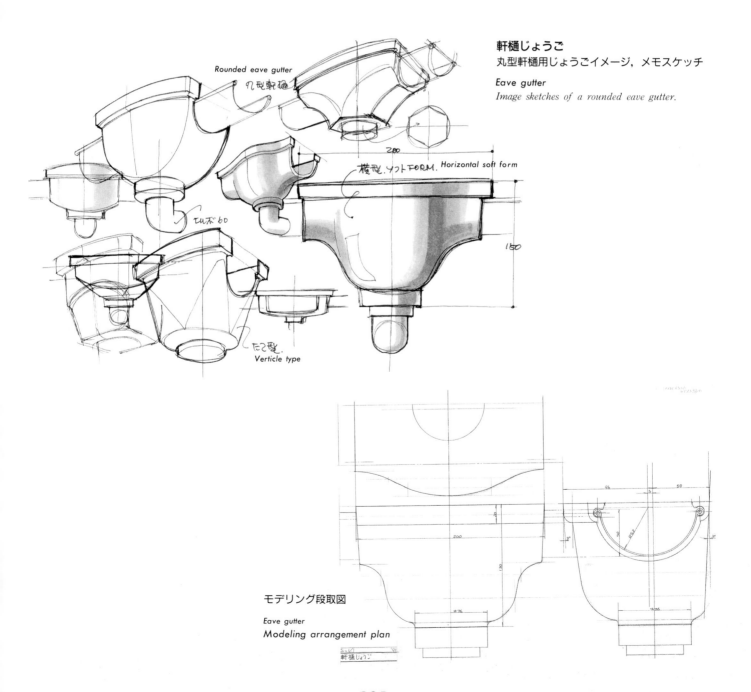

Rounded eave gutter

丸型軒樋

200

横型.ソフトFORM. Horizontal soft form

150

でんぽ 60

Verticle type

たて型.

モデリング段取図

Eave gutter
Modeling arrangement plan

❶丸型軒樋，たて樋との連接を考慮しながら，イメージしているじょうごより小さめのクレイ芯をスタイロフォームEKでつくる。

❶*Use styrofoam EK to make a clay core which should be smaller than the design image gutter, while taking into consideration the connection to the rounded eave gutter and verticle water pipe.*

❷ヒートカッター（プロフォームカッター）で切断したスタイロフォームブロックを両面テープで固定する。

❷*Fix the styrofoam block, which was cut out with a heat cutter (Proform cutter), with double-sided adhesive tape.*

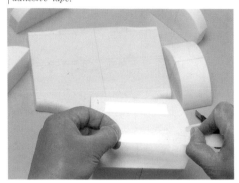

❸じょうごを逆に伏せた状態のスタイロフォームのクレイ芯ができる。

❸*A styrofoam clay core facing with the funnel on top.*

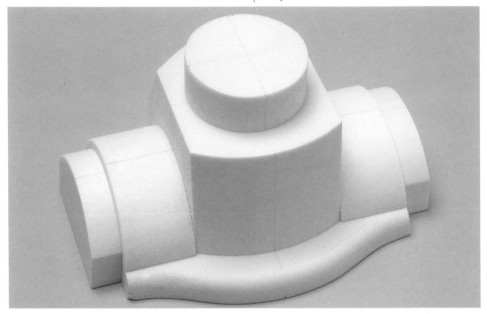

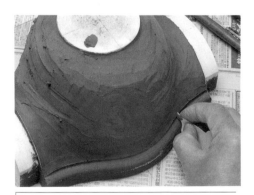

❼じょうご上縁のR（アール）付けはプラバン（t1.0mm）でゲージ（型板）をつくりオイルクレイを搔きとる。

❼*Use Plaban (1.0mm thickness) to make a gauge for the R-shape on the upper edge of the funnel and remove the oil-based clay with it.*

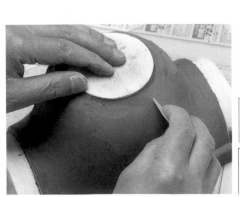

❽意図した形ができれば扱（しご）きヘラ（プラバン t1.0mmを種々の形状に切ったもの）でオイルクレイ表面を滑らかにする。

❽*Using hazing spatulas (various shapes cut from the 1.0mm thickness of Plaban), make the oil-based clay surface smooth once the design shape is completed.*

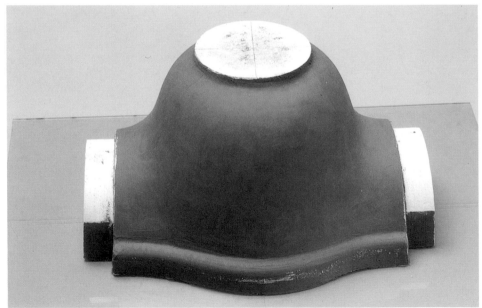

❾オイルクレイ原型のでき上り。芯の一部露出した部分は軒樋及びたて樋と嵌合する。

❾*The completed oil-based clay form. The parts revealing the core are going to be joined to the eave gutter and the vertical water pipe.*

❹芯にオイルクレイ（油土）がよくのり，また，スタイロフォーム粉がクレイに混入しないよう表面にジェッソ（リキテックス）を塗る。

❹*Apply a coat of Jesso (Liquitex) to make it easy for the oil-based clay to adhere and prevent the styrofoam powder from getting mixed with the clay.*

❻親指大にとったオイルクレイ（油土）を押しつけるように芯に盛り付ける。

❻*Take out a thumb-sized piece of oil-based clay and press it into the core to build it up.*

❺ジェッソが乾いたら石膏型取り用プラスチック板（t2㎜）にスタイロフォーム芯を両面テープで固定する。

❺*Once the Jesso dries, fix the styrofoam core to the plastic sheet (2mm thick) for making the cast mold with double-sided adhesive tape.*

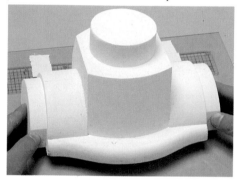

❿クレイ原型から石膏雌型を取るため離型剤（カリ石けん液）を表面に塗り，水を含んだスポンジでふきとる。これを2〜3回繰り返す。

❿*Apply some coats of potash liquid soap to the surface in order to make it easy to remove from the concave cast mold and wipe off the excess with a damp sponge. Repeat this process two or three times.*

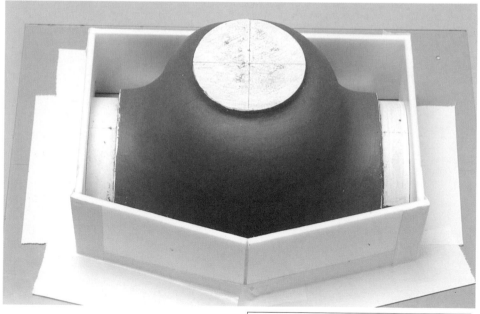

⓫注型枠をスチレンボード（t5㎜）でたてる

⓫*Build up a pour-on frame with a styrene board (5mm thick).*

⓬やわらかめの石膏泥漿を原型表面にかける。

⓬ *Pour the cast slip over the surface of the original form.*

⓭かけた石膏泥漿に少し粘りがではじめたころヘラでできるだけ均一な厚さになるよう盛りあげる。

⓭ *Once the cast slip becomes a little sticky in consistency, use a spatula to stroke it to an even thickness all around.*

⓱オイルクレイ原型表面を滑らかに仕上げたつもりでも石膏型に反転すると意外と凹凸している。細目のサンドペーパーで内面をさらに仕上げる。

⓱ *The cast mold might have some areas on the surface which are wavy, despite the smooth surface of the original form. Use a piece of fine grained sandpaper to give a yet another final touch to the inner surface.*

⓲石膏雌型に石膏泥漿を流し込むと硬化の際、石膏が膨張、雌型にヒビが入る。本体を傷めず脱型するためあらかじめ雌型に切目を入れる。雌型から複数個、型取りをする場合、抜きテーパーを十分に取り雌型にスタッフ（麻糸）を混ぜ補強する。また、条件が厳しい場合はシリコン雌型を利用する。

⓲ *During the process of hardening after the cast slip has been poured into the concave cast shape, the case will expand and crack the concave mold. In order to remove the main unit without any damage, insert a cut onto the concave mold beforehand. When more than one mold is needed to remove the concave mold, use a sufficient amount of tapering and mix resin into the concave mold to reinforce its strength.*
Use a silicone concave mold when conditions dictate it the better choice.

⓮オイルクレイ原型に石膏泥漿を被せ硬化する
のをまつ。

⓮*Cover the original form of the oil-based clay
with cast slip and wait until it hardens.*

⓰石膏雌型。

⓰*The concave cast mold.*

⓯石膏が発熱硬化すればオイルクレイ原型から
脱型する。

⓯*When the cast generates heat and hardens,
remove from the original oil-based clay form.*

⓴石膏泥漿を雌型に流し込む。

⓴*Pour the cast slip into the concave mold.*

⓳雌型内表面に離型剤（カリ石ケン液）を塗り，
水を含んだスポンジでふきとる。2〜3回繰り
返す。

⓳*Apply a coat of potash liquid soap to the surface of the inner side of the concave mold and
wipe off any excess with a damp sponge. Repeat
this process two or three times.*

㉑雌型表面に石膏泥漿がいきわたるよう雌型を傾ける。

㉑ *Tilt the mold to spread the slip evenly over the surface of the concave mold.*

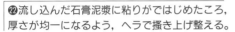

㉓型からはみだした余分な石膏をステンレススケールで掻きおとす。

㉓ *Use a stainless-steel scale to scrape off the excess cast.*

㉒流し込んだ石膏泥漿に粘りがではじめたころ，厚さが均一になるよう，ヘラで掻き上げ整える。

㉒ *When the cast slip begin to become slighlty sticky in consistency, use a spatula to spread it to an even thickness all over.*

㉖石膏本体を取りだす。

㉖ *Remove the main cast unit.*

㉗表面をサンドペーパー（#240〜#400）で軽く仕上げる。

㉗ *Gently rub the surface with a piece of sand-paper (between #240-#400) to finish.*

㉔流し込んだ石膏が硬化し，脱型する前に，本体内側の不要な石膏をノコ刃で削り落とす。

㉔*Before the cast completely hardens and is removed from the mold, shave off all unwanted cast from the inner sides of the main unit with a saw blade.*

㉕木槌で軽く雌型をたたき慎重に脱型する。

㉕*Give the mold a slight tap with a wooden mallet and remove the cast from the mold with great care.*

㉘底に石膏ロクロで挽いた部品を接着剤（エポキシ系）で固定する。

㉘*Fix the parts which were sawn off by the cast lathe to the bottom with an adhesive agent (epoxy resin).*

㉙丸型軒樋が嵌るよう溝を切る。

㉙*Cut the gutter opening to fit the rounded water pipe under the eaves.*

❸⓪丸型軒樋で嵌り具合を確かめる。

❸⓪*Check to ensure that the rounded eave gutter fits nicely into place.*

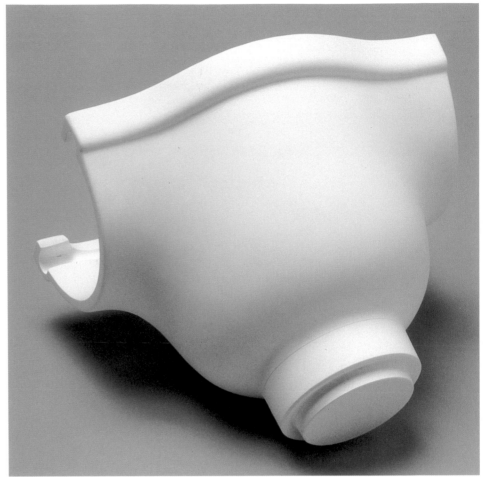

❸①軒樋じようご本体の完了。

❸①*The main unit of the eave gutter is now complete.*

❸②丸型軒樋，たて樋を取り付けてみる。

❸②*Attach the verticle water pipe to the rounded eave gutter.*

WITH REGARD TO CLAY MODELLING
クレイモデリング
造形手法

松田真次
Shinji Matsuda

クレイモデリングについて
About clay modelling

クレイモデリングは，デザインスケッチで描かれた2次元表現を立体三次元表現にし，造形的な質感・量感・全体バランスなどを観察・評価することを主とするため，造形表面に加工時の無数のキズが残っているとキズのため造形が見えにくくなる。今回の書では特にクレイ表面の面出し技法を中心に表現する。なお造形が見やすい色としては，白色（わずかな影の違いが表現できる）が最適であるが，現在市場に市販されているクレイでは明るいグレー色，α（アルファ）クレイを使用した。αクレイは造形的に見易いグレードである。なおクレイモデル評価時点で特別に色を付けたがるが，色調により造形の量感に変化が生ずるので，さけるべきである。また，造形評価時その場所で，造形的変更が表面クレイのみであれば，即対応できる点でもクレイは有利である。クレイ作業は基本的に作業者が動く（座っての一定作業は無理）ことが大切で，造形物を中心に作業者は造形物に対し，一番削りやすいポジションと姿勢を常に変化させることとなる。クレイモデルは人間が削る微妙な作業であり技術である。

※クレイ面の良さはクレイツール（レイク・フィニッシャー）が良く切れることが大切で，基本的には刃物でなければ良いクレイ表面はできない。

※クレイ作業はモデルの右・左どちらか片方を先行して進めると良い。片側での1次モデル評価後反対側の反転作業を行うと効率的である。

The main purpose of clay modelling is to enable one to evaluate the formative quality, volume and overall balance by transforming a 2-dimensional expressional design sketch into a 3-dimensional expression. It is therefore difficult to see the actual model if numerous stratch marks remain on the surface of the model from the processing stage. This book has been written to shine a special spotlight onto the technique of clay surfacing. White is the best color to show up the model clearly (as even the slightest of shade changes can be expressed), but here I have used α clay which is a high grade modelling clay that has the lightest hue amongst all grey clays available on the current market. In some situations clay coloring is added to the model at the time of evaluation. This act is not advisable, however, as the color will give different volume impressions to the model. One of the good things about α clay is its capability of corresponding well during evaluation should formative alterations to the clay surface be required.

The most important thing during clay work is to move yourself around the model to find comfortable positions in which to work (it is impossible to work well in one position). Clay modelling requires a fine touch and the techniques of human beings.

※ The quality of a clay surface will finally be decided by the quality of the tools, basically the edging tools.

※ It is more efficient to commence work on one side of the model and then move to the other side after the first evaluation has been completed.

1) クレイモデルとは（デザインクレイ）

デザイナーがデザインスケッチでは表現しきれない繊細な形をより速く具体的に表現する手法として，クレイモデルをつくる。デザイナーの意志を明確に表現し第三者に伝えるためである。クレイモデルは他の造形表現手法と比較し，削り，盛りが手早くできるためデザイナーとしての造形表現の時間的自由度と拘りを得るためにも，有利であり，現在時間的有効度として最適材料手法であろう。クレイモデル製作時にはわずかな曲線・端末Rの違いで大きくイメージが変化する。形を想像し製品化するとき，三次元，立体，造形をつくることなどを大切にしたいものである。また，クレイモデルをつくる際，数理的に造るのではなく，デザイナーの人間的感性を重視して造るよう心がけたいものである。デザイン造形は人間の視覚に訴えるのであり，機械部品ではないからである。

1) Exactly what is a clay model (design clay)?

Designers create clay models as one of the methods to express delicate shapes in designs which cannot adequately be expressed in 2-dimensional design sketches in a swift and bold manner in order to put across their ideas to a third party. In comparison to other formative methods, designers can easily shave off bits that are not wanted or add extra pieces if needed with the clay model method. Clay modelling is therefore a favored method with designers owing to it adding a flexibility to their formative expression. It could be considered one of the most efficient materials available in present times. A slight difference in the curved lines or terminal R can change the image greatly. It is important for designers to creat 3-dimensional cubic models to see the actual shape before the design is mechanized. Also, designers should try to avoid using mathematical calculations and instead rely on their own design senses when creating models.

In this way the end product is more likely to appeal to the visual senses of the beholder. Creations should not be machine parts.

2) クレイモデルの各種類

①**フルサイズモデル**：実物と同一寸法（1/1）でつくる。詳細な部分までリアルにつくり，造形的質感，量産バランスを見る。

②**スケールモデル**：1/10・1/5・1/4・1/2と分れる造形は基本的には1/1でつくるべきであるが時間，コスト的に問題が生じるため開発初期段階ではスケールモデルが合理的手法である。特に大物（4輪・鉄道車両等）開発時に使用される。

2) Clay model types.

1. Full-size models : An actual size (1/1) model, describing in detail the formative quality, balance and volume.

2. Scale models : Such scales should be kept to 1/10, 1/5, 1/4 and 1/2. Basically, full-size models (1/1) are more advisable, but time and cost problems involved in creation make the scale model a more rational approach at the early stages of development. This style is especially used for large objects (such as four-wheelers and railway carriages) during the development stage.

3) 開発手順，各モデル

量感・質感・造形バランスを観るためには，フルスケールモデルが一番良いが時間的，コスト的にも大きな物（自動車・鉄道車両など）は，開発初期段階ではスケールモデルをつくる。2輪車は大物ではあるが初期段階よりフルサイズ1/1モデル以外はつくらない物もある。

開発初期 イメージモデル・先行モデル　1/10・1/8

開発中期 スケールモデル　1/4・1/2→線図作成

開発後期 フルサイズモデル　1/1 ┌風力専用フルサイズモデル，
　　　　　　　　　　　　　　　　　 └線図作成→木型デザインマスター

①**アイデア**：調査・検討・分析→アイデア，スケッチ
②**立体**：スケールモデル→フルサイズクレイモデル
③**設計**：線図化→木型→レイアウト図化・単品図・ASSY図
④**生産化**：生産技術→生産フォロー

4) 基準

①工業製品のモデル製作時最も重要な作業は基準設定である。

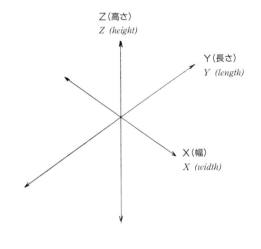

Z（高さ）
Z (height)

Y（長さ）
Y (length)

X（幅）
X (width)

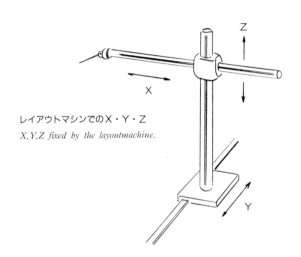

レイアウトマシンでのX・Y・Z
X, Y, Z fixed by the layoutmachine.

②基準 0（ゼロ）ポイントの設定は図面化，線図化の基本となる。なお 0 ポイントはメーカー製品により異なる。

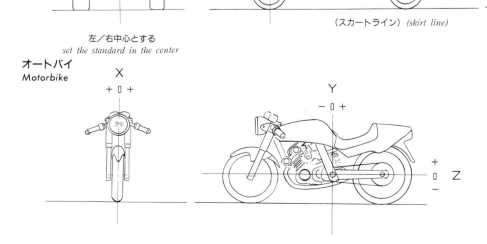

例）(Example)

自動車
Car

+ 0 +　　X

－ 0 +　Y

+
0　Z
－

（スカートライン）(skirt line)

左／右中心とする
set the standard in the center

オートバイ
Motorbike

X
+ 0 +

Y
－ 0 +

+
0　Z
－

---

3) The development process of each model.

Full-size models will provide a more precise idea of the design as one can use them to study the quality, volume and formative balance of the actual model, but when working on large models (such as four-wheelers and railway carriages), scale models can be used during the development stages. Two-wheelers also belong to the 'large model' category, but in certain cases they will be created in full-size from the commencement of the early development stage.

* *Early development stage : Image model. Tentative model 1/10, 1/8.*

* *Middevelopment stage : Scale model 1/4, 1/2 → chart making*

* *Late development stage :*
　　　1/1→Full-size model
　　　　→chart making → wood model design master

1. *Idea : Investigation, review, analysis → idea sketch*
2. *Solidity : Scale model → full-size clay model*
3. *Design : Line chart → wood model → layout drawing, individual part drawings, ASSY drawing*
4. *Creation : Creation technique → production followup*

4) Standards

(1) The most important part involved with the creation of industrial products is to set the standard points.

(2) The zero-point standard set will create the basis of the drawing and charting process. However, each maker will have its own point setting.

5) クレイの種類と使い分け

●インダストリアルクレイJ525　色調：ブラウン／加熱温度62℃±2°
冷えると硬くなる。よって精度が必要な物，大型モデルに適している。自動車産業で主力に使用している。

●桂油土　色調：グレー／加熱温度40℃±2°
冷えても多少やわらかい。加工性（カット・荒削り）に優れ，造形面出し状態も優れているが，面出し，フィニッシャー加工時多少技術を要する一部自動車産業にて使用されている。

●αクレイ　色調：明るいグレー／加熱温度45℃±2°
近年開発されたクレイであるが，インダストリアルクレイと桂油土の中間に位置し，幅広い用途に使用可能である。加熱温度も低く，また冷やした時点でもインダストリアルクレイよりやわらかい。加工性も良く，初心者にも十分適応できる。面出し仕上げ状態も非常に良いレベルに仕上がり，今後広い範囲で使用されることと判断する。
大物造形物（自動車など）～小物（カメラなど）まで使用可能であり，明るいグレーのため造形面が見やすい利点もある。

6) クレイ盛り付け方（クレイ作業基礎）

●基礎盛り

[○]多少高めの温度（やわらかい）のクレイを使用し，十分に中子（モデルコア）に付くようにする。
クレイを引き伸ばすように盛りつける。
※一度に多く盛り付けることはさける。

□Using clay with a slight high temperature, carefully press down on it until it adheres to the model core.
The clay should be spread evenly.
※Try to avoid using too much clay at once for the filling.

[×]硬いクレイを一つ一つ貼り付ける盛り付けを行うと，クレイが軽くハガレてしまいクレイ面に割れが生じる。

■The use of multilayered hard clay will create cracks on the surface which will result in parts breaking away.

●荒盛り

[○]基礎盛り時より一度に多く盛り付けることとなるが，やはり引き伸ばす方向で作業を行うと面が出やすくまたエアーも入りにくい。

□A greater portion of filling is needed than in the basic filling stage, but good surface work can be achieved by careful spreading. This will also prevent air from getting inside.

[×]荒盛りもクレイを貼り付けてしまうと面が荒れ，またクレイ内に多量のエアーが入りやすく，クレイが割れやすくなる。

■Should the clay be pasted on piece by piece, a rough surface will be created which will eventually crack as air will be allowed inside.

5) Type of clay and their proper uses.

●Industrial clay J525 : Color : brown／Heating temp. : 62℃ + 2
This type of clay becomes hard when chilled and therefore requires a high degree of accuracy when working. It is Suitable for largescale models and is mainly used in the field of industrial cars.

●Katsura oil clay : Color : grey／Heating temp. : 40℃ + 2
This type of clay remains slightly soft even when chilled, and is excellent for processing (cutting and rough shaving) and surfacing. However, a modicum of technique is required when working on the surfacing and finishing process. It is partly used in the field of industrial cars.

●α clay　Color : light grey／Heating temp. : 45℃ + 2
A newly developed clay. It can be placed between industrial clay and Katsura oil clay, and has a wide range of applications. It requires a low heating temperature and remains softer than industrial clay when chilled. It is easily handled by beginners owing to its generous processibility. It also creates excellent surface finishing. It is fair to suggest that the applicational ranges of this clay will widen in the near future. It is versatile for models from small to large and can therefore cope with such objects as cars and small cameras. It also has the advantage of availing a clear surface to the model owing to the lightness of its color.

6) Clay filling methods : CLAY FOUNDATION WORK.

●Basic filling

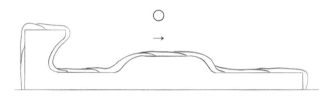

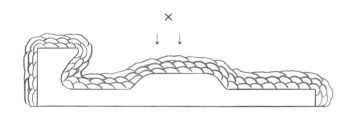

●Rough filling

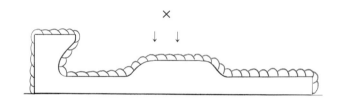

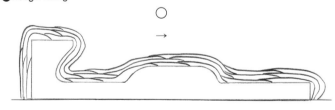

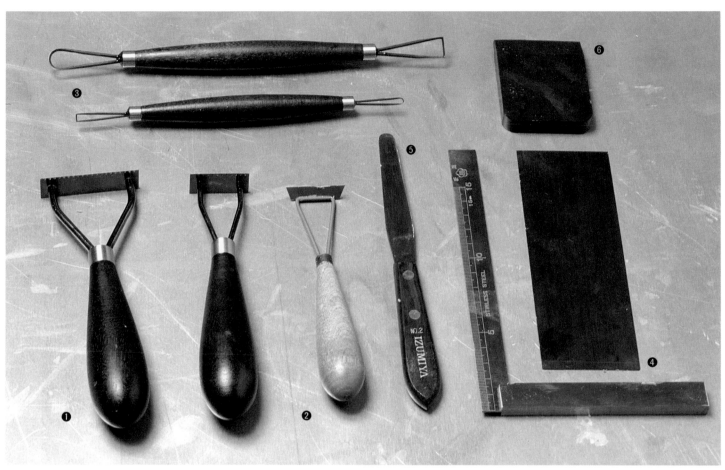

① レイク（直カキ） ┐
② フィニッシャー ├ 削り加工用ツール
③ ワイヤー   │
④ スチール板   ┘

⑤ パレットナイフ　ライン取り
⑥ ゴムベラ　面出し

※市販されている加工ツールをさらに色々と自分で改造すると使いやすい。

① Rake (direct scraper) ┐
② Finisher   ├ Shaving process tools
③ Wire   │
④ Steel plate   ┘
⑤ Palette knife   Liner
⑥ Rubber palette   Surface tools

Tools can be improved upon by various conversions to the originals purchased.

3. クレイツールの研ぎ方
Methods for sharpening clay tools

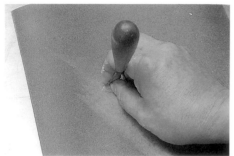

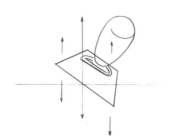

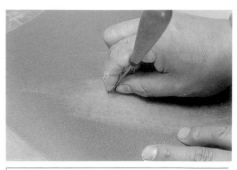

●フィニッシャーの研ぎ方
Sharpening finishers :

1.荒研ぎ　刃角を付ける　240#（サンドペーパー）
研ぐときはツールを45°斜めにし前後に動かすと
刃角が一定に保ちやすい

1. Rough sharpening.
Set the blade angle 240#.
It is easy to keep the blade at a certain angle
if the tool is placed at a 45° angle for shar-
pening and then moved up and down.

多少油を付ける
A small amount of
oil will be needed.

直線
Straight line.

2.中研ぎ　刃面出し　600#
600#で刃面を研ぐ。多少油を付ける。
研ぎ方は荒研ぎと同じ。

2. Inner sharpening.
Blade face production 600#.
The blade face is sharpened in 600# in the
same style as before.
A small amount of oil will be needed.

5.極細ペーパー作り（刃出しのため）
❶1,000#＋1,000#をこすり目をさらに細かくする。
❷油は付けない。

5. Superfine paper making *(for edging)*
1. Rub the 1000#＋1000# to create an even
finer 1000#.
2. Oil is not necessary.

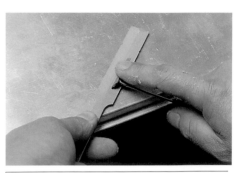

6.刃出し
●極細ペーパー面を多少力を抜き研ぐとき（油
は付けない）刃面が鏡面状態になる→返し研ぎ
1往復のみ（軽く）。
この状態になると良く切れる。フィニッシャー
は切れることが命。
[切れ味確認]
●右図に示すよう親指を切面に当て、手前に軽
く引きその指ざわりで判断できる。
※横に引くと手が切れるので注意。

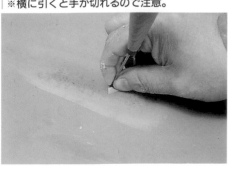

6. Edge sharpening.
When the blade is rubbed against the surface
of the superfine paper rather lightly, the sur-
face of the blade will resemble a mirror →
back-sharpening once only (lightly).
The blade will cut well after this stage.
The quality of the finish will depend on how
well the blade cuts.
Testing the sharpness of the blade.
As the picture on the right indicates, one can
easily test the sharpness of a blade by placing
a thumb on the sharp edge of the blade and
giving a light flick to-wards oneself.
※Injuries will occur if the finger is moved
sideways.

親指を引く
切れる物は鋭さを感じる

Pull the thumb towards oneself.
The cutting ability can be felt through
the sharpness of the blade.

7.特刃付け
●600#→800#で刃面研ぎ，返し研ぎ後細かい鉄
ヤスリ面に刃を乗せ，強く1回引き特刃を付け
る。
●荒削りと面出しの中間に中出しを行うと，良
い造形面が出やすくなる。そのために刃面に一
定のノコ刃状の刃を設ける。

7. Special blade making.
Sharpen the edge of the blade on the 600# →
800# and then back-sharpen it. Place the
blade on a fine iron cast and give a sharp
pull to create the special edge.
A good surface can be added to the model if
an extra
process is added between the rough shaving
and the surfacing. This will require a sawed-
ged blade.

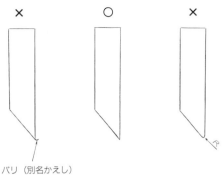

バリ（別名かえし）
Excess material (another name is 'return').

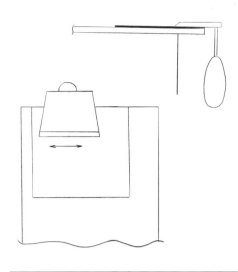

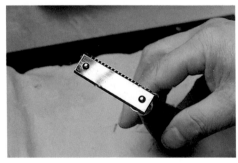

3.仕上げ研ぎ　刃面仕上げ　1,000#
1,000#にて刃面を仕上げる。多少油を付ける。

3. Sharpening finish. Blade finishing 1000#.
The blade face should be sharpened as in 1000# for completion. A small amount of oil will be needed.

4.返し研ぎ
600#で1往復，1,000#2往復のみで止めること。
返し研ぎは表刃を研ぐと裏刃にバリが生ずる。
そのバリを取り除く作業が返し研ぎである。
※返し研ぎを行わないと刃とはならないし，切れない。
※返し研ぎは研ぎすぎると裏面にRが付き切れなくなるので，1〜2回往復で止めること。

4. Back-sharpening.
In the case of 600#, sharpen from one end to the other and back. In the case of 1000#, sharpen from one end to the other and back, and then repeat once only.
The process of back-sharpening is carried out to remove the excess material created on the back of the blade after the front of the blade has been sharpened.
※Without the back-sharpening process, the blade will not serve its duty as it will not cut well.
※ This process should not be repeated more than twice as excess sharpening will produce an R on the back of the blade and make it blunt.

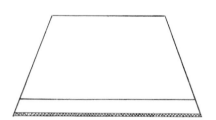

↑ 凹凸の深さは一定のこと
The depths of the ruggedness need to be regulated.

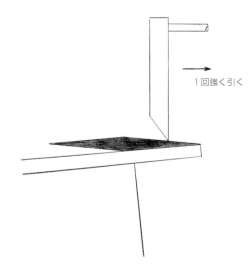

1回強く引く

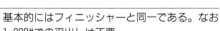

●レイクツールの研ぎ方
Sharpening rake tools.

基本的にはフィニッシャーと同一である。なお
1,000#での刃出しは不要。
240#　刃角を付ける
600#　刃面出し
800#　刃面仕上げ

Basically, the same methods as shown in the finisher are required. However, the 1000# process can be omitted.
240#　fix an angle to the blade.
600#　sharpen the blade face.
800#　finish off the blade face.

レイクツールの研ぎときも刃面にRが付くと切れ味が悪くなる。

The quality of the rake tool will decrease if the cutting edge has an R shape.

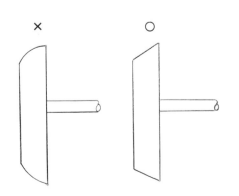

1. 削り出し

レイクの刃面で大きな凹凸面を削り取り，全体造形面をなだらかにする。

1. Shaving.

With the use of the blade face, scrape the large rugged surface of the clay to achieve an overall smoothness.

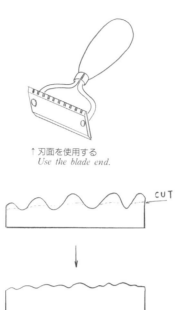

↑刃面を使用する
Use the blade end.

CUT

2-1. 荒削り

レイクのノコ刃面を使用し基本的形状を出してゆく。ツールの動かし方は一方向ではなく，ランダムに動かしてゆくと良い。

2-1. Rough shaving.

With the use of the sawedged end of the rake the basic shape should be formed. It is advisable to move the rake in random direction in order to achieve the best results.

2-2. 荒削り手順

❶❷レイクを引く方向に対し直角にし，削ることにより1回の削りしろが大きく初期レベルの表面状態時に有利である。
❸❹レイクを引く方向に対し斜めにセットし，削ることによりレイクの振れが安定すると同時に細く削り取ることができる。
❺レイクを引く方向を曲線状にしレイクも斜めにすることにより，より安定した削りができるが，削り量は少なくなり表面状態が良くなる。

2-2. Steps for rough shaving.

❶❷A large area can be shaved off by setting the rake at a 90° angle against the pulling direction. This is favourable during the early stage of surface treatment.
❸❹A steady sway of the rake can be achieved by inclining the rake to till against the direction of the pull. At the same time a more increased slanted shave becomes possible.
❺More steady shaving can be achieved by pulling the rake to draw a curved line and inclining it into a tilt. This will, however, decrease the amount being shaved, but the condition of the surface will improve.

クレイツールの動かし方，削り方
Effective ways of handling the tool.

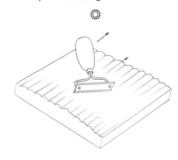

削り量は少ないが，凹凸面に対し，ツールが安定し良いクレイ面が出しやすい
The quantity being shaved is small, but the tool can be moved steadily against the rugged surface which enables ease of gaining a good quality surface.

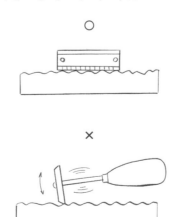

3. 面造りができた次に中仕上げ

特刃付けしたフィニッシャーでより細かな面を作る。この時点では造形上の仕上げ状態をつくる。
中仕上げ削り時は，ツールを軽くにぎり軽く削る（ツールの刃が切れることが大切）ようにする。きれいな面をつくるには強く押し削ることはさけよう。

3. After the surface treatment of rough shaving, we come onto the process known as the mid-finish.

The use of a finisher with a special blade attached will produce a much finer surface. At this stage the surface should be ready for work on the actual modelling.
Try to hold the tool lightly and give light touches to the shaving during the process of the mid-finishing (it is important for the blade to cut well). Avoid pushing the tool too hard in order to achieve a good quality of the clay's surface.

削り手順
Steps of the shaving process.

❶
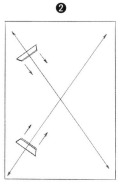

❷
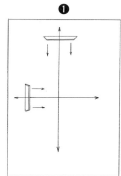

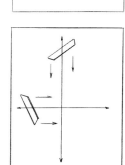
❸

❹
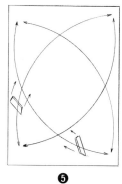

❺

注意　造形面が荒れている状態で面仕上げに入ろうと手順を急ぐと，面に波状のチャター現象が生ずる。

NB : The surface of the clay will end up with wavy lines if the surface finishing process is carried out too swiftly while the surface is still rough.

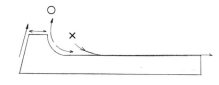

中仕上時のツールの動かし方のポイントは
1. 軽く持ち軽いタッチで削る。
2. ツールを面に接する時は軽くまた下図に示す流れで接する。
3. ツールの動きは多方面で行うこと。

Effective ways of handling the tool during this process are :
1. Grip it lightly and give light touches to the shaving.
2. It should be gently placed on the surface and moved as is shown in the picture below.
3. The tools should be moved in random directions.

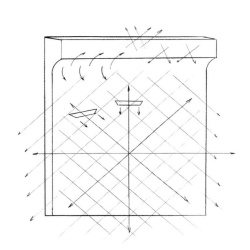

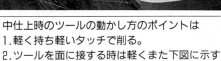

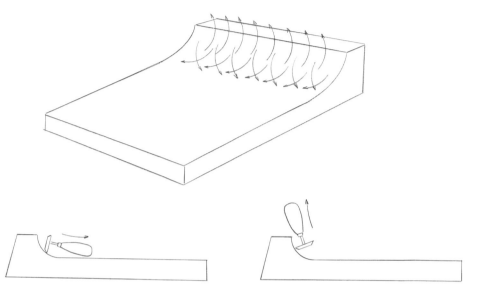

4. 曲面削り

曲面削りのときはツールの動きは下図に示すよう，ランダムに動かすようにすると良い。

4. Shaving curved surfaces.

The tools should be moved in random directions for shaving as indicated in the picture below for the treatment of curved surfaces.

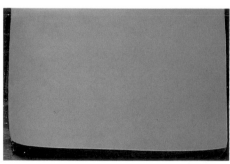

5. 面仕上げ──3つの方法

❶フィニッシャー特加工刃にて面出し完了後，フィニッシャーにて（良く切れる刃のこと）クレイ面を満遍無く面を仕上げた後，ゴムベラまた指，手のひらなどで面を連続させてゆく。

❷フィニッシャー特加工刃にて面出し完了後，ゴムベラ，指，手のひらなどで面を連続させてゆく。なおこの方法では多少面に細かな線が残る。（造形を見る時には支障なし）

5. Surface finishing. 3 methods available.

❶*Once the surface treatment with specially processed blades has been completed, the clay surface is once again thoroughly treated with a finisher (ensure the blade is sharp), a rubber spatula, the fingers and the palm of the hand to create a continuity to the surface.*

❷*After the surface has been treated with the specially processed blade of the finisher, use a rubber spatula, the fingers and the palm of the hand to give a continuity to the surface. This method, however, will leave faint lines on the surface. (This will not matter when the formation is checked).*

❸フィニッシャー特加工刃にて，面出し完了後フィニッシャーにてクレイ面を満遍無く面を仕上げた後，テレピン油をウエスにしみこませ表面をみがきその後，ゴムベラ，指，手のひら等で仕上げる。No.3の方法は玉，面，等三次元造形の急な箇所に使用すると良い。

❸*Once the surface has been treated with the specially processed blade of the finisher, a thorough treatment of the clay surface should be carried out with the use of a finisher. Then, soak a rag in terrapin oil and polish the surface before the final treatment with the rubber spatula fingers and palm of the hand takes place.*
The No.3 method is suitable for the treatment of steep parts of 3-dimensional models such as spherical surfaces.

6. フィニッシャー

クレイ表面はキズが無い状態に仕上り造形が見やすくなる。またこの後塗装を行っても十分耐える面状態となる。

6. Finishing.

The clay surface is completed with no marks, which make the formation easily noticable. The quality of the surface is good enough to take color.

❶デザイン，スケッチとレイアウト図をもとに縮尺レベルを決め，中子はデザインの自由度を与えるため２周りほど小さく作ると良い。中子をモデル寸法ギリギリで作ってしまうとクレイモデルでの削り自由度がなくなり，デザインクレイの意味をなくしてしまうのでさけるべきである。

※小さなモデル（300mm以下）では中子不要クレイのみで良い。

❶ Firstly fix the reduced scale level from the design sketch and layout plan. It is then advisable to make the modelling core two sizes smaller than the expected size of the model in order to retain some flexibility for alterations to the design. One should avoid making the core too close in size to the actual model as this will not leave much space to work on and a modicum of significance will be lost from the clay design.
A core is not necessary for small clay modelling (less than 300mm). The clay on its own will be sufficient.

1.クレイ盛り付け

❷盛り付けはモデル予定寸法より１周り大きく盛り付ける。盛り付けが荒すぎると削っている際にクレイがハガレクズレたりし，また面が出しにくくなるので，なるべく基本の形に忠実にしっかり盛り付ける。

1. Clay covering.

❷ Cover the model core with clay until the size exceeds the expected dimensions of the model. At this point the clay should be added to the basic shape of the core as closely and as tightly-packed as possible to avoid the clay losing its hold when the work commences. Such occurances will make the creation of the surface difficult.

2.基準線を入れる

❸クレイモデルをつくる際，必ず何かの基準となる線を入れること。２輪車，自動車，鉄道などはセンターラインと水平ラインを入れるようにすることがポイントとなる。

2. The insertion of the base line.

❸ Some form of base line should always be drawn with clay modelling work. One should make a point of drawing a center and horizontal line when working on clay models of bicycles, cars and trains, etc.

3.荒削り（使用ツール　レイク50）

❹荒削りは基本形状を出す事が主である。平行面，水平面，形を出す。
削るときは小さな物は人と物どちらも自由に動かし削りやすいポジションを得ることが削りのポイント。

3. Rough shaving.
(The tool used here is the Rake 50.)

❹ The rough shaving is needed to create the basic shape of the parallel and horizontal surfaces.
The important point in this process is to get a comfortable position in which the shaving can been carried out freely by moving either yourself or the clay model.

❺鉄道のように平行面が多くあるとき（側面）は、時々定規で面の平行面を確認しながら削るようにする。なお主力は造形作業であり形状を大切に。

❺ *During the process of making a clay model which has many parallel surfaces (flank faces) such as a railway train, it is advisable to check the surfaces occasionally with a ruler. The most important process here is the creation of the shape, therefore strong attention should be paid to these surfaces.*

4.イメージを出す

❻時々，パレットナイフを使用して基本的な外形の形状，艤装などを入れてみて全体イメージを描きながら削っていく。
※この時点では精度よりイメージを大切にするよう。

4. Image Creation

❻ *With the occasional use of a palette knife, draw in the complete surface image and outline shape for shaving.*
At this stage the priority should be given to the image creation rather than accuracy.

5.フロント周りの造形出し

❿デザインスケッチ，テープドロー・レイアウト図などを基本とし，パレットナイフラインを確認しながら削っていく。
※あまり長時間同じところを（フロント及びサイド）削っていると，一方向にイメージが片寄る。時々削る箇所を変えると良い。また時々手を休み多少離れて観ることも大切である。

5. Creating the shape of the front area.

❿ *Using the design sketch, the tape drawing and the layout plan as a basis, give occasional touch-ups with the palette knife and shave to shape.*
It is advisable not to spend too much time shaving the same area (front and sides) as there is the possibility that this will result in a partial image. An occasional position shift is recommended. It is also important to take regular breaks and view the work from a short distance.

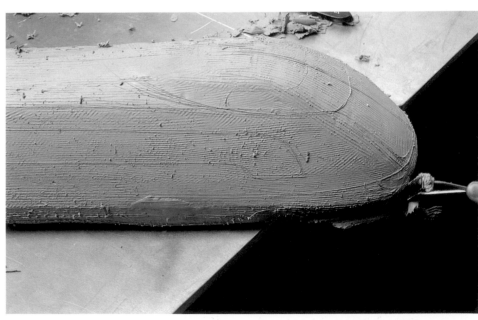

⓫削るとパレットナイフのラインが消えるので，時々造形バランスを見るために，再度パレットナイフでラインを描き直しては削り…繰り返し作業となる。

⓫ *The lines created by the palette knife will be erased during the shaving process, so the job of reapplying these lines should be repeated each time in order to maintain the overall balance of the model.*

❼パレットナイフでイメージしたラインを入れ，デザインスケッチテープドローなどで描いたイメージに対し，三次元造形時では，イメージが異なるときが生ずるのでパレットナイフで描いたラインを大切にすると，繊細なラインを描くことができる。

❼ *Use the pallet knife to draw in the image lines. The image of the design sketch will come in for a few amendments whilst one is working on the three-dimensional process. The lines drawn in with the palette knife will therefore help when it comes to adding delicate lines.*

❽パレットナイフでイメージラインを描き，削っていく。

❽ *Use the palette knife to draw in the image lines and the shave to shape.*

❾削るとイメージラインが消えてしまうがこれを繰り返し，確認しながら造形としての完成度を上げてゆく。
※なお基本となるレイアウト図などの確認も行うこと。

❾ *The image lines will be erased by the shaving process, but the repetition of this process and reconfirmation of these lines will bring the model to completion.*
The basic layout plans should also be reconfirmed.

⓬水平ラインは定盤等平面台の上にスコアなどでサイドラインを描く寸法等はテープドロー，レイアウト図を参考とする。

⓬ *With regard to the horizontal lines, use a score-like tool to draw in the side lines on a plane base such as a modelling board. The tape drawing and layout plan should be refered to for the sizes.*

⓮サイド面，ルーフ面を相互に削り込んでゆくことにより，それぞれの造形バランスを確認する。

⓮ *Check each modelling balance by shaving the sides and roof alternatively.*

⓯サイド面の削り出しを行っている。ルーフとサイド面は造形として重要な関連性があるので十分注意確認しながら削ること。
※サイド・ルーフどちらか片側の面が波打っていると，面の交わる箇所が波を打つ。

⓯ *This is the side shaping process. The roof and the sides have a very important relationship to the model, so a great deal of care and occasional checks are needed during this process.*
If the sides or the roof undulate, the area where the sides meet will also undulate.

⓭水平面確認後再度サイド面を削り出す。この時点では水平面とサイド造形両面の削り出し作業となり，レイク（レイク50）の動きも斜めにスライドさせながら削りを行っていく。

⓭ *After the horizontal surface check has been made, start to reshave the sides. At this stage both the horizontal surfaces and the sides of the model should be shaved to shape. Scrape the rake (Rake 50) diagonally against the shape.*

⑯サイド面，上面断面を確認すると両面とも微妙なRで構成されている。

⑯ *A check of the sides and the upper surface will reveal that both sides have been made up of a fine 'R' shape.*

⑰基本的造形が確認後，後部を直角にカットし面を出す。

⑰ *Cut the rear part of the model at an angle of 90° having checked the basic model to reveal the surface.*

⑱パレットナイフを使用して形状確認とイメージ出しを行っている。

⑱ *Use a palette knife to check the shape and create the image.*

⑲写真はヘッドライト周りのイメージを出し作業をパレットナイフで描いている。

⑲ *The photograph shows the process of creating the image around the headlights with the use of a palette knife.*

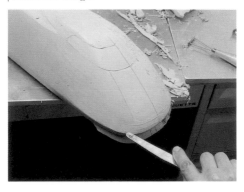

㉓フロントスポイラー端末バリ取り。軽くフィニッシャーにて削り取る。

㉓ *The front spoiler terminal finish. Shave lightly with the finisher.*

㉔サイド面の面出し。

㉔ *Shaping the sides.*

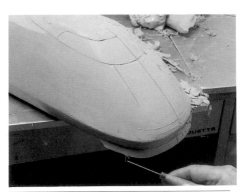

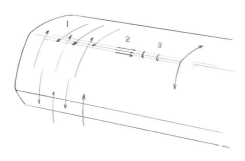

刃を斜めに
Move the blade diagonally to shape.

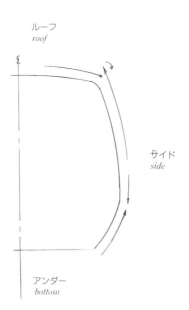

ルーフ
roof

サイド
side

アンダー
bottom

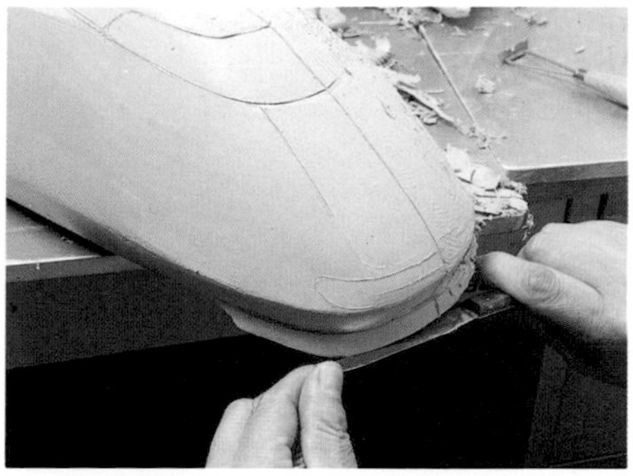

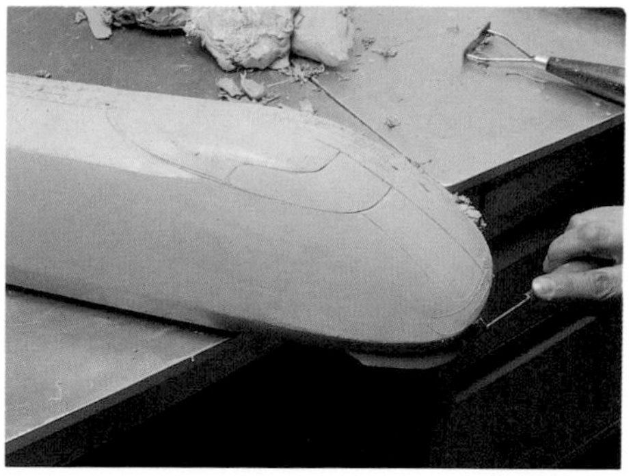

⑳フロントスポイラー端末処理を行っている物が小さいため，プレート（スケールスリーク）を端末部に軽く当て，R水平出しを行っている。

⑳ The terminal process is added to the front spoiler. Being small, a plate is lightly added to the terminal section in order to produce the horizontal 'R' shape.

㉑フロントライト下面形状出しを行っている。下から上に引くと良い。

㉑ This is the process of shaping the lower section of the front light. The best results can be achieved if one works from the bottom up.

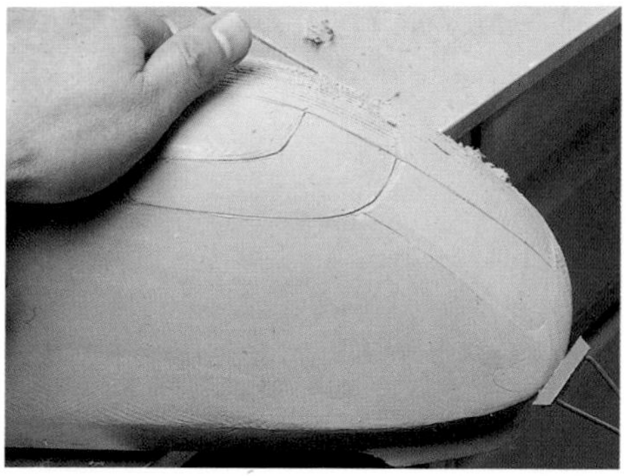

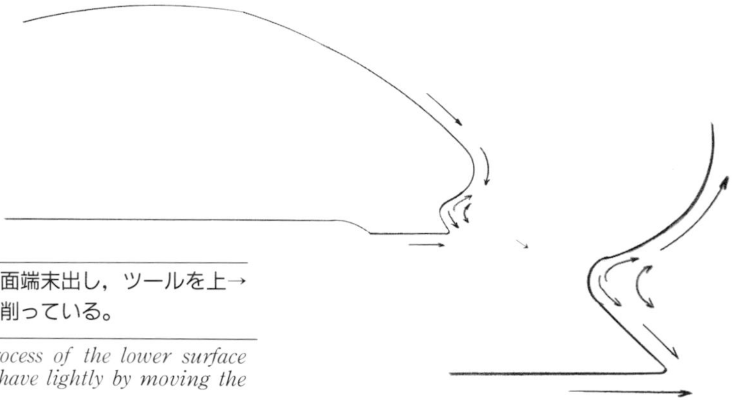

㉒フロントライト下面端末出し，ツールを上→下に斜めにして軽く削っている。

㉒ The terminal process of the lower surface of the front light. Shave lightly by moving the tool up and down.

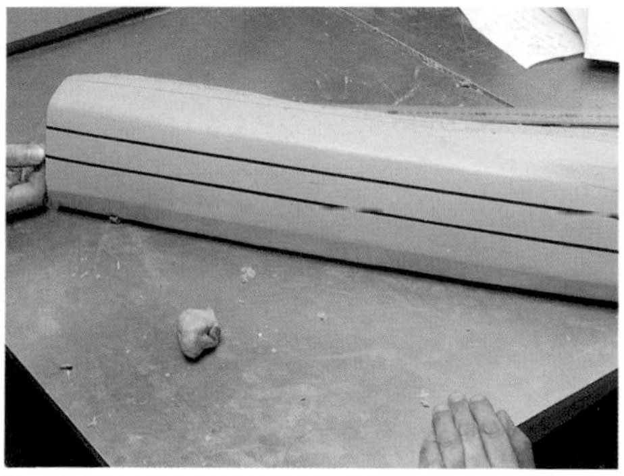

㉕イメージスケッチ，レイアウト図を基本にサイドウインドラインを0.5㎜テープで貼り付ける。
※なお，レイアウト図を基本とするものの，この時点でもデザインクレイモデルを中心にサイドウインドの位置も決めると良い。

*㉕ Using the image sketch and the layout plan as a basic reference, make the side window line by sticking on a 0.5mm side tape.
At this stage it is also advisable to fix the position of the side windows by looking at the whole balance of the design even though you still have to rely on the layout plan as a basis.*

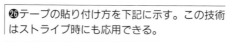

㉖テープの貼り付け方を下記に示す。この技術はストライプ時にも応用できる。

㉖ Stick the tape in place by following the following diagram. This method can be applied during the stripe process.

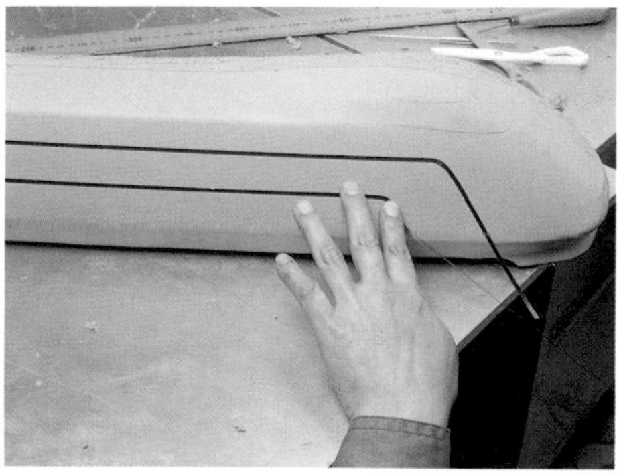

直線 *Straight line.*

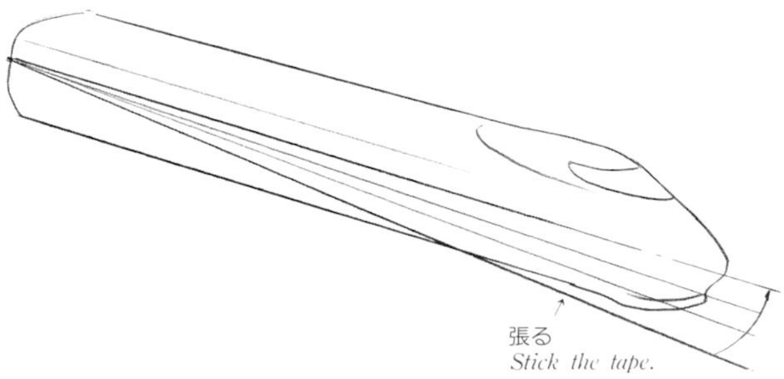

曲線 *Curved line.*

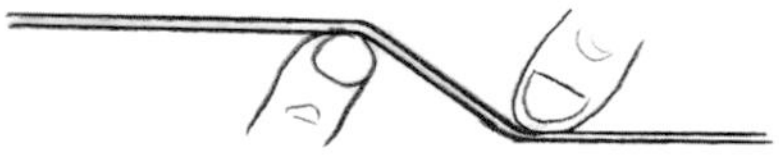

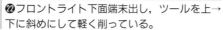

  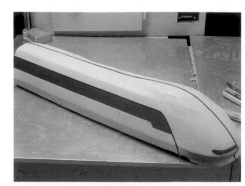

㉗パレットナイフにて，フロントウインド，フロントボンネットなど位置ラインを描き，バランスを確認する。

㉗ *Use the palette knife to draw the position lines on the front window and bonnet to check the balance.*

㉘テープラインが決定期指で圧着させること。

㉘ *Once the positioning of the tape has been decided upon, press in into place with the fingers.*

㉙カラーシートを貼り付け，サイドウインドイメージを出す。

㉙ *Create the side window image by sticking a color sheet in place.*

㉚鉄道車両1/30スケールモデルである。
三次元造形確認を線図のみでなくクレイモデル化し造形確認をするとよりリアルなイメージが出せる。

㉚ *A 1/30 scale model of a train carriage. A more realistic image can be produced if the 3-dimensional model is checked not only when drawing the line plan, but also during the actual construction of the clay model.*

㉛2両編成1/30スケールモデルを示す。
製作期間 4 日間

㉛ *The picture shows a 1/30 scale model of a two-carriage train.*
This model was four days in production.

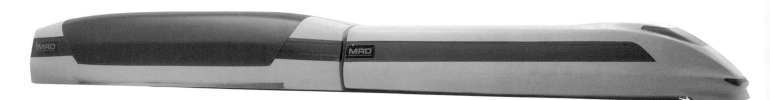

❶縮尺検討後中子（モデルコア）を作り上げる。２周りほど小さく作る事また，翼に当たる付根は胴体と一体とするか翼R／Lを一体にするか，中に鉄棒を入れるかする。翼の部分は薄くなるため中子状態で剛性を高めること。

❶*Create the model core once the reduced scale has been fixed. Ensure that the size of the core is two sizes smaller than the actual model. The joint sections of the wings can be connected to the body of the plane or inserted with the use of iron rods.*
Owing to the relative thiness of the wings, they should be properly strengthened at the stage of making the model core.

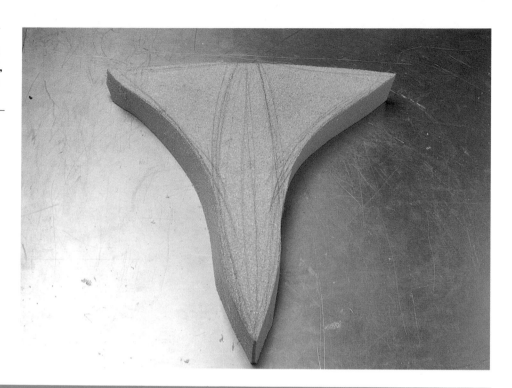

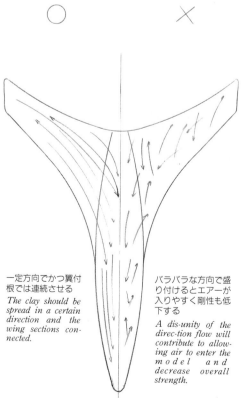

❷モデル中子加工に入るが，特に翼部分は注意を要する。また当製品は裏側もクレイ加工するので十分な中子形状にすること。

❷*Start with the model core process. The wings require special attention. The core needs to be well strengthened as it must also support the weight of the clay.*

❸基礎盛りを行う注意点として，翼部分周辺は一つの流れを出して引き伸ばし盛り付けを行うこと。

❸*Attach the basic covering. Note that the clay should be spread evenly to maintain a certain flow when working around the wings.*

一定方向でかつ翼付根では連続させる
The clay should be spread in a certain direction and the wing sections connected.

バラバラな方向で盛り付けるとエアーが入りやすく剛性も低下する
A dis-tion of the direc-tion flow will contribute to allowing air to enter the model and decrease overall strength.

❹裏面も表面と同一。

❹*The back should be done using the same method as the front.*

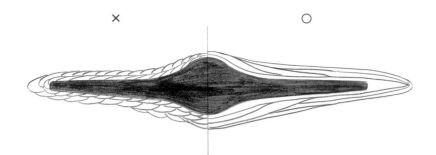

× ○

❺荒盛り，やはり翼部分の盛り付けに気を付ける。翼については多少やわらか目のクレイを一度に多く乗せ，一気に伸ばし盛り付けると一連性が増し加工時クラックなどが入りにくい。

❺ *Rough covering. Once again attention should be given to the wing joint sections. Best results can be attained by adding large pieces of clay each time and then spreading it quickly which improves a continuous smoothness and prevents the appearence of cracks.*

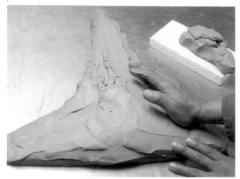

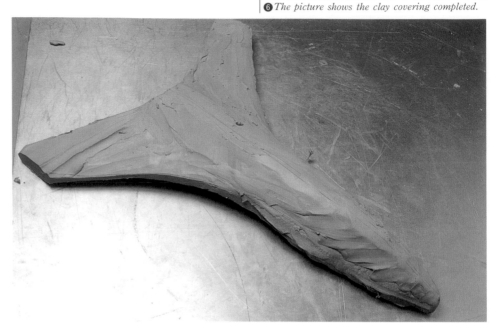

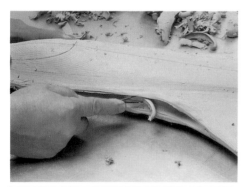

❿エアーダクトをワイヤーで掘る。凹部の奥加工はワイヤーの刃面に特加工を行いワイヤーにて削り加工し仕上げる。

❿ *Use the wire to dig an airduct. Then apply a special process to the blade face of the wire to treat the concave part. The wire should be used to shave and complete.*

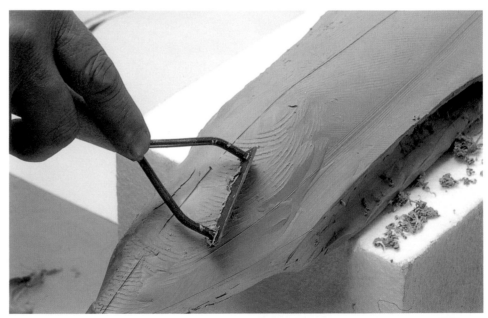

⓬操縦席スクリーン三次元部はツールを形状にそって斜め削りを行うこと。

⓬ *For the pilot seat screen, move the tool diagonally along the shape of it to shave.*

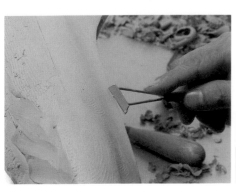

⓫胴体側面三次元部分の削りは，ツールを斜めに引く作業を多様し，仕上げていくと良い。

⓫ *Various styles of bringing the tool to the diagonal lines is advised in order to give the side parts of the body a 3-dimensional appearence.*

❼逆R部加工時まず，リングワイヤーツールで
加工するねらいの深さまで掘り込む。

❼*Use a ring wire tool to attain the reversed R
shape. Do not be afraid to dig in as far as is
necessary.*

❽フィニッシャー特加工刃を斜めに流しながら
削る。

❽*Move the specially processed finisher blade
diagonally to shave.*

❾翼端部の削りのポイントは翼の形状に合わせ，
流れるように削る。

❾*The edge of the wings should be smoothly
shaved.*

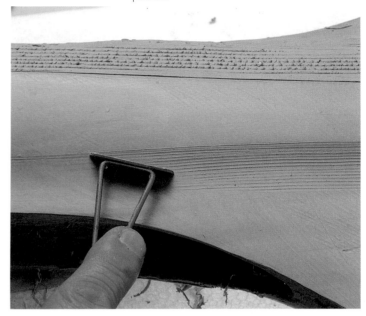

⓭翼端部の削りのポイントは翼形状に合わせ流
れるように削ると良い。

⓭*The edge part of the wings should be shaved
around in flowing movements.*

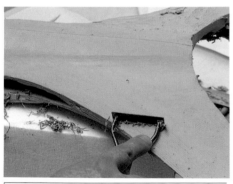

⓯翼表・裏両面が仕上がったところで端面R出
しをフィニッシャーで軽く削り仕上げる。

⓯*When the wings and both sides of the front
and back are completed, use the finisher to treat
the R shaped edge surface by shaving lightly to
complete.*

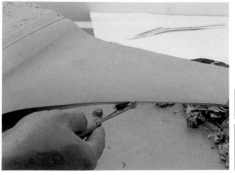

⓮上面削りと並行して裏面も削る。両面が正し
く削られることにより端面が美しく出る。

⓮*The back surface should also be shaved in
parallel with the upper surface work. Accurate
work given to both surfaces will bring out the
best results in the edge surfacing work.*

⓰操縦席三次元部及び先端周辺の造形仕上がり
状態を示す。

⓰The picture shows the completion of the 3-dimensional pilot seat and the tip area of the model airplane.

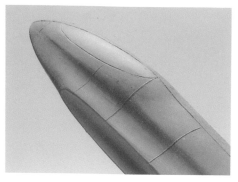

⓱エアーダクト上部ライン仕上がり状態を示す。

⓱The picture shows the line finish of the upper airduct area.

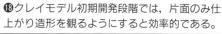

⓲クレイモデル初期開発段階では，片面のみ仕
上がり造形を観るようにすると効率的である。

⓲In the early development stages of clay modelling, it is more effective to complete one side first to check the formative shape.

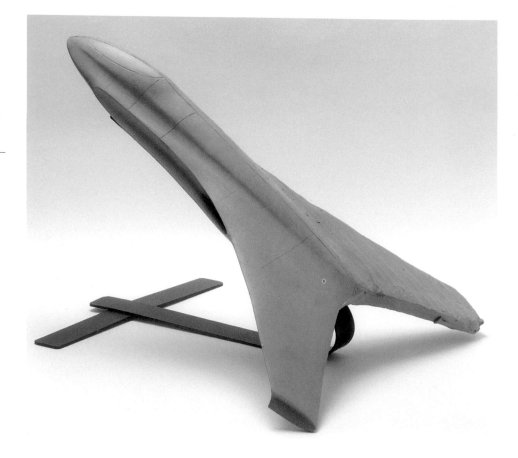

❶アイディアスケッチとレイアウト図をもとに縮尺レベルを決め、クレイモデル完成時予想寸法により、中子寸法（2周りは小さく）を決めカットする。

❶ *The level of scale reduction should be fixed through reference to the idea sketch and layout plans. The size of the core should then be decided and cut out while working from the conceptional drawing of the clay (two sizes smaller).*

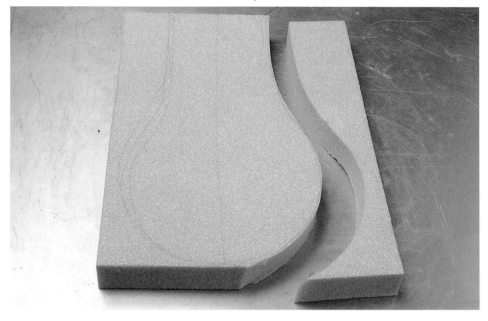

❷縮尺検討後中子（モデルコア）をつくり上げる。2周り程小さくつくること。

❷ *The core should be completed after the scale reduction has been confirmed. It needs to be two sizes smaller.*

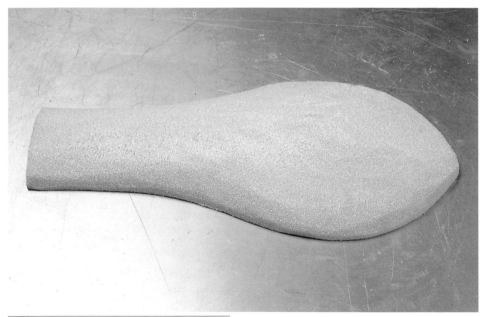

❹基礎盛りを行う。基礎盛りは多少やわらか目のクレイで行うと付きが良い。

❹ *Work on the basic clay covering. Softish clay should be chosen for the basic covering as it will adhere to the core easily.*

❸中子完成状態，表面にスケロールの切粉は取り除くこと。

❸ *The picture shows the completion of the core. Brush the styrene saw-dust from the surface.*

❺荒盛りを行う。荒盛りのコツはクレイを引き伸ばし盛り付けるとエアーが入りにくい。

❺ *Work on the rough covering. The secret of rough covering is to spread the clay in such a manner as to prevent air from entering.*

❼荒盛り完了状態基本外形より一周りほど大きいこの後削り作業となる。

❼ *The picture shows the completion of the rough covering. The model is one size larger than the basic external shape. Shaving will follow.*

❻裏面も入念に盛り付けること。大きい物でも同一です。

❻ *Work thoroughly on the back covering as well. The same treatment can be used for large objects.*

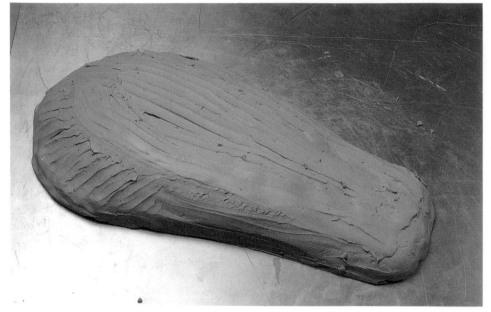

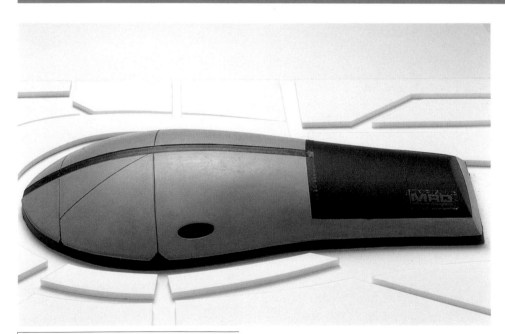

❿屋内競技場クレイ仕上がり状態を示す玉表面状態の面状態もクレイ表理で十分表現力がある。

❿ *The picture shows a completed clay model of an indoor sports arena. The round shape of the surface is well expressed by the clay.*

⓫リアルルーフ部分については，クレイ面に艶消黒塗装で仕上げたが，クレイ面直接塗装でも十分対応できる。

⓫ *The rear roof has been treated by applying a coat of black matt paint, but the surface is good enough to take a direct coat.*

❽球面荒削り時では，球面にそって流れるように削り込む。またレイク50により満遍なく削り，荒削り状態で基本的球面状態をつくり出すこと。

❽ *With the use of a rake 50, thoroughly shave along the curved lines of the spherical surface in the stage of rough shaving to create a basic spherical surface.*

❾荒削りでもレイク50で写真のような表面状態まで仕上げる。この後フィニッシャー特加工刃で面出しを行う。

❾ *With the use of a rake 50, give rough shaving touches to the surface until it resembles the one shown in the photograph. Then go onto the next process of surfacing with the use of the specially processed finisher blade.*

❿フィニッシャー特加工刃で表面出しした後，ゴムベラで表面をならし加工し面仕上げをする。

❿ *After the surfacing with the specially processed finisher blade is over, treat the surface with a rubber spatula to complete.*

⓫最後に手，指を使いより以上に面を出す（大物造形では無理であるが小物造形物ではこの作業はよく行う手法である）。

⓫ *Lastly, use the hands and fingers to improve the surface (such a method is not suitable for large models, but is used often on small models).*

⓮全体的に建築物をクレイモデルでの三次元スケールクレイで十分造形確認はできる。

⓮ *The formation of the overall building can easily be confirmed with the 3-dimensional clay scale model.*

8. 作例
Example of clay models

鉛筆削りフルサイズクレイモデル   *The full-size sharp-pencil.*

リアー周り
フルサイズモデルを短期間でつくるとき，クレイモデルは優れている。鉛筆削りは実質1日でモデルが完成した。

The front area and the rear area.
Clay modelling is an excellent medium for
making full-size models in a limited time period.
The time required in the creation
of this model was one day.

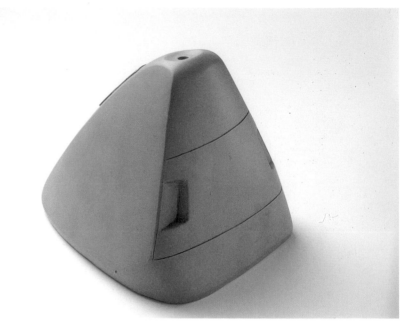

フロント周り

ハンドカメラ,フルサイズモデル   A full-size model of a handy camera.

手に持ってスイッチその他人間工学確認など造
形以外でも十分効率的であった。
製作期間　3日間

This is an effective model as not only the forma-
tion can be experienced, but also the shutter
switch and other areas that require human indus-
try can be fully checked by holding it in the
hand.
This model for three days in production.

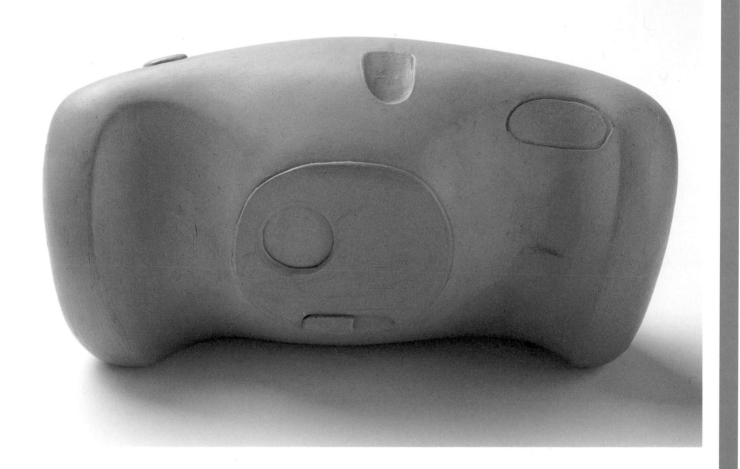

リアービュー
全体重量などは中子を調整することで十分対応
できる。

The rear view.
The entire weight can be adjusted in the core
making stage.

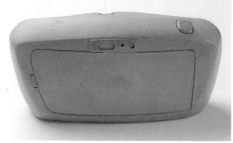

ビデオカメラ　A video camera.

クレイモデルにても細かな工作はできる。また
エッジ，ピン角の再理性加工もできる。
製作期間　1週間

*Details can be added to this clay model The
reproduction of the edges and the focus angle are
also processible.*
*The production period for this model was one
week.*

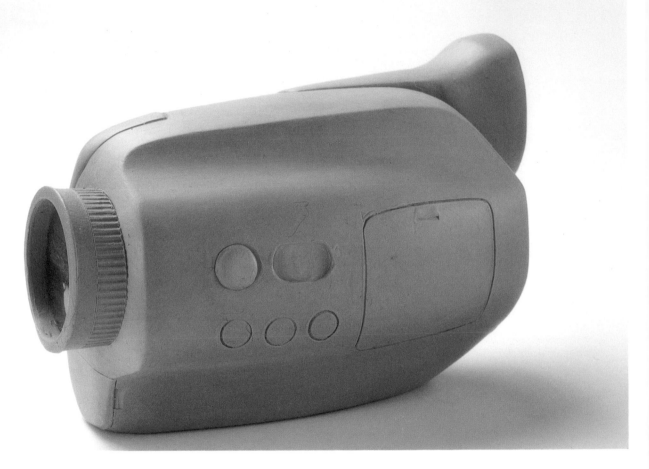

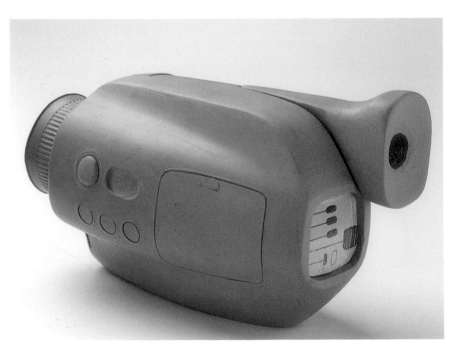

1/5スケールモデル *A 1/5 scale model.*

開発プロセスの一部 Part of the development process.

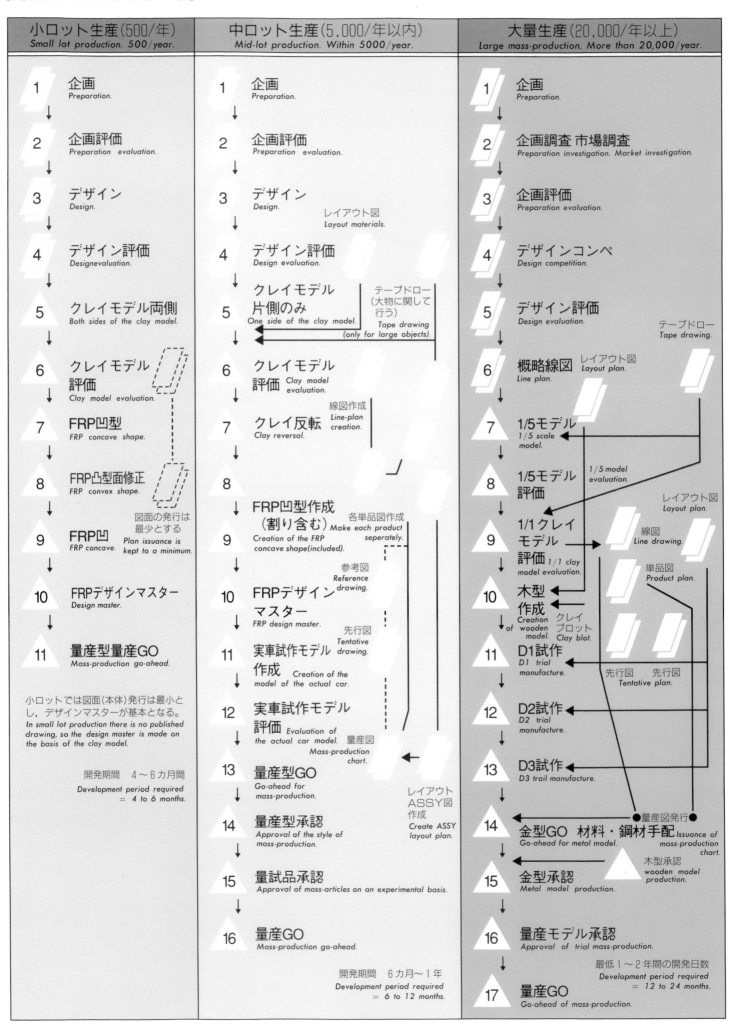

小ロット生産（500/年） Small lot production. 500/year.	中ロット生産（5,000/年以内） Mid-lot production. Within 5000/year.	大量生産（20,000/年以上） Large mass-production. More than 20,000/year.
1 企画 Preparation.	1 企画 Preparation.	1 企画 Preparation.
2 企画評価 Preparation evaluation.	2 企画評価 Preparation evaluation.	2 企画調査 市場調査 Preparation investigation. Market investigation.
3 デザイン Design.	3 デザイン Design.	3 企画評価 Preparation evaluation.
4 デザイン評価 Designevaluation.	4 デザイン評価 Design evaluation. レイアウト図 Layout materials.	4 デザインコンペ Design competition.
5 クレイモデル両側 Both sides of the clay model.	5 クレイモデル片側のみ One side of the clay model. テープドロー（大物に関して行う）Tape drawing (only for large objects).	5 デザイン評価 Design evaluation.
6 クレイモデル評価 Clay model evaluation.	6 クレイモデル評価 Clay model evaluation.	6 概略線図 Line plan. レイアウト図 Layout plan. テープドロー Tape drawing.
7 FRP凹型 FRP concave shape.	7 クレイ反転 Clay reversal. 線図作成 Line-plan creation.	7 1/5モデル 1/5 scale model.
8 FRP凸型面修正 FRP convex shape.	8 FRP凹型作成（割り含む）Creation of the FRP concave shape(included). 各単品図作成 Make each product seperately.	8 1/5モデル評価 1/5 model evaluation.
9 FRP凹 FRP concave. 図面の発行は最少とする Plan issuance is kept to a minimum.	9	9 1/1クレイモデル評価 1/1 clay model evaluation. レイアウト図 Layout plan. 線図 Line drawing.
10 FRPデザインマスター Design master.	10 FRPデザインマスター FRP design master. 参考図 Reference drawing.	10 木型作成 Creation of wooden model. 単品図 Product plan. クレイブロット Clay blot.
11 量産型量産GO Mass-production go-ahead.	11 実車試作モデル作成 Creation of the model of the actual car. 先行図 Tentative drawing.	11 D1試作 D1 trial manufacture. 先行図 先行図 Tentative plan.
小ロットでは図面(本体)発行は最小とし，デザインマスターが基本となる。In small lot production there is no published drawing, so the design master is made on the basis of the clay model.	12 実車試作モデル評価 Evaluation of the actual car model. 量産図 Mass-production chart.	12 D2試作 D2 trial manufacture.
開発期間 4〜6カ月間 Development period required = 4 to 6 months.	13 量産型GO Go-ahead for mass-production. レイアウトASSY図作成 Create ASSY layout plan.	13 D3試作 D3 trail manufacture.
	14 量産型承認 Approval of the style of mass-production.	14 金型GO 材料・鋼材手配 Go-ahead for metal model. 量産図発行 Issuance of mass-production chart.
	15 量試品承認 Approval of mass-articles on an experimental basis.	15 金型承認 Metal model production. 木型承認 wooden model production.
	16 量産GO Mass-production go-ahead.	16 量産モデル承認 Approval of trial mass-production.
	開発期間 6カ月〜1年 Development period required = 6 to 12 months.	17 量産GO Go-ahead of mass-production. 最低1〜2年間の開発日数 Development period required = 12 to 24 months.

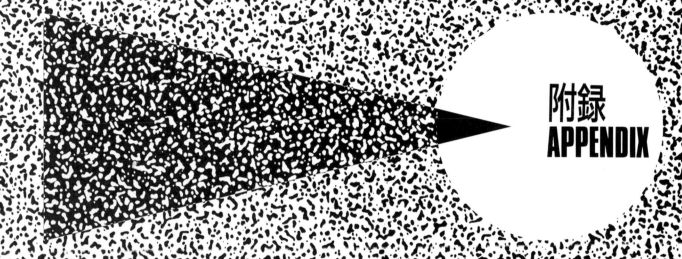

附録
APPENDIX

展開図・加工図を画く際の寸法のもとめ方

❶円周の長さをもとめる
How to measure the length of a circumference.

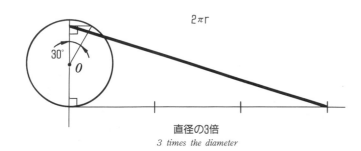

直径の3倍
3 times the diameter

$2\pi r$

❷半円周の長さをもとめる
How to measure the length of a semicircumference.

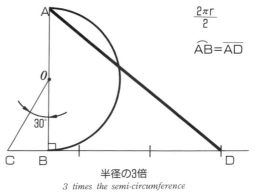

$\dfrac{2\pi r}{2}$

$\widehat{AB} = \overline{AD}$

半径の3倍
3 times the semi-circumference

❸-1 円弧の長さをもとめる
How to measure the length of a circular arc.

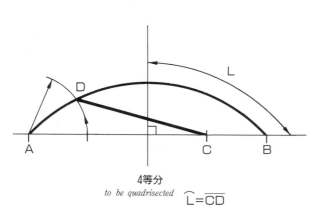

4等分
to be quadrisected

$\widehat{L} = \overline{CD}$

❹円弧上に直線の長さをもとめる
How to measure the length of a straight line on a circular arc.

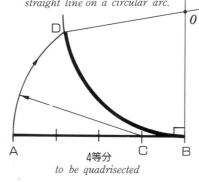

4等分
to be quadrisected

$\overline{AB} = \widehat{BD}$

❺角度・辺の長さをもとめる
Calculating an angle and length of a side.

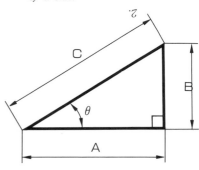

三角比 *trigonometric ratios*

$$\sin\theta = \frac{B}{C} \quad \cos\theta = \frac{A}{C} \quad \tan\theta = \frac{B}{A}$$

三平方の定理 *a theorem of three squares*

$$C^2 = A^2 + B^2 \qquad C = \sqrt{A^2 + B^2}$$

❸-2 円弧の長さをもとめる
How to measure the length of a circular arc.

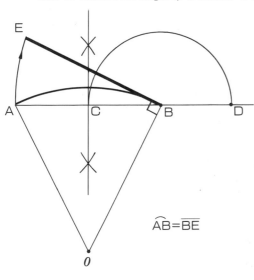

$\widehat{AB} = \overline{BE}$

❻円弧の半径・角度から円弧の幅をもとめる
Obtaining the circular arc's width from the angle and radius of a circular arc.

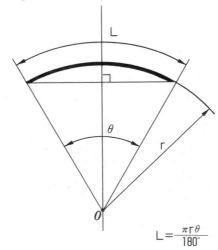

$$L = \frac{\pi r \theta}{180°}$$

❼円弧の幅・高さから半径をもとめる
Obtaining the radius from the height and width of a circular arc.

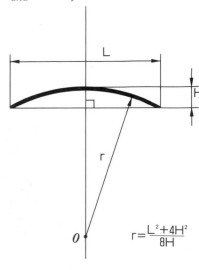

$$r = \frac{L^2 + 4H^2}{8H}$$

❽展開図を画く方法
How to draw an exploded drawing.

1.平行線法（平行線を用いて実長をもとめる）
  Parallel-line method. (To obtain an actual length using a parallel-line method.)

2.放射線法（放射線を用いて実長をもとめる）
  Radial-line method. (To obtain an actual length using a radial-line method.)

3.三角形法（二角形に分割して実長をもとめる）
  Triangle method. (To obtain an actual length by diving into triangles.)

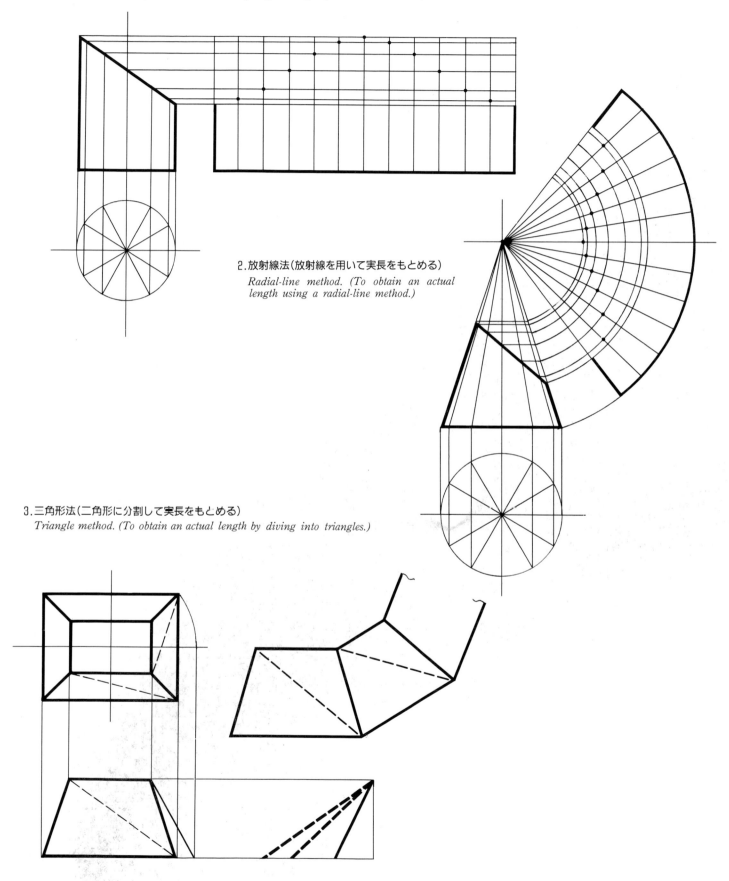

■あとがき

プロダクトデザインを学んでいる学生，新人プロデザイナー，デザイン教育現場から，多様な立体デザインモデル技法を，モデル制作スタートの時点から完成に至るまでのプロセスを，できるだけ細かく，段階的に分かりやすく解説した技法書がほしい，といった要望はかねてから多くあった。

そこで，これら関係者の要望をできる限り反映させ，まとめたのが本書であり，ちなみにシャープでジオメトリカルな造形処理を得意とする小島孝氏はペーパーモデルテクニックを，長年イタリアでデザイン活動した経験から，立体デザインはそのまま立体で展開・確認するがモットーの工業デザイナー田野雅三氏はスタディモデルテクニックを，カーデザイナーで日本におけるクレイモデリングの第一人者と評価されている松田真次氏はクレイモデルテクニックをそれぞれ各プロセスを追いながら紹介しているが，そのボリューム，技法解説密度の高さ，技法バリエーションの豊富さ等において他に類を見ない。

なお，関係者からの要望もあり，簡便なデザインコンセプトスケッチテクニック数作例を付加し，その一部のデザインを基にしてモデルメーキングにリンクさせた。

最後に，大変お世話になった編集部の山田信彦氏，カメラマンの工藤正志氏，ブックデザインを担当していただいた大貫伸樹氏とスタッフの皆さん，用具・用材を提供していただいた㈱いづみや様，この場を借りて心からお礼申し上げます。

1991年10月　清水吉治

AFTERWORD

There has been much demand from product design students, new professional designers and teachers in the design field for some time now for the creation of a technical book which covers full details on the process of various cubic design models from start to completion with full explanations on an easy step-by-step basis.

The book has been compiled to meet the strongest demands of these people. Within its pages are paper modelling techniques introduced by Mr.Takashi Kojima, the designer of home electronic appliances and an expert in the creation of geometrical models, study models techniques by Mr.Masazo Tano, the industrial designer whose motto it is to develop and confirm cubic designs with cubes and who gained much experience in Italy. The clay model techniques of Mr.Shinji Matsuda, a car designer who is now one of leading modellers in Japan. There are no other books to complete with the volume, quality of explanations and wealthiness of technical variation contained within these covers.

We have added a few examples of simple design sketch techniques by popular demand, and linked part of these designe into the actual model making.

Lastly, I would like to take this opportunity to express my gratitude to Mr.Nobuhiko Yamada, the editor, Mr.Masashi Kudo, the cameraman, Mr.Shinju Onuki and his assistants, plus Izumiya Co.,who kindly provided me with all necessary support.

Yoshiharu Shimizu
October 1991

■著者略歴

清水吉治 (しみず・よしはる)

1934 年長野県生まれ。1959 年金沢美術工芸大学工業デザイン科卒業後，㈱富士通ゼネラル D センター等を経て，Sutudio Nurmesniemi，フィンランド国立美術工芸大学留学。現在，㈶日本機械デザインセンター，㈶生活用品振興センター，㈶日本産業デザイン振興会，各企業内デザイン研修講師。埼玉県，石川県デザインアドバイザー。東京工芸大学，多摩美術大学，東洋美術学校講師。多摩美術大学二部，新座総合技術高校デザイン専攻科，OCA など特別講師。著書に「VTR 教材・マーカースケッチ」㈶日本機械デザインセンター，「工業デザイン全集第 4 巻」(共著)日本出版サービス，「マーカーテクニック」，「マーカーワークス in ジャパン」(編)グラフィック社など。1959 年毎日工業デザインコンペスポンサー賞(グループ)，1987 年特許庁㈶発明協会意匠賞，1988 年中華民国対外貿易発展協会より意匠貢献状，1989 年繊維機械デザインで金沢市長賞など各受賞。㈳日本インダストリアルデザイナー協会会員。

住所＝〒 350-12 埼玉県日高市武蔵台 5-29-12
　　　Tel.0429(82)1914

小島 孝 (こじま・たかし)

1962 年岩手県立盛岡工業高校卒業後，㈱ゼネラル入社。テレビ等各種家電製品のデザインを担当する。1983 年富塚光夫氏よりペーパーモデルの制作講習を受ける。1985 年 4 月より 1986 年 5 月まで㈱平渡総研において各種デザイン及び機構設計を手掛ける。1986 年 6 月 PMD 小島設立。各種デザイン，ペーパーモデル制作等現在に至る。

住所＝〒 167 東京都杉並区桃井 4-14-19
　　　Tel.03(3399)3505

田野雅三（たの・まさぞう）

1942 年和歌山県生まれ。1965 年金沢美術工芸大学卒業。
1969 年千葉大学工業短期大学部機械工学科卒業。1972
年 7 年間勤めた㈶柳工業デザイン研究会を辞め，夫人と
共にインド，中近東，ヨーロッパの旅に出る。1973 年
STUDIO COPPOLA（ミラノ）にて工業デザイン担当。
ALESSI，ARTEMIDE，TRONCONI 各社とテーブルウェ
ア，照明のデザイン開発を手掛ける。1978 年㈲田野デザ
インルーム設立。台所用品，洗面浴室ユニット，建材，
パブリックトイレ，装身具，CAR 用品，情報機器，ワー
キングチェア等企業とともに豊かな生活の形を求めデザ
イン開発を進めている。1988 年アクシスギャラリーで個
展。新座総合技術高校デザイン専攻科講師。プロダクト
デザイナー。

住所＝〒 350-03 埼玉県比企郡鳩山町楓ヶ丘 4-6-7
　　　Tel.0492(96)0356

松田真次（まつだ・しんじ）

1945 年東京都生まれ。昭和鉄道高等学校機関科卒業。
1965〜1971 年自動車重整備に携わり，2 級ガソリン・ジー
ゼル資格検査員 1 級整備士取得。1972 年本田技研工業㈱
本社技術部入社。ライフ，シビック，アコードの強度・安
全・認定・品質管理を担当。1977 年本田技研工業㈱純正用
品開発部門転勤，プロジェクトリーダー，チーフデザイ
ナー，造形・設計企画責任者となる。1982 年同社を退社
後，松田技術研究所設立。1986 年 5 月株式会社として現
在に至る。1980年㈱ホンダ用品研究所社長表彰，1981年
整備士講師会長表彰，1982 年㈱ホンダ用品研究所社長表
彰，㈱本田技術研究所社長表彰，1987 年中華民国対外貿
易発展協会クレイモデル講師協力受賞。小川テント㈱技
術顧問，㈱いづみや顧問，㈶日本機械デザインセンター
講師，長野県工業技術学院モデル講師。㈳日本インダス
トリアルデザイナー協会正会員，㈳自動車技術会正会員，
㈶日本機械デザインセンター正会員。企画・デザイン・設
計・クレイモデル・強度計算・全日本 2 輪 GP チーフメカ・
エンジンチューナー等マルチ開発者。

住所＝〒 174 東京都板橋区東新町 1-38-8
　　　Tel.03(3554)1030 FAX.03(3554)1033

参考文献

●糠沢・ジョセフ　アイデア・プレゼンテーション用ラフスケッチの要点　カースタイリング ’8　1974年
●ダブリンのデザイン透視図法　J．ダブリン　鳳山社　1980年
●清水吉治「工業デザイン全集第 4 巻・デザイン技法・スケッチ」日本出版サービス　1982年
●八重樫守（監修）CAR STYLING DESIGN　グランプリ出版　1982年
●清水吉治「マーカー・テクニック」　グラフィック社　1990年
●清水吉治（編）「マーカーワークス in ジャパン」　グラフィック社　1990年

モデリングテクニック

1991年12月25日　初版第1刷発行
1992年7月25日　初版第2刷発行
1993年5月5日　初版第3刷発行

著　者————清水吉治　小島　孝　田野雅三　松田真次ⓒ

発行者————久世利郎

印　刷————錦明印刷株式会社

製　本————錦明印刷株式会社

写　植————三和写真工芸株式会社

発行所————株式会社グラフィック社

〒102　東京都千代田区九段北1−9−12

Tel.03(3263)4318　振替・東京3−114345

ISBN4-7661-0617-2 C3052